Praise for Startup Rising

"This powerful and essential book will open your eyes to a new world of opportunity for people in the Middle East and emerging markets all over the world. Through vivid introductions to young entrepreneurs in the region and a compelling analysis of macro technology and economic trends, *Startup Rising* brilliantly demonstrates that peace and prosperity is attainable for the region."

—Julius Genachowski, Chairman of the United States
Federal Communications Commission, 2009–2013

"In this rich and incisive book Christopher Schroeder tells a fascinating tale about another Middle East, where new ideas, bustling startups, and promising ventures, as opposed to politics and violence, are shaping the future. A rare and eye-opening firsthand account that provides a powerful explanation for why the Arab Spring happened, and why its future may yet be brighter than headline news suggests. This book is a must read for anyone interested in the Middle East or how entrepreneurship and technology startups take flight."

—Vali Nasr, author of *Forces of Fortune*
and *The Dispensable Nation*

"Christopher M. Schroeder has done a service to the Middle East by highlighting the extraordinary energy and potential of entrepreneurs in the region. This area will be a hotbed of new ideas over the next 20 years, creating hundreds of thousands of jobs."

—Kevin Ryan, chairman and founder, Gilt

"*Startup Rising* powerfully articulates what we instinctively know to be true—each country, region, and society has the will and talent to determine its own future. Schroeder illuminates a Middle East poised for entrepreneurial growth, fueled by innovation, and ready to turn opportunity into impact and collective progress for both women and men."

—Alyse Nelson, President & CEO,
Vital Voices Global Partnership

"Christopher M. Schroeder has a message we should all hear loud and clear: To hell with pessimism about the Middle East. In *Startup Rising*, Chris's more than one dozen trips across the Arab world are woven together into a deeply personal and detail-filled narrative of how technology can transform social and political orders from the ground up. He convincingly shows Arabs rich and poor seizing the moment, and converting centuries of entrepreneurial spirit into disruptive and positive energy. The startups rising in the wake of the Arab Spring will ensure that the region isn't left behind."

—Parag Khanna, international bestselling author of
The Second World, How to Run the World, and *Hybrid Reality*

"*Startup Rising* shatters our stereotypes of the Middle East. You can just feel the dynamism bubbling up from below and sense the immense possibilities for the future. Schroeder's ability to tell this fascinating story of the breadth and depth of entrepreneurship in the region is stunning."

—James Goldgeier, Dean, School of
International Service, American University

"This is one of the rare books that will change how you see the world. Christopher M. Schroeder brings to life the emerging Middle East entrepreneurial ecosystems, providing a powerful understanding of entrepreneurship anywhere in the world and specifically of the Middle East's emerging generation of questioning risk-takers."

—Marvin Ammori, Bernard L. Schwartz Fellow,
New America Foundation

"Interest in entrepreneurship in the Middle East has never been greater, which reflects the critical role that new ventures can play in catalyzing economic change in the region. This book provides a lively look at the individuals and institutions behind these exciting and important developments."

—Josh Lerner, Harvard Business School and
author of *The Architecture of Innovation*

Startup Rising

THE ENTREPRENEURIAL REVOLUTION
REMAKING THE MIDDLE EAST

Christopher M. Schroeder

Foreword by Marc Andreessen

palgrave
macmillan

STARTUP RISING
Copyright © Christopher M. Schroeder, 2013.

First published in 2013 by PALGRAVE MACMILLAN® in the U.S.—a division
of St. Martin's Press LLC, 175 Fifth Avenue, New York, NY 10010.

Where this book is distributed in the UK, Europe and the rest of the world, this
is by Palgrave Macmillan, a division of Macmillan Publishers Limited, registered
in England, company number 785998, of Houndmills, Basingstoke, Hampshire
RG21 6XS.

Palgrave Macmillan is the global academic imprint of the above companies and
has companies and representatives throughout the world.

Palgrave® and Macmillan® are registered trademarks in the United States, the
United Kingdom, Europe and other countries.

ISBN: 978-0-230-34222-4

Library of Congress Cataloging-in-Publication Data

Schroeder, Christopher.
    Startup rising : the entrepreneurial revolution remaking the Middle East /
Christopher Schroeder.
        pages   cm
    ISBN 978-0-230-34222-4
    1. Entrepreneurship—Middle East. 2. New business enterprises—Middle
East. I. Title.
HB615.S37157   2013
338'.040956—dc23

                                                                    2012051291

A catalogue record of the book is available from the British Library.

Design by Letra Libre

First edition: August 2013

10   9   8   7   6   5   4

Printed in the United States of America.

*For the startups rising, their mentors,
their backers, their ecosystem builders,
and all, anywhere, who support them.*

*And for Jack, Julia, and Ben who will find
their own ways to help change the world.*

Contents

Eight pages of photographs appear between pages 120 and 121.

Foreword

I sure hope Schroeder is right.

In many ways he clearly is.

That software has taken over and changed many aspects of the global economy in less than a decade is now clear. Companies that are descriptively software enterprises—Google, Facebook (on whose board I serve), Twitter, Airbnb, Pinterest, and many others—have opened up human connections, access to knowledge, and new business models unforeseen before they existed. Software-powered startups have disrupted almost every traditional consumer-facing experience from books to music to travel to video entertainment and gaming to shopping to telephony and beyond.

But this is only a part of the story. Today almost every company is, in some form, a software company. Look at the dashboard of your car and consider how today's engines work. Think about the sophistication that allows you to safely bank online. Next time you buy a cup of coffee with a credit card, fill your car with gas, or shop at Wal-Mart, ask how remarkable innovation in software has allowed their logistics to scale. In 2011, I wrote in the *Wall Street Journal* that "software is eating the world," and software's appetite has increased dramatically since then. Traditional enterprises like Kodak and Borders that at best paid lip service to software innovation, at worst ignored it, are in an existential crisis—not in some theoretical future, but right now.

Schroeder is also right in describing the three forces that are driving tech innovation from unexpected corners of the globe and that a new generation of entrepreneurs take for granted:

1. How technology offers an irreversible level of transparency, connectivity, and inexpensive access to capital and markets;
2. How over two decades of experience in navigating emerging market investment has made regional and global capital more comfortable with political risk and understanding local market distinctions;
3. That with rapidly increasing access to technology there are large, untapped markets of consumers and businesses seeking greater software solutions.

To his three I would add a fourth: after twenty years of hard work by many talented people, all the technology required to transform industries through software finally works and can be widely delivered at global scale. And these are the earliest innings. I believe within a decade there will be five billion people using smartphones worldwide—the equivalent computing capacity of a supercomputer and the full power of the internet on everyone's person, all the time, everywhere. Schroeder notes that experts tell him to expect 50 percent penetration across the Middle East in three to five years. What this will yield in problem-solving and opportunity-building is limited only by one's imagination.

Schroeder is provocative and likely right, that we in Silicon Valley risk being hyper-focused on ourselves and our own echo chambers. There is no question that the network effect of talent—that world-class entrepreneurs, engineers, and design talent want to be with and are attracted by the best—has made Silicon Valley unique in the history of global innovation. That we historically have thought of emerging growth markets as either places to sell our products and services or relatively inexpensive outsourcing opportunities is limiting. If everything I have written here is true, innovation will clearly come from surprising places when great talent has access to software. Our answer has historically been to focus on such talents when we can bring them to Silicon Valley—which is why I have been an active supporter of a greater number of young entrepreneurs having access to the H-1B visa. At the same time, we will need to think differently if talent progressively wants to stay home and innovate.

Whether the remarkably talented entrepreneurs in the Middle East can scale and build regionally and globally competitive software at scale is still, for me, however, the central question—certainly a billion-dollar question, and ultimately a trillion-dollar question.

The stories of great entrepreneurs and ideas Chris describes are inspiring and potentially game changing. Middle Eastern entrepreneurs are spawning startups in education, crime prevention, traffic management, recycling, renewable energy, health, entertainment, education, and beyond, solving real challenges and finding new opportunities that can change societies. And they may change the world. Could, he asks, unique experiences in the region spawn globally adopted software in spaces like mobile, social networks, and solar energy?

Culture and ecosystem, however, mean everything, and these entrepreneurs face real headwinds. There are disappointingly few Middle Eastern governments and educational institutions seriously tackling the difficult decisions required to change downward trajectories in infrastructure at scale and speed. In fact, with a recent increase in internet restrictions in the region, Schroeder rightly points out that governments are not only hindering communication and transparency, but the very platform of economic growth that I believe will drive any successful country in the coming decades.

He raises an intriguing idea that regional entrepreneurial ecosystems are being built anyway, bottom up, enabled by access to software. There is a line that stands in my mind from one of the leading entrepreneurs in the region: there is no "*wasta*"—the system of favors and "Who do you know?" that has driven so much of life from getting into a good school to finding a good job—on the internet. A similar sentiment was expressed by the new regional head of LinkedIn, who noted that platforms like theirs emphasize transparently connecting job seekers based on their real skills and performance. Millions of people are using social networks, YouTube, and hundreds of startups in the region to take control of and improve their own lives. Perhaps this new generation will build new models of economic success despite the daunting challenges caused by political and institutional neglect.

The demographics of the Middle East are most telling to me—and are a double-edged sword. The vast numbers of young people coming into adulthood mean an unprecedented talent pool to create and innovate. Traditional business models simply cannot absorb them, and entrepreneurship will have to be part of the answer. If embraced by their societies, I'd rather have this challenge than countries now facing a decrease in youth. Ignored, however, the ramifications could be more generationally catastrophic. In many ways, emerging growth markets are making specific decisions about whether to embrace the new realities of the twenty-first century or hunker down in the missed opportunities often repeated in the twentieth.

I suppose if these entrepreneurs are not embraced at home, it's good news for Silicon Valley people like me. As Schroeder notes, there has never been a time in history where talent has been more mobile. Our doors are always open to great entrepreneurs who want nothing more than to build what was not there before.

But a unique opportunity is at hand for any society that actively embraces it. *Startup Rising* offers a remarkable narrative most of us don't consider when thinking about the Middle East. But it makes sense, and these courageous entrepreneurs and ecosystem builders are clearly on the right side of history.

Marc Andreessen
Palo Alto, California, 2013

Chapter 1

Celebration of Entrepreneurship

I sat, jet-lagged, in a small conference room, watching the desert sun sink toward the western horizon. It was my first trip to the Middle East in over a decade, and I had forgotten how hot it could get there even in November. Last time I had been a tourist—all antiquity, pyramids, and museums in Cairo. Now I was a seasoned internet investor, board member, and entrepreneur, attending one of the first region-wide gatherings of tech startups in Dubai. The looming skyscrapers and business towers before me had been barely an architect's dream during my last visit. Now, only the heat was familiar. By the end of this conference, virtually all my preconceptions of the Middle East would be thoroughly altered.

As if on cue, a flowing figure in black glided before me like a phantom. She sat beside me, shoulders proudly back, dressed in the traditional head-to-toe *abaya* that revealed only her face and hands. She said she was a university student in Saudi Arabia, and while there had designed a luxurious leather carrying case for mobile devices like smartphones and iPads—complete with a battery pocket to keep them charged. She asked whether I thought this was a good business idea.

I have happily listened to hundreds of ideas, investment pitches, and calls for mentorship throughout my career. It's inspiring to meet people trying to start something from scratch, with the odds so strongly against them, and it's gratifying to flatter myself that my nearly two decades of business experience might materially help these budding entrepreneurs. But on this day in 2010, my first mentorship experience in the Middle East was unnervingly different.

Fumbling for a coherent answer, I asked a few questions about her background and the genesis of her idea and offered some generic encouragement about following her dreams. She nodded politely, but with a palpable sense of boredom. "Thank you for that," she said. "It is very helpful. But I should have been more precise. I have a pre-order for a thousand units, and this leaves me with a dilemma. There are four low-cost manufacturers in China who are enthusiastic about doing business with me, but I am nervous about having my suppliers so far away. Should I risk manufacturing my idea with people I don't know very well, or should I raise the roughly $45,000 I'd need for machinery and then hire a young woman I know locally to handle production?"

I was stunned. Before me was a young, Saudi Arabia–based, tech-savvy woman entrepreneur looking to expand her operations globally. This was not the Middle East that I had been taught to expect. It was not the Middle East that my Western peers, even the most sophisticated businesspeople, knew. In fact, her story shocked even many of my skeptical friends in the region when I later described her.

One of the other young entrepreneurs in the room, the founder of a computer animation startup based in Syria, sensed my amazement. Eerily resembling a younger Leonardo DiCaprio with a ponytail, he winked at me. "There's a lot going over here, right sir?" Right.

I was in Dubai because I have been a successful entrepreneur and sometimes successful investor in many startup companies. I've played the roles of leader, board member, mentor, and amateur psychologist. I know the high of watching customers flock to a new product, and the gut-wrenching terror of realizing that even a small mistake on my part could cost my employees their livelihoods. When I talk with young entrepreneurs so passionate about technology and the internet that they can't imagine doing anything else, I am conversing with a sister or a brother. I know what they're in for, and I applaud them for it. It's a life of bold choices; one that, as the legendary founder of Netscape and venture investor Marc Andreessen reminded me at the beginning of one of my ventures, yields only two emotions: total euphoria and abject fear.

I was there primarily, however, because of an unusual journey.

In the United States, I am frequently asked why I care about the Middle East. My answer is usually a baffled, "Why don't you?" It's hard to name two regions of the world whose mutual needs, tensions, misunderstandings, and mistakes have had more impact in shaping their fortunes than these two. When I was growing up, when we thought about the Middle East at all, we generally lumped its unique cultures and histories into some simplistic context framed around the Israeli-Palestinian conflict or the Iranian Revolution. In college, I had a brilliant roommate who had recently escaped civil war–torn Lebanon with his family. When our late-night bull sessions turned to the Middle East, he tried patiently to teach our dorm-mates about the nuances of the region and how we were viewed there. One night, one of our classmates turned to him, as if the West had had no responsibilities for the region's challenges and said, "There is no hope. We should build a wall around the region and let you just figure your own shit out." There was embarrassed silence, but none of the rest of us had anything more sophisticated to offer our exasperated friend.

In the following decades, America's economic and strategic connectedness to the Middle East continued to increase. The accompanying tension and confrontation reached their apex in the terrible and brutal shock that was September 11. By that time I was a well-travelled executive. I understood that engagement and problem-solving anywhere required sensitivity to the countless big and small distinctions on the ground—that the most creative solutions were rarely one-size-fits-all. I had just joined the Young Presidents Organization (YPO), which has nearly 16,000 CEO members from around the world. The group's mission is less about business networking than building connectedness and understanding among senior executives. In 2003, a fellow U.S. member introduced me to other members from the Arab world. We collectively decided to form a sub-group of U.S. and Arab CEOs to help each other learn and understand our various cultural perspectives.

"The purpose of our group," as one Arab member more colloquially but accurately described later, "was to convince one another after September 11 that we're not all assholes." About two dozen of us met as often as three times a year—once in New York or Washington, once in Europe, once in the region. We got to know each other personally, and debated with outside experts. Most importantly, we learned about the unique problem-solving under way in both regions, well below the radar of the broader political narrative of economic aid and potential military conflict.

Two members of this remarkable group stood out. Lebanese-Jordanian entrepreneur Fadi Ghandour had built Aramex, the region's largest FedEx-like logistics and transportation company. Just over 50, he has the lean figure and tenacity of a man who swims two miles each morning regardless of what time zone he's crossed that day. Arif Naqvi had founded the Abraaj Group and built it into one of the largest private equity investment firms among all global growth markets. His legendary twenty-hour days underscore his insatiable curiosity about newly opening and changing worlds. They met when Arif invested in Fadi's company, and soon became close friends. They shared a passion for the broader societal impact of business, and led innovative corporate social responsibility initiatives around the Middle East. And as they compared notes on their teenage sons, how their lives were structured around and changing due to technology, they became convinced that they were witnessing an age of unparalleled historic opportunity.

During our YPO gatherings, they championed the rise of young tech-driven entrepreneurs throughout the developing world—especially in the Middle East. They believed that there were now significant opportunities for young people to create and build businesses that did not exist just a few years ago. A rising generation was demanding a different and better life than their parents', they argued, and they expressed these demands through the businesses they were creating. For Naqvi and Ghandour, embracing these entrepreneurs was nothing short of embracing the potential for a new Middle East. And they are putting their money and time where their mouths are. Both are leading go-to figures in the region, investing in, mentoring, and connecting regional tech-based startups. In the summer of 2010 they joined forces to hold what they called the region's first "Celebration of Entrepreneurship" in Dubai, an event that perfectly symbolized their beliefs. "You have to come and see this for yourself, man," they emailed me in invitation. I was skeptical, but most of our group knew we needed to be there.

The sold-out gathering had all the earmarks of a typical Silicon Valley event: more than 2,400 eager entrepreneurs and investors—most of them young and tethered to their mobile devices—sharing, debating, and connecting. There was the requisite hip music. Been-there/done-that speakers mixed with kids who were new to the game, dashing out ideas on whiteboards and rallying each other to new ventures. Yet the participants weren't familiar U.S. internet startups but a new generation of entrepreneurs from the Arabic-speaking Middle East. The music wasn't LA hip-hop but Arif Lohar, a leading Pakistani folk/fusion artist, whose band's vibrant rhythms combined with the vocals of Meesha, a stunning pop singer and top star in the region. They rocked the house with Urdu lyrics expressing love for and thankfulness to God.

Nobody discussed politics, religion, or historic obstacles. Instead, all they wanted to do was invent and build new businesses.

The Celebration of Entrepreneurship set me on subsequent journeys beyond Dubai—to Cairo, Amman, Beirut, Istanbul, even Damascus—and I saw similarly talented, successful, and intrepid entrepreneurs by the thousands, all driven to build, all willing to face the cultural, legal, and societal impediments inherent to their worlds. Just as importantly, I saw major global private equity and venture investors and tech companies like Google, Intel, Cisco, Yahoo!, LinkedIn, and PayPal among others making significant bets, and doubling down on earlier investments, despite uncertainty in the region.

Fadi's and Arif's instincts were, of course, prophetic. Only three months after the Dubai event, many of these same young people we met were protesting in Tahrir Square and other cities throughout the region, demanding open societies that would allow them to prosper.

∾

*Before Dubai, my own instinct was to summarily dismiss the likeli-*hood that Ghandour and Naqvi were right. In retrospect, I attribute this not only to my own regional bias, but also to the fact that I ignored everything I was witnessing in my own daily work running internet companies. I knew—as well as anyone—what level of innovation individuals are capable of when they build connections and share collaborative experiences through technology, no matter where they live. I should have known better.

My start in the early days of the internet was deeply personal. Within eighteen months in the late 1990s, I learned that my best friend suffered from crippling bipolar disorder and my mother-in-law was diagnosed with lung cancer that had spread to her brain. I am the grandson of Italian immigrants, so depression was not a disease, but something to "suck up." Cancer was only discussed in hushed tones among family and left in the hands of the doctors. Shocked by what turned out to be death sentences for both people I loved, I turned to the internet to try to understand things outside of my comfort zone.

This was nearly a decade before social networks, but I found small communities of people online who were going through similar experiences. We never knew each other, but in the months to come we taught each other, pointed each other to resources, and supported each other in troubling moments. When my loved ones lost their battles, these communities helped me process and mourn. I was a smarter, better informed, more sensitive support to my family and friends because of these connections. And I had no doubt that technology was unleashing not merely tools of convenience, but entirely new ways to share insight, build relationships, and take action. "You are not alone. You are not crazy. Actions you take can make a difference because others like you did the same." This has since become my stump speech on what this technology means for us. It was empowering and signaled a power shift. We as individuals could demand the transparency and make the connections to help us act. The world would change.

Some years later, a group of like-minded entrepreneurs and I decided to put our personal and professional experiences to work. We launched one of the first social platforms in health, HealthCentral.com, to aggregate "patient wisdom" in safe and trusted environments. Our company consisted of nearly fifty individual web and mobile sites where people who had "been there" could share their condition-specific experiences. We convinced some of the leading investors in the internet and media worlds to back us. Through the tumultuous ups and downs that characterize most startups, our platform grew to engage over 15 million people monthly. We were inundated daily with stories of people emboldened to step up, help each other, and better their own health as well as that of their loved ones.

It was on a chance trip during my tenure in my previous company—Washingtonpost.Newsweek Interactive—that the global ramifications of technology and collaboration hit me like a two-by-four. The *Washington Post*'s gracious and forward-thinking chief executive Don Graham asked me to visit Tokyo, Seoul, and Helsinki to get a closer look at these rapidly changing and advanced broadband and mobile societies. I spent several weeks with established CEOs and upstarts, thinkers, business professors, and students to see how they bought and used technology.

The cultures, histories and approaches in these countries are quite different from those in the United States. But the groundwork for social networks, mobile e-commerce, mobile texting, and shared video were well laid there several years before they became the norm here. My greatest epiphany, however, was that in expecting to see everything technology—a tech-powered, *Jetsons*-like world—I was unprepared to see almost nothing. Technology in these societies had become like water or electricity. People assumed its availability and simply embedded it in their day-to-day lives. Many were puzzled as to why I had made these trips at all. A diffusion of innovation—due to exponentially increasing access to information technology—was allowing entrepreneurs to create, collaborate, and affordably scale business to solve local, regional and even global problems as never before.

These societies were electrifying. And I began to wonder even then: what will happen when *every* country has similar access to these technologies?

The West tends to look at the world through the prism of its own successes, and believes that it has a monopoly on innovative ideas and entrepreneurship. Nothing amuses the entrepreneurs I meet around the world more than when some U.S. politician refers to entrepreneurship as a "leading American export," as if other, thousands-of-years-old entrepreneurial cultures have only recently discovered it. And one of the most common questions I hear from American entrepreneurs, investors, and policy makers as they consider looking at new growth markets is, what will be the "next Silicon Valley" of a certain region or country?

For all the hype, hubris, wealth, and celebrity associated with "the Valley," it remains an extraordinary place. It stands alongside Periclean Athens or eleventh-century Andalucía or Renaissance Florence for its raw, competitive, innovative zeal, which has utterly changed the world we live in. One cannot avoid stepping off a plane there without almost feeling the ubiquity of drive and innovation in almost every conversation in every restaurant, coffee shop, or bar.

Ben Horowitz, the former CEO of the tech juggernaut Opsware and co-founder of one of the most successful venture capital funds, Andreessen Horowitz, told me that what people most often underestimate about the Valley is the pure network effect of talent that is drawn to it. "Extraordinary engineering, product, creative people tend to attract the same," he told me, "to a point now that every company is tripping over themselves to attract the best—and the best really are in control of their own destinies here because of it." Mike Moritz, chairman of the legendary Sequoia Capital—a pioneering venture capital firm responsible for backing the likes of Apple, Google, Cisco, PayPal and LinkedIn which are among the other most successful technology companies in the world—agrees: "We try to find the most promising companies but if they are even a few hundred miles away—say Los Angeles and San Diego—our number-one challenge is to get the best people to move there."

"Interesting businesses are and will be created outside of the Valley, in the States and around the world," Horowitz readily concedes. "But think of the movie business. Great films are made in many locations, but there is a reason that the vast majority of successful films—certainly in aggregate dollars—come from Hollywood. That's where talent wants to be. There is Bollywood in India but it pales in comparison. In fact, how many technology startups outside of Silicon Valley or the U.S. have built multi-billion dollar businesses?" When I pushed venture capital investors who have opened up offices in emerging markets about why they do so, two consistent themes arise. First, they look for large market opportunities—one may lose money in a place like China, but for all its challenges it's too big to ignore. Second, emerging markets offer outstanding engineering and call-center talent, invariably much cheaper than in the United States.

As for opportunities for regional or even global innovation from the emerging worlds? "It happens all the time, especially for services aimed at local or even regional needs, which explains Alibaba, Tencent, and Baidu in China," notes Moritz. "But Silicon Valley has always been a magnet for immigrants. It's the place where raw technical abilities will always be embraced by successful companies and worldly leaders."

But what happens when the vast majority of talented people don't want to move—when they not only want to stay home, but are driven by almost patriotic passion to make change where they come from? The real question going forward won't be whether Silicon Valley is the only game in town or where the next one will crop up. Rather, it will be how rapid and inexpensive access to its innovations in software and devices will create new, multiple "hubs" of innovation in every corner of the globe. This will also challenge the West's definition of "innovation" as only the next shiny new thing. The word has different ramifications in emerging markets that are gaining ubiquitous access to software and devices for the first time. These markets create innovative solutions for their own challenges and opportunities. From their unique experiences and circumstances, in fact, their solutions may one day be adopted globally.

What if information technology could make geographic proximity and network effects of talent less important? We know this is already happening in our day-to-day lives. Skype, group chat, social networks, collaborative software, and other, ever-advancing video connections are already mainstream and improving daily. They have had clear impact on the social and political dialogue in every country where they are embraced. They create hubs of action in many walks of life—like the health seekers on HealthCentral—unimagined even five years ago, and tweaked by individuals to better attune them to local and regional cultural needs and norms. These experiences may not yet be as ideal as face-to-face proximity, but for a new generation raised on them, and by breaking down barriers of distance, might they be plenty good enough?

There is precedent for how local need-solving becomes globally competitive innovation in the hardware business. Certainly no one in the early 1980s would have expected Japan or Korea to become a dominant player in mobile devices and consumer gaming. Who would have imagined that Finland, a country known mostly for wood products, would create Nokia—a company that first used mobile communication to facilitate connections between forestry and milling locations hard to reach with traditional telephony?

Safaricom in Kenya (40 percent owned by Vodafone) in 2011 launched the first step in a global roll-out of smart phones for less than $90. Their screens are smaller than the iPhone's, their processing speeds lower, but they are genuine computing devices in the hands of people who never had access before. Over 350,000 were sold within several months. Basic cell-phone penetration in Egypt, a land of 80 million people with annual per capita GDP under $6,500, is over 115 percent. The penetration numbers hold true throughout the Middle East. Yet currently only 8 to 12 percent of these users have access to smartphones. Can we fathom what kind of innovation may come from countries—those that never even knew landlines—that attain mobile smartphone computing access of 50 percent or more of their citizens?

Mobile experts told me we could see $50 smartphones within three years to help drive this adoption. Should we be surprised that Kenya, with no legacy of wired telephone service and limited banking services, would be the birthplace of the mobile payments company M-Pesa—representing today nearly half of *all* mobile payments in the world, and processing 20 percent of the country's GDP?

Moritz concedes upon further reflection, "I've found in my travels that if you put great entrepreneurs from any corner of the world in the same room with each other, they are quite similar even if their mother tongues, religions, and colors are different. They look at the world, problems, and opportunities the same way. Their minds, their energies, and their desires to succeed are a *lingua franca*. They talk to each other as if they've known each other their whole lives."

Peter Thiel, the provocative but undeniably successful venture investor—an early backer of payment innovation companies like PayPal and Square, as well as social networks from Facebook to LinkedIn—seeks what he calls, "unobvious connections." Comfortable in the narrative of its own entrepreneurial success and relative absence of clear new competitors outside of its borders, the West may be missing an "unobvious" opportunity of historic proportion. We see innovation being harnessed in corners of the world all but until recently written off economically. We see rising middle classes across emerging markets. The ramifications should be clear.

∽

Is any of this, however, truly possible and scalable in the Middle East? In the face of brutal oppression in some nations and political uncertainty throughout the region, it's hardly an idle question. Added to political instability, the gap between the mega-wealthy and the desperately poor throughout the region remains shocking; education and literacy offer profound challenges. Corruption, high unemployment, heavy reliance on government largesse, archaic and often indecipherable rules of law, and cultural resistance to investing beyond fixed assets are all daily realities. For all the enthusiasm that came with the Arab Spring, Arabs are still debating vehemently the kinds of societies and governments they will create, what role religion and women will play, and how business practices will be proscribed. One need only spend a few days in Amman or Cairo, going through metal detectors in every restaurant, hotel, and tourist destination, to sense how the political and social realities can keep risk capital—and, indeed, business itself—sidelined.

There is no doubt that the political apparatus and context still matter greatly. As Arif Naqvi told me, "The direction of the Middle East will be determined by whether regimes in the region realize that twenty-first-century developments should not be met by a nineteenth-century mindset—that political reform will be matched by the unquestioned economic reforms and opening-up processes of the past few years."

But while we must take these concerns seriously, they can also mask the three-fold hurricane-force wind these entrepreneurs have at their backs.

First, technology offers an irreversible level of transparency, connectivity, and inexpensive access to capital and markets unprecedented only five years ago. A new generation in the Middle East, as elsewhere, has never known a world before information technology, and they have a keen understanding of how others like them live and create opportunity for themselves. They assume easy access to inexpensive technological, social, and collaborative tools to create businesses and affordably access once unreachable customers and markets regionally and abroad.

Second, this generation benefits from regional and global capital now more comfortable with political risk. Twenty years of experience in other emerging markets such as the BRICs (Brazil, Russia, India, and China), all but dismissed as economic engines less than a generation ago, has laid important groundwork. Nearly all of these countries were, and remain, equally marred by political uncertainty, opaque governments, corruption, and weak infrastructures. Yet significant investor returns there have established a comfort level with emerging markets across all sectors, and suggests sustainable economic opportunity could happen in the Middle East even more rapidly.

Third, changing market dynamics, growth, and opportunity in the Middle East were in motion well before the uprisings. As Vali Nasr, dean of John Hopkins School of International Studies, wrote in *The Rise of Islamic Capitalism,* his recent book on the macroeconomic rise of the Middle East, the demographics are staggering: "In 2008 the GDP of the economies of five of the largest countries in and around the Middle East—Egypt, Iran, Pakistan, Saudi Arabia, and Turkey, with a combined population of 420 million—was $3.3 trillion, the same size as that of India, which has three times the population." He adds that the Arab world alone has over 350 million people, nearly twice the size of Brazil; a GDP larger than Russia and India, and per capita GDP nearly twice China's. Disposable income has grown 50 percent over the past three years, to over $1 trillion in 2012. It's a young market, with over 100 million people under the age of 15, who love their connectivity and mobile phones.[1] Social media usage passed 25 percent in 2011, growing 125 percent year over year. The region has a tradition of entrepreneurship thousands of years old, and today more college and graduate students and engineers are turning to startups and medium-sized ventures than ever before. Even in countries with broader macroeconomic challenges, entrepreneurship has not only been a question of innovation but one of survival.

And this new generation is hungry. If there was one universal sentiment that connected every young entrepreneur I met it was this: their revolution was not merely about overthrowing longstanding dictatorships, but challenging a generational premise and complacency of their parents that things could not change. "Why should we accept mediocre jobs in lumbering large companies or the government—assuming we can even find those?" one Jordanian founder told me. "In fact, I don't understand why my parents accepted it!" One of the most common themes in emails I received during and after the Arab uprisings was a disdain for the word "stability." As one Egyptian executive wrote me, "It's not that we don't appreciate stableness—that the most successful ecosystem for entrepreneurs has this at their foundations. It's that the word 'stability' was used by the regimes and our parents as an excuse for accepting an unacceptable status quo. We can be better."

Even with all its fits and starts, recent events in Tunisia, Egypt, and elsewhere in the region have only convinced this generation that what once seemed impossible is, in fact, attainable. The protests have unified them in the conviction that what they are building is part of national and cultural missions. As one of the Egyptian entrepreneurs texted me from Tahrir Square during the protests, "I have always been proud to be Egyptian, but this is the first time I love my country. My work is Egypt's work." Another tweeted me more recently, "I will keep on saying this. Youth entrepreneurship is key in creating a long lasting impact in the Arab world!"

These entrepreneurs come from every walk of Arab life. They are women and men; devoutly religious and culturally Islamic; college educated and self-taught; young and old and from literally every country in the region. They are above all realistic about the odds against them, yet unfazed by the political and infrastructural barriers. They view the recent political change as an unprecedented opportunity and, in some cases, confirmation of their efforts over many years. They are unleashing social and economic forces that will create the foundations of a new Middle East. These forces will build and evolve over years, but will be accompanied with a speed and transparency through technology that will hold any leadership, and themselves, to instant accountability. These entrepreneurs are not naïve. They expect setbacks. But they believe they are on the right side of history.

So to me, the most interesting question of all is, why *wouldn't* the Middle East be ripe to unleash a new era of tech-based entrepreneurship and innovation of the sort that has driven growth and job creation around the world?

∽

I first began to piece together these questions sitting in the "network café" at the Jumeirah Hotel conference center on the second day of Celebration of Entrepreneurship, soaking up a large cappuccino amid young people head down over their BlackBerrys and iPhones. Dubai is a strange blend of familiar and surprising, a place one of my friends who recently moved there called "Vegas on steroids." Everything in the city is new and opulent, and as convenient and organized as a newer American city. Western shops are fronted by elegant billboards plugging regional cell phones, airlines, and hotels. A nearby luxury hotel has that view of the Gulf with a helipad seemingly suspended in mid-air, famous from luxury magazine ad campaigns with celebrities like Tiger Woods hitting golf balls over the edge.

Our conference center, like much of Dubai, was a wind-swept desert less than two decades earlier. Dubai City had grown from a few hundred thousand people to over two million in the same amount of time; currently less than 20 percent are indigenous Dubains, while the balance of the population hail from a hundred other countries. In a short time this multiethnic society had built the world's largest skyscraper and indoor ski complex, and an artificial reef filled with luxury villas that is shaped like the world when viewed from space. It was almost impossible to find a restaurant featuring local food, and my hosts scheduled me for successive nights of Chinese, Thai, and French cuisine, and the first Argentinian *churrasco* I'd had since my last visit to Buenos Aires. Dubai is an entrepreneurial city built by and for entrepreneurial dreamers. It was a perfect setting for this gathering.

At a table across from me was a young Kuwaiti, still amazed that more than a million people had downloaded his mobile game apps over the past two years—apps he'd created for his own amusement. He sat across from a 19-year-old coffee entrepreneur from Yemen who insists that every aspect of his operations (including packaging, which most producers outsource to China) be done in his own home community. Joining me for tea was that young, ponytailed DiCaprio lookalike whose Damascus-based computer animation company creates cheap, elegant short films for television, the web, mobile devices, and social networks. Running to a session speech, I was cornered by a stocky, affable thirty-something Egyptian entrepreneur with a shaved head who has developed technology to blend air into shower water in order to dramatically reduce water consumption, an obvious advantage in the Middle East. He handed me his business card, of which I'd received over 100 in my first day, because he wanted to pitch me later and talk about how best to gain patent protection. I never found that young Saudi woman with the luxury charger in the packed crowd, nearly a third of whom were women with their own ideas.

As I wandered through the long hallways lined with young people, I noted the energy of everyone—some in suits, others in jeans, still others in traditional Arab business dress and head scarves, all in animated chatter among themselves or on their mobile devices. There was a mobile text question-answering founder who wondered how much money he could raise. There was an entrepreneur with an innovative way to send and confirm documents securely on computing and mobile devices wondering when and how to staff up ahead of sales. The inventor of an iris-recognition technology wanted to know the best partnerships and reasonable business terms allowing him to offer his services to airports. All shared the common worries—do I have enough time? Will I make the right trade-offs? What if I fail?

Upon my return to the United States, I wrote an article for my former bosses at the *Washington Post* describing what I had just seen. The reaction to the piece was one of the largest and most moving of anything I had written. Experts in the Middle East economies and policies from leading "think tanks" and successful global venture capitalists and investors asked me if what I saw was large-scale and sustainable. Countless people in the region wrote in appreciation of the piece, all saying in some form, as one entrepreneur from Ramallah did: "Finally someone is telling our story."

Apparently the U.S. Department of State was also paying attention, because a month later, I was invited to return to Cairo by State's Global Entrepreneurship Program to be a judge for one of the first startup competitions there. My fellow judges included Austin Ligon, entrepreneur and founder of CarMax; Seth Goldstein, a successful serial Silicon Valley and New York entrepreneur and blogger who subsequently co-founded one of the hottest new music blog companies, DJZ; Faysal Sohail, a leading Palo Alto venture capitalist; as well as a top New York investment

banker, an MIT management scientist, and other emerging market investors, among others. All were widely traveled, and had a sense that
something new was happening in the region. Most had seen and even
successfully invested in entrepreneurs in other emerging markets with
their own versions of infrastructure, corruption, and cultural barriers.
Over the course of four days we drilled into 32 presentations to find two
winners, culled from hundreds of applications of web, mobile, and hardware startups throughout the country. The narrative I had seen in Dubai
was in full force in Cairo.

On January 17, 2011, I had an experience that suggested how the
nascent entrepreneurial revolution in the region is interconnected with
something bigger. I left my fellow judges in Cairo after the competition
to visit Damascus, a historic city with its own brewing narrative of entrepreneurship. Young entrepreneurs were harnessing remarkable technology, despite government restrictions on mobile access for data and social
networks like Facebook. Notwithstanding these limits, when I walked
past the desk of the warm and stylish boutique hotel in the old city—one
of over 65 that had been opened in recent years—I invariably saw young
people with their Facebook pages opened. I remember one internet advertising startup founder telling me, "The rules are a pain, but we figure
it out." That evening, I met several young Syrian entrepreneurs and more
senior business executives for drinks at the sleek, modern Four Seasons
Hotel below the hills and a few miles from the Old City. The large bar
area was thronged with a noisy crowd of executives from many countries,
buzzing over their interests and dealings. All at once, silence fell. People
studied their mobile devices, mouths agape. There was a pause for what
may have been seconds, but it felt like minutes. Then everyone started
speaking at once, saying the same thing in different languages: "He's
gone. He's really gone."

Zine el Abidine Ben Ali, Tunisia's dictator for more than two decades, had boarded a plane almost certainly leaving Tunisia forever.
Within minutes, I received a text from Ghandour: "This is the biggest
thing to happen in the region. Watch it closely. Bigger than your Iraq
invasion. Bigger than the '67 Arab-Israeli War. People want change, and

this will change things everywhere." A few weeks before, a young, educated man with few economic prospects and no job had set himself on fire in protest to being fined for merely trying to open a fruit stand without a permit. That one act had spiraled into this moment. All my drink-mates were in awe that a seemingly small protest could lead to this. Anything seemed possible.

Two days later I returned to Cairo for a last dinner before I was to fly back to the United States. At the table were experienced business professionals in their forties or older, a few government officials including representatives from the U.S. Embassy, and two young entrepreneurs from the competition. Tunisia was the central topic of conversation. "Sure this is big," one U.S. official told me, "But Tunisia isn't Egypt. Mubarak isn't Ben Ali. The army will never allow anything like this to happen here." I looked over at the young entrepreneurs, and one leaned over and said, "I don't know. Maybe they are right. But I'm not certain why we are that different."

Within a month, after 18 days of demonstrations, Mubarak resigned as president. A year later, he was serving a life sentence in an Egyptian prison amid rumors of his imminent death.

Syria, of course, is also the cautionary tale—a country of globally competitive talent and passion stifled first by government control and then squashed, for now, by government brutality. The most talented and creative entrepreneurs I have met there have either left for Dubai or other countries in the region or have dived deeply under cover. Some have been killed. The narrative of civil war and sectarian violence, the go-to expectation of so many in the West, seems to be playing out—and may very well win. But I do not bet on this over time.

"I have found that in the long run over history, when societies have a choice between taking their own destinies into their own hands or national suicide, it's not a good idea to bet on the latter," author and global policy expert Parag Khanna told me over a long afternoon of tea in the spring of 2012. He knows of what he speaks. Having lived in and traveled to almost every corner of the world—on the road 300 days a year—his books like *The Second World* are almost prophetic regarding the rise of emerging markets as central players on the world's stage. "What so many fail to understand," he says, as he stares hard into my eyes, "is that psychological barriers are dropping all over the world. The conspiratorial legacies of the Cold War—especially in the Middle East, Africa, and Latin America—are yielding to a new expectation of greater self-reliance." He added with a smile, "When you no longer think of yourself as just pawns in a superpower battle, or playing a rigged game, you want to step up."

Clearly something is afoot. Business, investment, and political leaders in the region and around the globe have a historic, and perhaps unprecedented, opportunity to embrace these young entrepreneurs as good investments on the ground floor of a much bigger world. At the same time, they can embrace these innovators and risk takers as central to truly new societies and economies in the Middle East. They have an ability to side with a new generation which is tirelessly and unrelentingly committed to offering paths to different and better lives. And in the active encouragement of this new era of entrepreneurship in the Arab world lies the foundation of global innovation for and from the Middle East.

Personally, I will look at the modern history of the Middle East as beginning at that conference in Dubai. While economic success is hardly assured there, the rise of a new generation of business entrepreneurs cannot be ignored. I decided to dedicate a year of my life to exploring the strengths and limitations of the rising entrepreneurial ecosystems of the region, and to shining light on a few of the thousands of young entrepreneurs. They are all not only innovating local, regional, and global enterprises, but they are also working to solve some of their long-ignored social and infrastructural challenges. I wanted to better understand the surprising power of the role of women and religion among these entrepreneurs. And I wanted to learn more about why many global technology juggernauts are doubling down in the region during this time of uncertainty. I hope that this book will encourage others to take a deeper look at this historic regional change and in turn provide the "a-ha!" moments I have experienced, and open minds to the unprecedented possibilities arising in the Arab world.

As such, *Startup Rising* opens itself up to challenges. As a matter of scope, I have focused on the Arab worlds—primarily Egypt, Jordan, Lebanon, Saudi Arabia, and Dubai—but mean in no way to give short shrift to similar remarkable and significant activities happening in the other Emirates, North Africa, the Gulf, Turkey, and even Iraq and Iran. The extraordinary ecosystem that is Israel has been well examined in Dan Senor's and Saul Singer's definitive *Start-up Nation* and many research studies and articles. Even so, experienced Middle East scholars and broader political scientists may argue that what I have seen represents a small fraction of Arab society and will be a sideshow to the traditional power politics of the region. Thoughtful economists and experts on emerging markets may well add that tech entrepreneurship cannot create enough jobs regionally fast enough, let alone compete globally with the more open societies of the West. Successful investors in emerging markets may argue that there simply are safer bets in other developing countries. And they may all be right.

But they should reconsider.

I offer no crystal balls here but, rather, hope only to challenge the traditional narrative of the Middle East in light of substantial and swiftly growing access to rapid technological change. To seek precedence and parallels in the past is safe, easy, and comfortable. But it is also what led some of the greatest minds to predict the strength of Mubarak's position just weeks before he fell. As the great automotive visionary, Henry Ford, is said to have, perhaps apocryphally, noted, "Had I listened to the market at the time, I would have built a faster horse."

Contrasting the potential of these entrepreneurs with tumultuous and unsettling events in Cairo, Baghdad, and Aleppo, I have often thought of a quote in a different context from a more recent visionary and descendent of Syrian immigrants, Steve Jobs: "And no, we don't know where it will lead. We just know there's something much bigger than any of us here."[2]

Chapter 2

Work-Around

"ENTREPRENEURSHIP ISN'T NEW TO THE MIDDLE EAST"

One of the most entrenched hurdles to entrepreneurship and innovation in the Middle East can be summed up in a single word: "wasta." I heard it for the first time when I visited the large and leafy campus of the American University of Beirut. It would, however, become one of the most common refrains whenever people described what it has traditionally meant to get ahead in the Middle East.

It is ironic that I learned it here. Situated on a beautiful bluff overlooking the sea, the well-groomed campus—a mix of over 60 stately, ultra-modern, eco-friendly buildings—conjures Palo Alto or Cape Town. It is hard to fathom that civil war raged outside its gates for two decades and that sectarian identity is still very much part of the student experience today. It seemed, and in many ways is, an oasis of independent thinking and perspective.

Founded in the mid-nineteenth century by American missionaries, AUB is still considered among the most highly esteemed educational institutions in the region and the world. It has remained true to its focus on a traditional liberal arts education, but boasts outstanding medical, engineering, and, recently, business programs. The school's original motto remains inscribed on the gates in Latin: "That they may have life, and have it more abundantly." When I was there, however, it was in the midst of a re-branding campaign perhaps more attuned to the Arab uprising times—"Leadership and Transformation."

I visited the campus to meet its gracious president, Peter Dornan, a leading Near East scholar who had made his name at the University of Chicago. He had arranged for me to spend time with some of their leading business school faculty, but it was a later, ad hoc sit-down with a dozen or so undergraduates that really grabbed me. Respectful and measured, students from across the region and of all disciplines described their passions, dreams and goals. But the cordial dynamic shifted when I asked them how many planned to pursue their careers in Lebanon.

In one voice they shouted, "No!"

Startled, I asked why? And, again, as one they barked: *"Wasta!"*

They were incredulous that I had not heard the word.

I had, however, encountered the concept. It meant, roughly, "a display of partiality toward a favored person or group without regard for their qualifications." But this literal translation belies the level of emotion it conjures among the new generation. Every student had his or her own example. Try getting a summer internship or a job interview, or navigating some regulatory permit process, they said—it was all about whom you knew, whom your parents or mentors knew, what favors they could cash in or bank for a later day. When the stakes were higher, it could mean outright bribery and threats.

"It's not only about getting in the door," one aspiring banker told me, "It means once you are there you have to work under layers, generations, of people who are there *not* because they deserve it but because of *wasta*. This is the best we can do?" He then urged me to put the concept to the test in my own travels. If I'm ever hassled by someone for any reason, he suggested, I should pick up my mobile phone and pretend to call some-one. More often than not the hassler will back down in case, in fact, I do know someone.

It is easy to get excited by the potential of startups in the Middle East, but impossible to ignore the legacy of *wasta* they have inherited in the region's often corrupt business environment. Entire books have been dedicated to the intricacies of these regional economies, and each coun-try has its unique history and experience. What they have shared—from wealthy oil sheiks in the Gulf to the benign and not-so-benign dictators elsewhere—is a history of governments using *wasta* to constrain capital and maintain political control. Regimes have survived for decades by allowing a select few to aggregate wealth and impeding others' access to capital. "Oil has obviously compounded this," one regional investor told me, "What incentive was there ever to diversify beyond oil and trade? And for those few who made their fortunes here, what incentive was there to share the wealth?" He paused for a long moment, "I'm not justifying anything, but before World War II, Japan and Europe had a long history of industrialization and manufacturing. After the War, the United States pumped billions for decades to help create diversification there. Hell, even after the War we were mostly Bedouins!"

The net effect, in economic terms, has been that while the income share held by the highest 20 percent of wealth concentration has been comparable to other emerging markets over the past decade (hovering between 40 and 50 percent),[1] overall economic prosperity has been much more stagnant. Outside of oil exports, real GDP growth rates in the 2000–2011 period have averaged almost 5 percent for the Middle East/North Africa region, which is much lower than that period's average growth rates for high-performing countries like China (10.4 percent) and India (7.7 percent).[2] In terms of real per capita growth, the Middle East/North Africa region as a whole performed the weakest among all regions in the world over the past two decades, with the exception of sub-Saharan Africa.[3] In addition, as the United Nations Development Program notes in its 2011 Arab Development Challenges Report, against a poverty line of $2.00 income per day, the Arab region has a 19 percent poverty rate, which is 60 percent higher than the rate of Latin America. Moreover, the region holds the highest overall unemployment rate among developing regions, and more than double the global average of youth unemployment rate: a stark 24 percent.[4]

The net effect, culturally, has been an entropy of acceptance that there only could be one way of doing business. One older executive told me, "When you thought about it, you felt terrible about it. You knew that in accepting this, in being close to the powers that be, how damaging it could be for society in the long run." But what, for years people argued, was the choice? *Wasta* can mean the difference between success and failure, or at its extreme even imprisonment. In most of the countries, government is the largest source of jobs and job creation, often with low performance expectations and little reward for those who take extra initiative. The upside, such regimes have long argued, is "stability." Growth may be slower, economic reform more gradual, but that is better than revolutionary Iran. "Some deal," one entrepreneur wrote to me, via email me during the Tahrir Square protests. "I hate the word 'stability.' I get the importance of 'stableness' from the perspective of having some day-to-day predictability for our families and businesses. But all my life the regime used that word to scare us, to keep us quiet. It suppressed our imaginations."

Yet despite all this, great entrepreneurs in the region still rose, even before mass access to information technology. What was it like for them? I began my investigation a little less than 150 miles southeast of Beirut, in Amman, Jordan.

The Fixer

Mohammed al-Ajlouni hates being called a "fixer," but that's what he was to major U.S. news organizations that came to Jordan in the early 1990s to cover the pending first Gulf War. "You have to understand, covering war was entirely different than it is today," ABC News correspondent and *NightLine* producer John Donvan recalls. John and I had become friends both in the news worlds, and later when our boys went to the same school. On one of my first trips to Jordan he told me I had to meet

Mohammed. Remembering those early days, he told me: "There were no mobile phones, no laptops or iPads, no easy ways to get, edit, and distribute video feeds on the run. You needed a permit for everything, needed to talk your way around everything. You needed someone on the ground that could just make things happen. When I met Mohammed, I knew I had lightning in a bottle."

Mohammed's belly laugh makes heads turn in any public space, and he almost fell out of the chair when I asked him for his version of how he got started. "To Americans," he caught his breath, "everyone is a 'fixer.' If I was a white boy, I would have run ABC. I simply knew more than they did." Ajlouni had started with the major local Jordanian TV station only a few months before as a young engineer. Because all the networks needed access to his studios and satellite uplinks, they were willing to pay handsomely for it. "We had already booked our two studios exclusively to CBS, but I recognized Donvan when he walked in with a colleague who spoke Arabic—about ten words," he laughs again. Wanting to help, he offered to improvise studio space in an extra storage room and lifted a prayer carpet behind Donvan as a back-drop. "Hey, it looked Middle Eastern," his eyes twinkled as he recalled. It was very difficult to get satellite signals from Iraq, and Jordan had limited satellite connectivity. But Mohammed made it work, and he quickly became the key point for all footage for CBS and ABC. He and Donvan formed an immediate friendship, and Ajlouni began working regularly on the side for ABC News. "I felt like I was royalty, making an additional $100 a day to do whatever they needed. I can tell you ABC got their stories up better and faster than any of the others." His experience convinced him to set up his own shop, Jordan Multimedia Productions, which, over the next two decades, became the largest source of television and studio access and equipment for the entire Middle East and North Africa.

Mohammed's background would not have predicted this outcome. He was born in a small town on the border of Syria, to one of the most important religious leaders and judges in the region. His family is said to have descended directly from the Third Caliphate, one of the successors of the prophet Mohammed. "My father was unique," Mohammed recalls.

"He wanted all of his kids to study in English—though he spoke none—because he believed the future lay in English." Born in 1936, his father had watched as England, a small island nation, expanded its empire around the world, and he read every day. "It was rarely religious books, but histories and thought leaders like Gandhi," Mohammed noted. "But he also insisted that we emphasize the sciences, as they would provide a better future than the humanities." His father visited a priest affiliated with a nearby Roman Catholic School, where his nine children would attend as the only Muslims. "And we did all right," Mohammed adds, "My siblings are doctors and engineers and professors. My path, let's just say, was different."

Mohammed's story is the stuff of improbable fiction. A restless, distracted and underperforming student in high school and at the local university, he heard from a friend about a program to study in Fort Smith, Arkansas. He had never been outside of Jordan (except for one trip to Syria at age fifteen), nor had he ever been on a plane. "Pictures of Fort Smith, all desert and flat buildings, looked like Jordan, so why not?" he recalled. He and his buddy filled out applications, secured visas and were accepted to the engineering program there. "This was the late 1970s, and our first lesson in America was all Trans Am sports cars and the TV show *Smokey and the Bandit*. We needed to make money, and we soon realized to extend our visas we needed a longer-term university affiliation. We heard that the cheapest opportunity was in Louisiana, and they had accepted sixty Arab students already. So we flipped hamburgers all the way down there."

His first encounter with *wasta* came after he received his engineering degree and returned to Jordan for his required four-year military service. Privates did the hardest work, and were paid the equivalent of $30 a month. With a well-placed connection, however, he became an officer at $700 a month and was assigned to cushier jobs in research and intelligence. "I really didn't know what I wanted to do when I got out," he recalled, "but something about TV in the States stuck with me; I wanted to do something with film." His father helped him get a job in a photo shop, where he worked in the darkroom. There was nothing particularly creative or artistic about his duties there, but he soon realized he loved the operations and, again through connections, landed a job in the back room of the largest local Jordanian television station.

His experience during the Gulf War led to an offer to run ABC News' newly-opened Baghdad operation, which he did until 2008, though he always maintained side projects of his own. "I learned that so many television media companies really had what were temporary needs," he recalls. "If you're going to do a story in Somalia, why buy and lug expensive equipment or build studio space? I bought cameras and rented them to media companies. I started printing cash on the side doing this, and setting up temporary 'studios' in hotels by building cheap temporary high walls with a big door." He was tempted to return to the West and learn more about best practices in news production, but realized the Middle East was where he had the edge. "You just couldn't find people like me easily in the region," he notes, "In the U.S. they wouldn't have given a fuck about me, but in the region, Peter Jennings never traveled anywhere for fifteen years without me." Mohammed decided to use his unique leverage to found his own company, Prime Television.

"Let me tell you what it meant to start a business in Jordan in the mid-1990s," Mohammed laughed. "It simply couldn't be done if you didn't know people. In fact, it holds true today, at least for businesses they understand and think will make money. You can't do anything in film without a permit—a physical piece of paper to film anything anywhere. It doesn't matter if it's in a public location. If you know the right people, each piece of paper each day takes ten minutes. If you don't know the right people, you simply won't get the paper at all. Do you know that the same guy is at the permit office 20 years later that I dealt with the first time?"

As he built a client list ranging from the BBC to one of the region's largest media companies, other local business executives began to wonder if Mohammed was getting "too successful." Mohammed wisely inoculated his business from his competitors by working the governmental system in two ways. First, he hired the son of one of the leading ministers as a partner, and second, he became indispensable to his clients.

"Jealous local media business types tried to screw with me, keep me from getting permits, etc. Hell, once I was thrown in jail for a few days and I still don't know why—just to show me they could, I suppose. But when you do great work for big media companies and become needed, that tends to be the best protection against the system you could have."

The protection, in a world of *wasta,* worked well and the business thrived with no questions asked. But what *wasta* gives with one hand, it takes with another. The very partner he chose to protect him in the system, knowing Mohammed had little personal money, told him he'd have to sell the company to him for a fraction of what it was worth. "I was pressured to take whatever price he offered, and there was no way to win on this, because he was so connected. So I had to take the deal."

Ajlouni chuckles when he recalls that the minister's son not only soon ran the business into the ground, but his father was summarily fired when the Jordanian king changed governments. The new prime minister had been an admirer of Mohammed's, and helped him establish a new news service business, with full licenses and permissions to function throughout Jordan. But at a price. In order to get uplinking satellite licenses with the Jordanian television company he had to, yet again, bring on a "connected" partner. "So I gave up a chunk of my company to a guy I didn't know in order to play big. But look, one day I had nothing, the next day my time had come," he guffawed. "But what kind of way is this to do business, truly?"

He established ABS Network in 2003 to offer reporting, satellite, and electronic news gathering facilities. By 2005 he had operations in Jordan, Iraq, Afghanistan, and Lebanon; the following year he opened studios in Dubai. Five years later, the Arab uprisings came and changed the dynamics again. "After the Wars I learned that newer markets were good places to start—places like Iraq and Afghanistan and now Libya and Tunisia and I hope shortly the rest of Africa—because the rules of *wasta* either were thrown out or would have to change. Maybe new rules would be set up, but for a time there are no rules, none of that nonsense, so I could just leverage my existing structure and do things." He also argues that after the uprisings, *wasta* may finally be in its waning days.

Regimes anywhere looking for their piece are simply more hesitant. "I think the effect on the old ways of business-as-usual are huge in all this change, in all the transparency brought by technology," he argues. "Before, in Egypt, you needed Mubarak's son as a partner to do almost anything in business, especially as a new entrepreneur. If the new President Morsi had a son who tried this, no chance."

He has been operating in Libya and Tunisia for a year and has encountered almost no red tape, and he wonders whether Egypt will open up. In Saudi Arabia and the Gulf, however, it's business as usual, at least for now. "The numbers and deals are always moving around—you never know what you have there without your influencers." And he still looks over his shoulder, just like anyone else his age raised in the Middle East. "The reality of my life always has been, and it hangs over your head now, if they are going to unplug you they will unplug you." But he believes equally that the business environment for entrepreneurs, for all the political uncertainty, is just easier than when he started two decades ago. "Of course the internet has really changed things I think for good. If you want to truly understand that transition, however, you need to talk to your friend, Fadi Ghandour."

The Ecosystem Builder

All roads from the past to the future of entrepreneurship in the Arab world seem to pass through Fadi at some point. His story is different from Ajlouni's, but offers equal insight in what it has meant to be an entrepreneur in the Middle East, and the transition that is coming.

At 53, Ghandour's groomed stubble of a beard has turned slightly gray, but his daily two-mile swims give him the taut look of someone much younger. His eyes often dart as he processes questions and makes connections in his mind. I had met him through YPO in 2003, and we have since debated world politics and social justice. Sitting down for a long breakfast in New York City in the summer of 2012, however, was the first time we compared notes about what it meant to be an entrepreneur in the Middle East. His answers were deliberate, but his voice rose with passion when he wished to make a point. "I didn't ever know I was an entrepreneur, just a businessman," Ghandour reflects on his earliest days, shrugging. "But I can tell you, man, it was hard," he sighed before his eyes quickly lit up and he laughs. "I felt then, as I do now, that doing something new had its advantages. You could get a lot done before the system understood that you might be changing the whole business ecosystem."

Ghandour is the son of Ali Ghandour, an entrepreneurial icon who, in 1962, founded Royal Jordanian, Jordan's national airline. A graduate of NYU's aeronautical engineering school, Ali Ghandour first met King Hussein of Jordan in 1957, when the U.S. Federal Aviation Agency referred the king to him to get his American plane fixed. (At the time, Ghandour was the FAA's sole authorized inspector in the Middle East.) He had also been the senior vice president and head of engineering at Lebanese International Airways, Lebanon's first private airline. Politics would reunite the King and Ghandour in 1962, when Ghandour received a death sentence for his alleged part in that year's coup against the Lebanese state. The King learned of Ghandour's political troubles, invited him to Jordan, offered him protection and asked him to set up the country's first national airline. Over time, the professional collaboration would grow into a political one, making Ghandour—despite being a staunch democrat—one of the King's closest confidants over the course of three decades.

Fadi's father ingrained in his children a broad sense of social justice tempered by a can-do pragmatism. Fadi recalled, "We learned early on that you cannot be neutral in anything you do. He believed if you see something in your nation that is not working you *have* to fix it. There is no place for idle people—every citizen is a beholder of the law, but you don't need the law to tell you what to do or to wait for the law to do things." Not only did the household buzz with discussion of politics and business, but Fadi got to witness his father in action. "One of my early memories was in 1969 when a faction of the PLO downed a Swiss Air flight. My father was the head of the Arab Air Carriers Organization and became the chief negotiator among all parties. This included the IATA (the International Air and Travel Association) because there was a call by some European airports to boycott handling the Arab airlines, and they met at our house. I heard it all. I saw his unwavering commitment to finding a solution. It was much like the way he raised us."

However, he also learned the hard lessons of trying to effect real change through government. His ideals and his pragmatism seemed destined to clash in the conservative country. "In many ways my father never wanted to be in politics, but he always was an activist, he always wanted to make things better. He believed that in politics in the end, you always lose because you can't change government easily, small people will try to hurt your reputation—there is no fun in it. More often than not you just get hurt." He paused and looked into the distance. "I'm sure his being sentenced to death loomed huge in our family for all the obvious reasons."

His father insisted that his children study in the United States. "There was no discussion about it. If you had the means in the Middle East in the '70s, you just did it, assumed it was the best." He was accepted to George Washington University in Washington, D.C., where he lived with his mother and two sisters, who had to relocate to the United States to address his youngest sibling's hearing impairment and learning disability. His other sister attended Holton Arms, a top private high school. "It was not a normal college experience in this way," he recalls. "But we all made it work."

Despite how he was raised, Fadi did not seriously engage in politics, let alone social activism, until he got to the United States. College was the first time he really had to engage with other opinionated people, gather facts, and argue his position outside of his family. It was a culture shock. "The campus didn't have many students from the Arab world, and those who were from the Middle East were made up primarily of Iranians (the Shah was still in power at the time) and lots of American Jews. I had never really known a Jew except for television and, other than some family vacations to Lebanon or Cairo, I really didn't have much contact with the rest of the Middle East. They loomed large in the political debate on campus on the region. And they were really smart, and really prepared. I wasn't. It triggered something in me."

He studied engineering at first because it and medicine were considered by many in the Middle East to be the clearest path to a prestigious job. After almost failing, however, he turned instead to political science and became a leading campus activist for Arab issues. Soon, everything he touched took on a serious intensity. "My father and his friends all thought I was a revolutionary. I just didn't do what others did, especially others like me from the region." Notwithstanding, Fadi initially thought he might return to Jordan and enter politics, but mostly he was drawn to do something new, to work around existing systems, to have impact. These desires sparked a life-long passion for entrepreneurship.

"In many ways I had no clue what I wanted to do. What I did know is I wanted to make impact and didn't have any patience for the bullshit of the systems around me. *Wasta* was everywhere, and even while I had all the connections of course," he frowns, "I hated all of it." His father wanted him to work as a central bank employee in Amman, but from the first interview, no aspect of the job seemed relevant to him. They told him to come back for a second interview and take a test. They never saw him again.

Back at college, Fadi had begun to hear about a relatively new logistics company called Federal Express. One night he and a classmate had a long conversation about the potential in the company, and how behind the postal system was in the Arab world. He didn't give it much more thought until some months later at the Paris Air Show, where he met up with Bill Kingson, an old family friend and successful entrepreneur. Kingson was establishing a business to deliver canceled checks in the United States and was contemplating doing the same in the Middle East. It was 1981 and the 22-year-old Ghandour became increasingly intrigued by the opportunity in logistics in the region. He joined a rental car company in Amman, mostly as a home base from which to research courier services. He took two weeks off to travel to the United States to meet all of the early services at that time—FedEx, Purolator, Burlington Northern—and was inspired. "We barely had decent post offices in the region," Fadi recalled, "So the bar of expectations was low. No one in government really knew what the logistics business was, so I knew I could start building by moving fast and not having to worry about all the bureaucratic stuff until I started getting successful. I knew I could do this." In 1982, Fadi envisioned building a company that would own no aircraft but serve as a wholesaler—a general contractor of sorts—in the Middle East for the logistics players in North America. Aramex was born.

It has since become the largest logistics company in the Middle East and North Africa, and recently acquired operations in South Africa. But the early years were full of near-death experiences. "Every problem an entrepreneur could face we had—mistakes because we were just start-ing, mistakes in hiring, mistakes in firing, regulatory hassles in getting goods shipped among countries in this region, running low on cash." Growing to become the first local company in the region to go public in the NASDAQ in 1997, going private again in 2002 in a management buy-out with the Abraaj Group, and a subsequent new public offering in Dubai solidified the company's position.

Preparing for the company's twenty-fifth anniversary in 2007, Ghan-dour found a copy of his mission statement from the early 1990s—a time when success was hardly guaranteed. He was startled to find that back then, years before "corporate social responsibility" or CSR came into vogue in Western business schools and corporate publicity cam-paigns, he had written: "We want to be the leading corporate citizen in our region." As we'll explore later, Aramex—and Fadi himself—have more than proven true to CSR, but the mission statement's meaning also reflected practical lessons. "There is no *wasta* in stepping up to the com-munity. It is the right thing to do, but as there was so little tradition of it in the Middle East, we stood out by embracing our role in the community. Why are we here? To build a great business, sure. But what future are we really creating for our kids if the communities around us aren't building as well?"

If Ajlouni was about taking the punches of *wasta* and keep tena-ciously coming back, the same could be said for Fadi or any entrepre-neur trying to start something. But Ghandour proved that a lot can get done playing on a brand new field, where *wasta* didn't yet exist—or would be slow to catch up. "You had to know people, as I did, you had tons of paperwork to get any business going, but logistics was new—we could get really far just by moving faster than the system, and dealing with the ankle weights when they rose. We became leaders in corporate social responsibility because no one had heard of it, no one knew what to make of it, so we just did it." He paused, smiled, and looked straight at me. "So when the internet came I knew it represented change for not only the new generation of entrepreneurs who got all over me about it, but all of Arab society. There is no *wasta* in the internet."

"Business in the Middle East will be seen as before and after Maktoob."

"It really is hard to understand where we've been in the Middle East and where we're going without sitting down with Samih Toukan," Fadi told me, "He is at the core of the ecosystem today—a founder, a torch-bearer, even an adventurer. He comes from a respectable family, but he is totally self-made, totally an entrepreneur." Samih and his partner Hussam Khoury founded Maktoob in 2000, one of the first all-Arabic internet portals, in Jordan. It made headlines in 2008, when Yahoo! bought it for $175 million. No other internet company in the Arab world had been sold for a fraction of that amount. "The exit was great, don't get me wrong, but there is bigger learning here," Fadi cautions. "If anyone understood that there was no *wasta* in the internet, it was Samih. No one in government understood websites then. There was no legal jurisdiction—it was a gray zone without rules. He built it on independent investors and never felt beholden to government for anything. He is representative of an up-and-coming middle class that will change things because they are not beholden to anything other than their ambitions."

Samih doesn't like to overplay the point, but he absolutely believes his experience gave other young startups a sense of hope, that an entrepreneurial ecosystem could be created in spite of the old ways of doing business. "We have a long way to go still," he told me over an early breakfast at the tony Grosvenor Hotel in Dubai. Toukan brings his own energy field with him. Tall, lean, and intense, he looks almost professorial in his wire-rimmed glasses. "It's ten times better today. There is real independent money available, people who've been there willing to mentor, and more examples of successful startups. But what really happened in the region was an explosion of ideas. It took us almost a decade to have our 'overnight success' with Maktoob. It's all moving much faster now. In fact some of our employees have spun out to build their own businesses. Those businesses are encouraging others to do the same."

I began to think there was something to my professor analogy when I learned he came from a family of academics. He was born in Amman, Jordan, the son of two economists trained in the West, his father a successful banker. His sister and uncle are both economists, but Samih was drawn to science and engineering. He earned a degree in electrical engineering, and later an MBA, at the University of London, and returned to Amman to be an IT consultant for Anderson Consulting. "Most of what we did then was systems integration advisory work, and I learned that firstly I was good at it, and secondly there was a lot of demand. I hated working for a big company, so I decided to break off and start my own."

In 1994, and against his parents' wishes, he left Anderson with a colleague to start his own consulting company, Business Optimization Consultants (BOC). They found it difficult to find customers because they no longer had the vaunted Anderson brand. There was, however, one exception: Fadi Ghandour had worked with his team at Anderson and liked what he saw. "They had done a lot of great re-engineering work for our sales processes," Fadi recalled, "So I was happy to keep using them." In some ways, Samih really didn't know what services to offer until one weekend he read Michael Hammer's *Re-engineering the Corporation*. "So that Monday, that was my pitch to Fadi—we need to do some re-engineering for you." Not knowing exactly what that might mean, Samih sat down and began to whiteboard with company executives and learned that they had become a traditional, department-run organization. "We made them work in customer teams—green team, red team, across all services. Really became organization change agents for them." Fadi loved it and became an investor in BOC as well.

Other clients followed, but Samih and the team weren't satisfied. "Most of us were born in and around 1969," he recalls, "And we had strong feelings about our region, that our worlds and the world more broadly could be a better place. It's hard to do that by selling hours. Being a consultant is like reading a book, you finish it and move on. We wanted something sustainable, something of higher impact." He and the team brainstormed a series of ideas, but it wasn't until a trip to London that the switch truly flipped. He and Hussam visited their first internet café—a hole in the wall with exasperatingly slow service. For the first time, however, they were finding what seemed like an infinite array of content—articles about Jordan, photos of Petra, the world at their finger-tips. They stayed for hours. And they kept returning. On the plane ride back they both agreed: the internet was it.

Back in Jordan, where there were no internet service providers, it was all but impossible to log in other than through an expensive long-distance modem. "We spent $2,000 a month," Samih laughs now, "But it was a good investment. We found Hotmail and created an account, but of course, there was nothing in Arabic. This gave us ideas for what would become Maktoob."

They began by developing the first websites for their corporate clients. Aramex, in fact, launched its first website in the Arab world through them. "We watched these sites get traffic for no reason. Custom-ers just found our sites—first a few hundred, then a few thousand," he remembered. "And by 1998, we knew Hotmail was hot, but that for our region, language was crucial. Maktoob means, literally, 'a letter,' but also means 'written' or 'destiny.' And it was easy for English speakers to pronounce." They launched the first email service in Arabic for the public and received 5,000 users in their first month. In those days that number seemed impossibly high, and BBC sought them out for an inter-view, skeptical of the figures.

What of government bureaucracy or headaches? Samih laughs. "We built the first website for the late King of Jordan, but no one really knew what we were doing so we just moved." He discovered, however, that with speed came a long-standing cultural challenge of mistrust. "People liked what we offered, but really didn't trust the internet. What does internet 'service' mean? You are with the Secret Service?" Interestingly, though,

American internet brands were instantly trusted, so his company also packaged and sold Netscape as part of their offering.

By 2000, they had reached 100,000 users, and other companies began to appear—like Arabia Online, the first purely Arabic content portal across all subjects. Samih and the team, however, believed focus was the key. Email was the killer app, and they drove hard here, raising $2 million from regional investors to drive users even before they had a business plan beyond the corporate website-building business. By 2003 they had broken the million-user mark, and it nearly killed them. "We were 30 people, and everyone was doing tech or customer service. There were no server farms then, no cloud. I can remember my partner Hussam literally carrying servers on his shoulders to hook them up as fast as he could to ensure clients weren't down too long." And they constantly plotted ways to educate their audiences and make it easier for them to come on board. "There were no Arabic keyboards then," Samih told me, "So at our own expense, we sent thousands upon thousands of Arabic stickers people could put on English keyboards to help them type in Arabic— people never forgot us for this."

At the million-user mark they began to experiment with other services. They introduced chat and group rooms, and encouraged local celebrities—singers, politicians, actors—to host weekly chats, which helped the company's credibility grow. News and sports soon followed, and forums and user-generated discussion boards. Internet advertising was in its infancy, and they made a little money in sponsorships, but they still had no clear revenue stream, despite their tremendous audience. When the global tech bubble burst after September 11, they were lucky to have met Fadi's investor, Arif Naqvi of the Abraaj Group. "I watched my own kids," Arif told me later, "I knew the internet was going to be huge." They invested for 20 percent of the company that helped Samih roll up other smaller online companies that were growing in different countries. "These other companies had great audiences, but no business plans or home for revenue, usually one guy somewhere. We could buy them for a few hundred thousand dollars, more than they ever guessed they'd be worth, and we would continue to aggregate audiences large enough to get the advertising dollars that had to come one day." Rolling up the largest women's content site in Saudi Arabia, the leading sports site in Jordan and others, they grew their audience first to five million, and then ten million by 2005.

The following year, though they were not consciously looking to be bought, they felt the scale they had achieved could yield interesting business development possibilities with the large U.S. players. Samih recalled, "Some responded to my calls and emails, others did not. AOL did not. Yahoo! did." He was first approached by their team in Singapore, which led Yahoo!'s efforts in emerging markets, and they immediately understood Maktoob's potential. In a subsequent trip to Mountain View, California, Samih met then-CEO Terry Semel at Yahoo!'s headquarters. However, China was the only international priority on his mind.

Their discussions went dark until several years later, when Yahoo! Singapore called on Samih once again. By coincidence, Tiger Management, a leading investment fund from New York, had recently invested in the company, and the South African e-commerce company Naspers had also started courting them for partnership or even buying some of their assets. "We had recently taken the Abraaj money and weren't looking for any of this. But Tiger offered a valuation for something like four times what Abraaj had invested, and we figured they would be well connected in the States and could move our stalled business development desires." The activity made Yahoo! even more interested. "I think Naspers thought we were bluffing," Samih recalled, "Because Yahoo! got very serious all of a sudden, and finally wanted to negotiate with us exclusively." What had started as a business development conversation became a bid to acquire them outright. "Everything was normal for me until the day it happened," he adds. "Even my family didn't know all this drama until the day the deal was signed."

Yahoo! had taken only their portal and email business, and Samih was left with four or five experimental companies Maktoob had started on the side—Souq.com, the e-commerce platform; CashU, the cash payments company for e-commerce and several internet gaming properties. "I knew within that first week that my role in life would change substantially. I had some money now. I had these small companies with great potential. Once, my mission was to grow a company. Having seen what I had seen with startups throughout the region, I knew now I could play a role growing an industry and to support the entrepreneurs." He found separate CEOs for each of his companies, and launched the first internet holding company and investment firm, Jabbar. He raised additional capital, for these assets and for a war chest for future acquisitions and new company launches. And they offered entrepreneurs common resources like office space and financial, strategic, and legal help so that they could focus on creating ideas.

"Let me tell you," Samih stares hard at me. "We do not have a lack of ideas or a lack of innovation. We assuredly have the people. We have large markets and can be gateways to larger markets. What we don't have yet is the support infrastructure at scale and we don't, culturally, fully believe in it yet." He shrugs and continues, "Imagine if ten years ago some kid in the Arab world came up with Facebook? Maybe his friends would have told him he's stupid. Maybe his Dad wouldn't let him quit his 'safe' job." He pauses for a long time, "But I'm telling you it is changing. I see it every day. Spend time with our companies and many others like them. You'll see. Spend time with these new companies!"

And, of course, I did.

Chapter 3

The New Breed

While the development and sale of Maktoob was a signal event, it also paralleled broader consumer adoption of technology in the region. In October 2012, Booz & Company and Google released extensive research on what they call "The Arab Digital Generation," or ADG. Focused on three thousand digital users in nine countries, all born after 1997, their findings were striking, suggesting that the Arab world's internet appetite has been moving at a clip to rival any other region in the world.

While the region lags others in internet penetration, the number of internet users in Arab countries has been growing faster (23 percent annually versus a global 14 percent), and it's expected to exceed 140 million next year. As mobile penetration exceeds 100 percent in almost every country, and smartphone reach is expected to break 50% percent within three years, online access will accelerate. Those who are online tell a remarkable story of change over the last five years, with clear ramifications for the future. Eighty-three percent use the internet daily, and half of those for at least five hours a day. A whopping 78 percent said they prefer the internet to television, and 44 percent say that they spend less time meeting friends face-to-face than online or on their mobile devices. More than half want to pursue their own ambitions in both education career. Unsurprisingly, over 40 percent would like to start their own businesses.[1]

What kinds of businesses are this new breed of entrepreneurs creating to meet these new market dynamics? In these still early days, startup ideas have for the most part fallen into three categories. *Improvisers* are enterprises that have adopted models already proven successful in English-speaking markets, and have Arabized the experiences both in language and cultural sensitivities. *Problem Solvers* are entrepreneurs who see local and regional challenges, once thought of as government's role to solve, and make businesses out of solving them. And those in the third category, *Global Players*, know from the beginning that they are developing unique companies that can reach and have impact in any market.

Improvisers and the Rise of E-commerce

Attend any startup conference in the Middle East, and you will feel utterly at home. Familiar enterprises abound—not knock-offs per se, but companies that address similar consumer needs to their Western counterparts, only sensitive to the unique local market and culture. Maktoob, of course, was a leading example but there are hundreds across any vertical. Jordan's Altibbi.com would remind any American of WebMD, but it uses additional anonymity in message boards to protect female users in the region. ArabMatrimony.com is the leading "dating site" in the Middle East, though I am regularly corrected by locals that in the Middle East there are no "dating sites," only "marriage sites."

Some of the most visually alluring and innovative games in the world are now being developed quietly in the Arab world, while drawing global audiences. However as *Falafel Games* founders Radwan Kasmiya and Vince Ghossoub note, you will not find "any U.S. Marines fighting their way through war-torn Beirut in our stories." Since 2008, they have released dozens of browser-based games attuned to their experiences growing up in local cities or countrysides, perhaps touching on local food and music. Lebanon's Game Cooks focuses on mobile gaming, UAE's Tahadi

Games and Jordan's Maysalwar embrace and expand social gaming, and Egypt's Nezal Entertainment leverages the founders' experiences in Tahrir Square with a Facebook game that uses those eighteen days as a backdrop. And now, to keep up, international players like the U.S.-based Zynga are supporting Arabic in their new releases, and Turkey's successful Peak Games is targeting the entire Middle East region.

We in the West tend to think of innovation as the next, new, shiny thing and some investors look down on the improvisers. But in emerging growth markets, new access to existing technologies (e.g., higher-speed broadband, mobile phones, smart devices), can not only reach sizeable markets, it can lead to fresh and surprising thinking about local and regional problems. "This stage is normal and to be expected," enthused Samih Toukan, whose Maktoob was often called the "Yahoo! of the Middle East" even before it was acquired. He believes that improvisers have the easiest path to success and are natural building blocks that conservative investors here can understand. "You were never going to have Facebook in any growth market on day one," he notes. "It takes time to build belief in an ecosystem, and success breeds success." He believes that people outside of growth markets like the Middle East do not understand that these businesses are actually innovative for their regions and help build up the regional tech environments. "Fine by me," he smiles. "I get to see all the best companies first."

No area of opportunity generates more excitement locally, and has as much immediate and future market opportunity, as e-commerce. Statistics vary among studies, but the size and potential are clear. The growing consumer population in the Middle East is spending over $1 billion online, expected to more than double over the next three years. Gaming has historically represented about 40 percent of online purchases, and with women representing a relatively small 32 percent of online shoppers, a shift to broader consumer categories is expected. In fact, two-thirds of online consumers say they use the internet to research products and services for purchase on and offline. Total current value of the offline retail sector in the Middle East is roughly $425 billion, and Google estimates that fewer than 15 percent of Middle East businesses yet have n online presence. When even a small percentage of these come online, the growth estimates expand significantly.[2]

Encouraging as these statistics are, they belie two key historic and cultural barriers that have limited e-commerce growth in the region to date. First, each country has its own unique—and often opaque—shipping regulations. "E-commerce has blown out in the United States, but that is because of the easy free flow of goods across every state," Fadi told me. "Imagine if every state had its own customs, its own numerous bureaucrats checking every package, making delivery and tracking unreliable for whatever reason, adding fees and taxes every step of the way. That has been the Middle East through today, it is the greatest challenge." In fact, the Booz/Google study found that the "considerable regulation of cross-border trade means that tariffs and duties tend to be relatively steep. It can be cheaper to buy an item from the U.S. and ship to Dubai, for example, than buying from Dubai and shipping it to Riyadh (Saudi Arabia)."[3] Street addresses and address systems also vary by country, making it difficult to deliver packages even after they have finally cleared customs.

Second, credit card usage in the region is among the lowest in the world, even for in-person store and restaurant transactions. Statistics vary, but it is estimated that in a region of over 350 million, fewer than 10 percent have credit cards and while significantly more have debit cards, holders do not actively use either online. E-payments like PayPal, not to mention mobile payments, are in their early days even by African standards. The result is that well over two-thirds of all transactions in shipping in the Middle East is cash on delivery, or COD. Fadi Ghandour laughs when he considers it. "I can't tell you how many times customers deal with Aramex drivers delivering goods like they are the merchants! Arabs love to haggle, so they want a discount or find something wrong with the good or simply say they don't want it." The costs of finding addresses and dealing with repeat visits alone can add 3 to 5 percent to the cost of delivery. Returns in the region hover at between 17 and 25 percent due to COD, and is four to five times less when payments are done online.[4] Beyond that, Fadi notes, there are cultural sensitivities around the mere act of delivering a package in some places. "In Saudi, we tried to deliver during regular hours, but the men are at work and the women are at home alone. You can imagine what that brings up. I've had drivers tell me they had to escape from husbands coming home threatening them at gun point!" Even those in the digital generation prefer to deal with an actual salesperson, and see a product before they buy it. They are reluctant to use credit or debit cards online, concerned about fraudulent websites and/or payment theft.[5]

However, this is changing, as illustrated by the GoNabit story. As a Canadian pioneer in the interactive couponing world in the Middle East, Dan Stuart has a unique worm's-eye view to the challenges and changing opportunities. He and his local partners built the first Groupon-like deal business, GoNabit, in Dubai in May 2010. The company was acquired by Groupon competitor LivingSocial in June 2011, who later shut down the business to focus on more mature markets like Spain, Australia, and Canada. I sat down with Dan in Dubai shortly after their decision. "I respect their focus, and they have treated me and the team exceptionally well," Dan told me at the top of the Media One Hotel, which overlooks the growing Dubai skyline. Tall, lean, and athletic, his warm smile and casual air belie his status as a hardened veteran of Middle East startups. "It's a shame though. Our recently landing our first $1 million customer and that we spawned dozens of direct and indirect competitors here, tells you how much is changing."

GoNabit's business, like other "virtual goods," never had to deal with the shipping concerns of other e-commerce players. But they all wrestled with the resistance caused by cultural uncertainty. "By definition, we had to be very hyper-focused on the relatively smaller number of credit card holders across the region, and this differs widely from the UAE to Lebanon to Egypt. We had to tease out those who really wanted to buy things and cared about getting the most from their money and discovering new local places," he recalled. Credit card buyers were a good place to start, because such buyers, while relatively small in number, were wealthier and willing to pay. Their marketing strategy was simple, based on two questions: how can we reach people already online, and do they have the means and mechanisms to pay? "We learned though, that having a credit card and money didn't mean conversions right away. Trust really is a central issue, as the market had little when we got there. It's changing, but in 2010 people didn't think or trust to go online when thinking to buy, because almost nothing was being sold online in the region."

Much of this uncertainty, he believes, was a timing issue, reflecting lack of education and experience among the customer base. Dan had an epiphany two years ago as he arrived at O'Hare airport in Chicago, where he saw that ads for online sites were everywhere. Taking the subway into the city, on every platform advertisers were pushing waiting passengers toward dot-com opportunities like online food ordering at local restaurants, and posters for Facebook apps covered the walls of the airports, including ads for app developers on the baggage carousels. "I knew that this was the case in the States, but it reminded me that the internet is so pervasive here that one can advertise offline and outdoors and safely assume the people seeing the ads are online, and have the means to pay online. I can tell you that a billboard on the side of a road in Cairo promoting something dot-com would be seen by a huge number of people, but have little, if any, commercial impact." He recalled that, in their first research questionnaire as GoNabit, over 25 percent of GoNabit users said that their first online buying experience took place the previous month. "We were the entry point for so many people to buy online. People used to say years ago that eBay was like training wheels for e-commerce for sellers—helping them get online. Guys like us needed to be the training wheels for buyers." Further, he argues, the enterprise security companies have done a great job of spreading fear among consumers. "Semantic, a huge enterprise software security company, has the resources and has done well selling to people's fears and have been way ahead of the e-commerce companies in 'educating' the market."

But over the last two years, GoNabit began to see the light. They partnered with banks that already had credit card users or were hoping to encourage new ones. And they found they could grow their email lists at a third to a half of the cost in the United States, building a database of hundreds of thousands of potential online buyers they could sell to and educate. The challenge was mining these member lists for qualified buyers and activating as many people as possible. "There is still a glass ceiling of e-commerce buyers and sellers to reach in the Middle East. One can't just spend and spend and hope people will convert to whatever you are selling. But the glass ceiling is quite rapidly moving up as more people become comfortable, as entrepreneurs are taking care of the challenges of delivery and payments and creating great online offerings." And for e-commerce sites moving real goods, he believes that logistics companies like Aramex are taking the complexities, if not the sticker shock, out of shipping across borders, while new payment solutions are springing up. "When I started there was barely one passable payment solution, and few brands in the region had any interest in investing money here." Dan pauses and smiles. "The biggest difference today is that both buyers and sellers are asking *me* daily about how to transact online. Logistics and online payments are still expensive, but now brands and entrepreneurs alike are stressing systems to make them work. Investment is increasing and e-commerce is seeing more interest as people are spending real money online. It may not be ready to explode, but there's an industry now that's waiting for smart people to make it more efficient."

Hassan Mekail, one of the leaders of Aramex's e-commerce group, could not agree more. Tall, broad, bald, and wearing sunglasses that could not mask his intense gaze, Hassan has the energy of an American football player. He speaks rapidly and with authority. "I see the numbers every day. I know that we are shipping in 2012 300 percent more than over a year ago, all driven by online orders. Is it still too difficult to move packages through customs? Sure. But that is our expertise." We were driving through the desert from downtown Dubai to the newly opened Dubai Logistics City (DLC). Currently focused on cargo, the DLC will be the next home of the new Dubai airport. Looking out the window, I imagined that the flat, dry terrain, punctuated by the occasional small office building or mall, is what all of Dubai must have looked like only a decade or so earlier. Then, on the horizon rose two 40,000-square-meter warehouses emblazed with the red words "Aramex." "Wait 'til you see this," Hassan smiled. "We have the knowledge, infrastructure, and flexibility to help businesses scale, cost effectively, and not deal with the country by country hassles. That is a problem we are taking on."

I entered the newest of Aramex's six major cargo hubs, which span the world, from Kennedy Airport to the Middle East. Through this network, they launched a program they call "Shop and Ship," which allows customers to order products from nearly any e-tailer in the United States and China and soon the Middle East. It's a seamless process: Aramex receives the ordered goods at its facilities, takes care of all the bureaucratic headaches, and then delivers the goods right to the shopper. Modern and climate-controlled, Aramex facilities are immaculately clean, stacked nearly thirty feet high with pallets of goods, each box technologically tagged and monitored. Their 30-year history of doing business throughout the Middle East and Africa, as well as their recently increased physical presence on the ground, opens a sorely needed logistics platform for the rising e-commerce world. Fadi notes, "Setting up regional warehouses where there is the highest volume of purchases—like what you saw—has enormous ramifications. Businesses can deliver faster within a country and return faster all while they save on the shipping costs by consolidating volumes versus sending individual consignments back and forth." Every Aramex driver is equipped with the latest mobile capabilities to accurately monitor every package. The regular two-way communications between Aramex and buyers and sellers greatly enhances accurate delivery locations, and digitized maps mean more reliable and efficient delivery times. It is hard to imagine why any other e-commerce player would want to replicate this when they can plug into Aramex's infrastructure as if it is their own. For a price, of course.

Aramex is taking much of the friction out of shipping goods, but they have also determined that payment issues—requiring connections to banks and credit card companies—are not their expertise. Besides, nearly a dozen other innovators have entered the market here with new ones appearing regularly—among the first and leaders, a spinoff of Samih Toukan's Maktoob, called cashU.

I skyped with a cashU founder with the improbable name of Martin Waldenstrom—a Swede whose Skype profile photo is wool-hat clad and clearly recently off the mountain slopes. Coming off of a successful career in foreign exchange trading and banking from Sweden to London to Singapore to Dubai, Martin garnered an expertise in finance information technology and founded his own IT consultancy. On a chance call from a headhunter, he met with Samih Toukan of Maktoob in 2006. Samih was wrestling how to address the payments challenges in the Middle East, because he believed there would be significant opportunity once cracked. "They were starting very simply, with digital goods like ringtones," he told me, "But so few people had credit cards. I started researching the issue and found people, especially kids, wanted to shop but they had no means to do so." CashU had begun talking with Aramex about partnering with their dispatch centers, where people could come in and buy PIN-protected cash cards. Like gift cards in the United States, all buyers had to do was type in the PIN number and shop to the fixed denomination limit of the card. "They were doing maybe $50,000 a month tops at the time," he smiles, "It was clear it was easy, secure, and with internet penetration so low then, there was fantastic potential."

Shortly after he joined, Martin negotiated a deal with a local Jordanian MasterCard issuer to connect the relatively small credit card base with potential online transactions. Over 30,000 people registered within a month. As an introduction to another challenge of the Middle East as this business took off, however, his Jordanian partner received a phone call from MasterCard in the United States. Because at that time cash cards required no identification under $500, some wily entrepreneurs bought hundreds of cards for $499 and sold them in many corners of the region who had no access to them, including Iran and Syria, for as much as $2,000. "So the good news was, we were right about how desperately people wanted to buy things online," he paused, "But the bad news was Iran and Syria were on the State Department 'watch lists' so we had to shut the whole thing down." Confirmed of the demand, however, cashU pivoted to create what they called "Closed cashU System" or CCS, where merchants and buyers would share information to buy and sell on the platform. "When it was the only game in town, it answered the challenge," Martin notes, "But we knew over time people want to buy from any store, not just the ones who agreed to be on CCS. In 2007, Skype joined our platform, and that gave us great growth, but we would have to pivot again."

Today, cashU still has the pre-paid account/closed-loop system and they have integrated their service with logistics company drivers' personal devices so that, Square-like, they can accept immediate "cash" payments when they deliver goods. Aramex now handles 20 percent of their COD deliveries this way. He understands, however, that as more and more consumers demand commerce online, they are in the midst of a shift in demand for a true e-payment system which they have begun to offer. "COD will be with us for a while," Martin notes, "But I receive a call every week from some startup not only offering an e-payment solution but now an m-payment—for mobile devices. We are entering an era where people will want their secure mobile capability to buy what they want where they want to, online and off. And they want convenience— enter nothing complicated, just buy and click."

Few people understand this shift better than Elias Ghanem, who became the general manager of the newly created PayPal Middle East and North Africa region in the summer of 2012. He knows something about solving payment challenges. Born in Lebanon, he and his family of four kids are truly global citizens. Ghanem studied in Beirut, Paris, and Miami and has worked for global financial companies like Visa in Miami where he covered all of Latin America. Before returning to the Middle East he was in Singapore, where he joined PayPal's Asia-Pacific operations to lead their expansion in Southeast Asia and India. All told, he returns to Beirut in his new role after more than 30 years overseas.

"The first challenge in building a new business is accepting the need to change mind-sets and the traditional way of doing business," he explained to me. "It initially takes courage, energy, and vision. Very few stakeholders are willing to do it at the beginning, but slowly and surely, one after the other, everyone comes to understand the benefits of new technology and embraces it." Along his career, he had several opportunities to confirm this thinking. As a young executive at Visa, he led efforts with the three largest banks in Brazil and the government to move the nation's extensive food voucher program from paper to a smartcard-based solution. The benefits in efficiency were clear. Paper vouchers were easily lost, and the government had little way to track their proper usage. Traditional providers put up a tough fight against the new technology, but Elias and his partner banks insisted and worked their way to build customer awareness and trust. Today digital vouchers significantly outpace paper. "I learned a clear lesson then and have seen it repeatedly in emerging markets around the globe: launch new products with the right technology, ensure that what it offers is simple and meets a clear consumer need, partner with the right players committed to make it work, and you have a perfect recipe for success." Interestingly, the Egyptian government similarly shifted nearly 14 million paper food stamps to smartcards in 2005. An investor familiar with the project estimates the government saved nearly $200 million per year.

PayPal, which is owned by online auction juggernaut eBay, has built a global market of 100 million active consumers across 190 countries with a simple proposition. "We are e-commerce enablers," Elias told me, "We take any friction out of e-commerce by offering a safe and convenient payment platform for buyers and sellers to connect their buying needs and their payment instruments (credit cards, bank accounts, balances). We have a trusted global brand and reputation that makes people feel secure in doing business online." Despite the country-by-country challenges in the region and consumer resistance to credit cards, Ghanem could not have been more thrilled by what he discovered when he returned home to the Middle East. "In all the markets that I've launched consumer financial products, I've never seen so many people starting a meeting with us saying, 'Finally, you are here.'"

In only his third month at PayPal Middle East in the late fall of 2012, Ghanem gave me a quick tour of how he saw each country in terms of e-payments. The United Arab Emirates and Qatar are relatively the most mature markets in terms of e-commerce. "Governments and business are aligned in their eagerness to make things happen. They are extremely active, dynamic, and innovative." Saudi Arabia is the place to watch. It is by far the biggest market, with a large and strong consumer population. The nascent e-commerce market is growing fast in this country and in the next few years will have enormous impact. The rest of the Gulf is also moving in the right direction, albeit more slowly. Jordan and Lebanon are smaller markets, but also clear leaders in developing entrepreneurial e-commerce solutions. "Young people in these markets build new products and test them in their own markets hoping to deploy them in the UAE and ultimately Saudi Arabia. It's a good strategy, as Dubai and Saudi are so large, and successful ideas can become blockbusters there." Finally, Egypt is one of the largest under-banked countries in the world—investors have told me less than 10 percent of the population has bank accounts. "The opportunity here is to bring all the under-banked populations to online business," he adds.

For Elias the first opportunity is to engage the local authorities in each market (the regulators, central banks, ministries of trade, small and medium-sized businesses, trade associations) to help them seize the potential of e-commerce. Regulators have a unique opportunity to structure the e-payment landscape and regulate it in a way to help it grow while keeping it flexible and adapted to the high speed of innovation in technology. Central banks historically understand how to regulate banking and money transfers transactions, but an e-transaction really combines both, as goods or services are sold across the globe without face-to-face interaction. "The regulatory environment in each market in the region is evolving to define the right framework for these new capabilities," Elias explains. "Things will change in the Middle East and my job here—as it was in every new market I've entered—is to be humble, to listen, and mostly be an advisor as needed to the regulators to help them understand the huge e-commerce opportunity lying ahead in each market. There is a significant opportunity for merchants of all sizes to join the global e-commerce trade and serve billions of people constantly connected online through a PC, a phone, or a tablet somewhere in the world."

Elias believes strongly that in the end e-commerce will thrive or stall based on trust and safety. "Paying at delivery, known as 'cash on delivery' or COD, at its essence" he argues, "is a very basic human desire to see the goods before signing the check or swiping the card. So if it's a normal behavior when we go to a store, why would we be surprised that in the early days of e-commerce here, people have the same desire when the store comes to us—which effectively it does online." In every market he has entered, Elias has seen lack of trust for credit cards used online, everyone seeming to have a bad story of some friend cheated in an online transaction.

He believes that there are four pillars in the e-commerce ecosystem: the regulators; the merchants (from the entrepreneurs to multinational companies); technology and logistics needs; and payment enablers like PayPal and other global, local, or regional payment solutions. From his experience, when the four pillars come together to educate consumers that online is as safe, if not safer, than physical commerce, e-commerce grows steadily. Each player has to do his part to build confidence. PayPal, as an example, has a "Buyer Protection" program in which consumers are protected if the goods bought online and paid with PayPal are not delivered or are not as described on the website. PayPal reviews the transaction and reimburses the buyer. He recalls that in Malaysia, PayPal sponsored a very successful "Month of eSafety" in conjunction with the government to provide tips to consumers on how to remain safe when shopping online. He told me that in the Middle East, merchants across all business verticals are debating not offering COD as a payment option at all. He notes, "They know this may slow their growth in the short run, but in the long run they will by educating the customer to use the most efficient and safe payment option."

Talk to anyone concerned with e-payments, and to a person they will tell you the final game-changer will be mobile. Aramex's Hassan Mekail, effuses: "M-commerce and e-commerce will eventually be part and parcel of the same thing. You are a point of sale wherever you are, whatever you see you are instantly connected to your ability to pay." Ghanem agrees. "Mobile is by far changing the way we do commerce as it has blurred the line between the brick-and-mortar store and the pure online commerce. Nowadays you need to be able to access your mobile wallet, while your safety is protected, and pay through multiple channels, in store, online, on your phone, soon on your TV, at a kiosk in the street." Why not buy while waiting for the subway or walking along the streets of Dubai, by scanning a QR code on a billboard? The PayPal account known as the "digital wallet in the cloud" offers its customers the unique way to access a universal payment solution for all customer needs. Ghanem notes, "Imagine entering a store, selecting the nice pair of shoes you've been dreaming of, scanning the barcode, leaving the store . . . and voila, the shoes are at home, even before you! All thanks to your phone and digital wallet!" He adds that PayPal went from $300 million in mobile transactions in 2010 to $4 billion globally in 2011 and expects to reach $10 billion in 2012. "These are still the early days of m-commerce and the numbers are already stunning. Who can predict the m-commerce growth in the Middle East when smartphone penetration breaks 50 percent, which will probably happen in the next couple of years?"

Today nearly every retail operation is finding ways to transact online, and the entrepreneurial community has launched hundreds of platforms, from virtual goods such as music and gaming rewards to fashion and technology retailers to food delivery. Three, however, have jumped out at scale. While their numbers are not public, Souq.com and Marka-VIP—both broad online marketplaces—are expected to gross over $100 million in 2012, and Namshi, the online shoe boutique that Germany's Rocket Internet invested in, also took a subsequent $20 million round from blue-chip U.S. investors J. P. Morgan Chase and London-based Blakeney Management, and most recently in early 2013 the U.S. venture capital firm Summit Ventures joined.

Souq.com was the first spin-out from Maktoob after Yahoo!'s purchase, and founder Ronaldo Mouchawar is a longtime partner of Samih Toukan. Intense, tenacious, and given to punctuating almost every sentence with a statistic, Ronaldo was raised in Syria, where he learned to sell agriculture equipment alongside his father. "You learn humility, you learn to shut up and listen doing this," he recalls. Following the lead of his uncle who studied medicine at Harvard, Ronaldo found his way to Northeastern University in nearby Boston. Completing a degree in computer engineering, he first worked in tech operations in the early days of video for Electronic Data Systems (EDS), but soon switched to sales. He discovered he had the gut for it. Wanting to return to the region, he met Samih in the late 1990s through a mutual friend and was intrigued by his vision for Maktoob. But it was in the Maktoob offices in 2000 that he was struck by Samih's larger commitment—to improving the Arab world. "Samih had built into his culture a sense of identity; their mission statement quoted the Palestinian Darwesh's poem on being Arab. The team worked hard, they respected each other, they knew technology cold and they knew where they were going. They believed in empowerment for the Middle East, and e-commerce really is all about empowerment. To sell, to create a business, to offer businesses and customers choices, to build an employee team where you didn't micromanage them but empower *them*—it was fantastic, and forward-thinking."

At first, they thought eBay was the model to replicate. They had a growing and engaged audience with Maktoob, so why not create an Arabic auction site? E-commerce was in its infancy, with a series of small startups and only one site out of Jordan, Arabia.com, having any scale. It would subsequently close its doors when the first tech bubble burst. Their auction business did well initially, but also had its limitations in scaling. Yet both he and Samih knew that Middle East countries were large consumers, and with time and trust, things could move their way. They made three crucial decisions. First, they focused on Dubai and the Emirates, whose internet penetration, at 20 percent, was the highest in the region, which averaged 2 percent. Second, they focused their product offering initially on mobile devices. "Then and now people change their phones every few months, and the rate of new mobile users had long been significant," he recalls. Third, they gave up on auctions and moved to fixed-price sales. But within months, their growth became so rapid they expanded into books, media, apparel, and other IT. They became Aramex's first e-commerce partner in 2006, and together the two developed a "safe pay" program to facilitate cash payments to thousands of merchants. Souq.com today is the largest e-commerce site in the region, boasts over 500 employees around the region, and is one of the 13 largest websites in the region, reaching over eight million shoppers each month. Every day they create new offerings in high fashion and services like daily deals.

Souq.com is not alone. Rocket Internet, the German online and e-commerce conglomerate with holdings around the world, is known for its emotionless, analytic—some would say brutal—approach to entering and exiting markets. In 2012 they exited Turkey, viewed by many as a leading internet capital in the broader Middle East, because their numbers told them the market had matured and was saturated with local e-commerce companies. In the same year, they not only doubled down their bet in Dubai, but encouraged the global investment bank, J. P. Morgan, to join them in investing expansion capital there and around the globe. In January 2013, venture capital firm Summit Partners joined them. Muhammed Mekki, a former Dubai-based McKinsey consultant and Iraqi-American born co-founder of their investment through the end of 2012, Namshi, is pretty matter-of-fact about it: "The numbers are there, and the wind is blowing at our backs," he tells me. Namshi is something like the Zappos of the Middle East, and is rapidly expanding beyond shoes to broader fashion items. When I visited Aramex's facilities in Dubai, which does the logistics for the company, several enormous rows of inventory were all Namshi's and I was told it had grown exponentially over the past year. However, Mekki walks humbly as well. "Namshi will never take anything for granted. Plenty of other e-commerce companies are in or circling the region."

Mekki began conversations with Rocket shortly after joining McKinsey to explore potential sectors in e-commerce. The Arab uprisings brought these explorations to a temporary halt, but by the fall of 2011 Rocket came back more interested than ever. "I didn't have the background or passion for fashion prior to this, but Zappos' success in the States was clear and consumer demand in the Middle East spoke for itself," Mekki recalls. "There was no competition at the time, Rocket had had success throughout Europe and elsewhere, they had a technological platform built I knew I could leverage and knew we simply could move faster than anyone." He signed on as CEO in September, and by

December Namshi was out in the marketplace. "There is a reason why they are called Rocket," he smiles. "It is a rocket culture, very different in the Middle East, but I knew it would not only be a competitive advantage for us but also push others around us to be the same." They went from Mekki himself to 145 employees in less than a year, and house 30 alone in the Aramex shipping facility to ensure packaging, distribution, and customer service. They now sell over 500 brands, 12,000 styles all stocked in the warehouse I visited. "It is hard to explain how different things are in over the past year," he notes. "At first, many of the brands we dealt with really didn't understand e-commerce and wanted to know where our physical stores were. Without a physical presence, even if we offered them cash, they would not send goods to us. But within a few months our reputation took care of that. Consumers showed up at higher rates than we expected. Initial focus on Gulf countries limited regulatory differences as they share very similar rules, and Aramex helped us in any event. COD remains a challenge, but we are seeing an increase in credit card usage every month. There is no question in my mind that e-payment companies like PayPal and others will change things significantly."

And this is just the beginning. Aramex's e-commerce guru Hassan Mikkail is as passionate about what's to come as he is about the present. To discover and support future innovation in e-commerce, he and Aramex have launched a new kind of startup incubator (they prefer "Business Maker,") in Dubai he calls eHouse. Instead of funding startups with seed capital, eHouse focuses on online retail companies that have gotten some traction. "What do they need more than anything?" he asks rhetorically. "They need to focus on their innovation and getting their brand known and connecting to buyers. They don't need to waste time at this stage with all the back-end hassles and costs. That's where we will come in." Like a traditional incubator, eHouse will offer office space, legal, financial, and human resources, and technical support. But unlike an incubator, they will charge the new businesses a modest fee for these services, and for significant warehouse space on the premises to manage their inventory. Aramex will handle all inventory management, logistics, and delivery. After the test run in Dubai, Hassan hopes to open eHouses wherever Aramex has facilities. The first eHouse is located in a large business park near downtown. It is large, open, modern and wired. Hassan walked me around the last of the construction debris, pointing out rack after rack of storage shelves next to the sleek, spare offices. "Arabs are the most innovative and entrepreneurial sellers on earth," he says, as if to himself. "We will help hundreds of businesses, and hundreds of businesses will spawn hundreds of others. That's how you build an ecosystem."

The Problem Solvers

The difference between entrepreneurs and so-called "social entrepreneurs" is blurring today. The former once connoted hard-nosed money making; the latter nonprofit, or at least not solely for profit, enterprises. But now in almost every business pitch I hear in almost any industry, the entrepreneur is thinking about the societal impact of product, or a socially responsible way in which to run their company. In the Middle East, the Arab uprisings have found a deeply socially conscious, often nationally proud expression in business ideas. Mostafa Hemdan is an engineering student at Tanta University, a small school two hours outside of Cairo. "My generation is outraged by so much that we have inherited," he tells me. "We simply want to fix it. Why wait to see if someone else will?"

Tanta is a working-class town and, like so many other cities in Egypt, suffers from intermittent and unreliable garbage collection. At school Hemdan noticed a lot of unaddressed waste—the metal and material left from computers and consumer electronics. Schools and businesses just seemed to let the debris stack up in warehouses or at garbage dumps. One day, while doing homework on a leading global engineering website, IEEE TV, he discovered a collection of videos under the heading "The Green Environment." One was a documentary about how a new company built a business separating precious metals—gold, silver, copper—from discarded computers and selling both the metals and scrap material to separate recyclers. Hemdan watched the film dozens of times and showed it to his closest friends. What, he asked them, if we found "green" recyclers of the precious metals or other parts of value and cut a deal with local scrap metal shops to take what was left? "I knew nothing about recycling," he explained to me, "but it was clear no else really knew either. Not my professors, not even people I met in the two local scrap metal businesses, who had never given a thought to consumer electronics. There was a gap, and I thought we could not only build a significant company, but also build a culture of recycling in Tanta and throughout Egypt." He launched RecycloBekia that week with twenty students—two founding classmates and dozens of his fellow students who volunteered to help.

"I first tried to look for something similar in Egypt to learn from," he said. "We found a few guys recycling in bottles and glass, but that was it." He tried in vain to find the person who posted the video for advice on how to create a startup recycling facility. Finally, he decided to simply post a question on one of the leading global business-to-business websites, alibabba.com: "I have old computer components to sell if there are any green buyers." Almost immediately he was contacted by businesses in China, the United States, and England. He was shocked. "They all wrote me how they were eco-friendly and wanted to know the price. I didn't even have the computers yet, and hadn't thought about price at all; I was happy to take whatever they offered. But they all told me, 'You're the seller, tell us your price.' This was a good lesson for me."

So he went back on alibabba.com pretending to be a buyer of used computers, to see how others priced the parts. He then chose one of the online buyers from China, who wanted 6,000 hard drives. He spoke to his school and local businesses about procuring the old computers cheaply or even free if he took them off their hands. He researched how to ship materials and set up safe online banking. He partnered with a local scrap dealer to separate the parts, committing to the "cleanest" way to do so—and they shipped the hard drives. The money appeared in his account the day they were received. "That was my first $1,000, our first capital," he recalls, "We asked for a loan from one of our professors to help us to buy those hard drives and after receiving the money we gave him his percentage of profit. That's how we launched the company." Other buyers soon appeared, and almost immediately Hemdan received local press attention. Within the first year of operations, he won numerous local awards and raised $150,000 of additional capital.

With this investment he decided to move his operation, now nearly 30 full-time employees strong, to Cairo. "We could lease a modern space cheaply there, and Cairo is a much larger tech center than Tanta, so the demand to move used equipment is higher," he told me. RecycloBekia targets universities, multinational corporations, and high schools, and hopes to eventually get everyday Egyptians thinking about how to recycle their used computers. "Many schools and companies give us the old computers for free. Corporate Social Responsibility is becoming more than a buzz word, and people take it seriously." He pauses and then laughs. "But I'll tell you, we still have to pay for some of these computers because we Arabs care about the value of everything we have. Even if the thing is useless, we want to know what you will give me for it." The team is mapping out an investment in what would be their largest e-waste recycling center. "Our hope, of course, when we get greater traction in Egypt is to take the concept throughout the entire Middle East. We plan to be the largest company to collect, cleanly separate, and recycle old computers."

Recycling is only one of a myriad of challenges that rapidly growing cities in the Middle East have long wrestled. A veteran of driving the Beltway of Washington, D.C., and Highway 110 in Los Angeles, I was utterly unprepared for Cairo traffic. According to a recent World Bank study, among other studies, Cairo traffic alone costs the economy roughly $8 billion, or 4 percent of Egypt's GDP per year, and accounts for over 7,000 deaths (over 20 percent of which are pedestrians) and over 100,000 injuries.[6] Cairo now sprawls to a population over 18 million and at 14 million cars on Egypt's roads, the ratio of cars to kilometers of road is one of the highest in the world. Public transportation is antiquated and not keeping up with these demographics. The Cairo subway system is half the size of D.C.'s metro, though it carries four times more passengers per kilometer of line. While the new Egyptian president Morsi has declared Cairo traffic as a top priority, substantial infrastructure changes will require significant prioritization, investment, and years to implement. The prime minister's economic plan for 2012 didn't even mention traffic at all.

Software and social media–based startups, however, are not waiting. The crowd-sharing Bey2ollak mobile app, launched in October of 2010 in partnership with Vodafone Egypt, currently has over 350,000 users per month to share updates on real-time traffic patterns. Available for all mobile platforms (Blackberry, Android, Nokia, Windows Phone, iPhone), it also remains the only SMS traffic capability, supported by a multiyear development and marketing relationship with Vodafone that includes text and social media campaigns. At its size and scale it has become one of the leading mobile advertising platforms in the nascent mobile marketing worlds in Egypt, and won top honors at Google's first Ebda2 startup competition in the country, receiving the $200,000 prize. Another startup, Emokhalfa, makes crowdsourcing in traffic more personal by building community pressure around reckless driving. Users can report any vehicular misbehavior—double-parking, driving in the wrong direction, road rage or aggressive driving, even sexual harassment—by texting the license plate number, posting a photo, or calling a designated hotline. Emokhalfa has partnered with local nongovernment agencies and other groups that are under the Ministry of the Interior to aggregate data about individual misbehaviors as well as information that may impact traffic flows. In the meantime, anyone—a parent about to put a child on a school bus, for example—can check the license number for previous violations. Find it impossible to find a taxi in Cairo? There are no dispatch services today. Startup Ogra is an Uber-like software app that seekers can use to find the nearest participating taxi and order a car without long waits. In addition, as the app is GPS enabled, using an Ogra-discovered cab can allow loved ones to ensure a customer's safe arrival to his or her destination. Ogra's Cairo-based co-founder Edward Disley explains: "Ogra has major technical differences and is more than a simple application connecting clients to taxi-drivers like Uber—it is a complete smart solution for the entire taxi industry. The need is so great and unaddressed." He hopes to expand through the Middle East and one day even Europe and the United States.

As one venture investor in the region told me: "Governments are going to have to step up, but as we've seen around the world there is no reason to wait. Almost any problem can find a software solution today."

The Global Players

As mentioned in the first chapter, I was invited in 2011 to be a judge at one of the largest startup competitions of that time. Hundreds of young people from around the country had come at their own expense to Cairo, to be weeded down to the 35 finalists we would meet. There was something gnawingly familiar about a thoughtful but quiet presentation by a founder of a team of app developers from Alexandria, Egypt. Alexandria sits on the northern coast, and as the country's second largest city is a bustling metropolis and active tourist destination. Nothing remains of the legendary library created in the third century BCE during the reigns of the first two Ptolemys, but the tradition of learning continues in what some consider one of the leading tech entrepreneurship hubs in the Middle East. I really couldn't place why this pitch felt so familiar until I looked down at my iPad and realized I had downloaded his most successful offering months earlier. It had since become the largest paid weather app in the world, WeatherHD. I check it every day.

Amr Ramadan is the kind of entrepreneur investors look for. That he described starting his company, Vimov, with exactly the Egyptian equivalent of $1,060—not "about a thousand bucks"—told me he watches every dime. He began his investor pitch to the Cairo judges by openly admitting the failure of his first product, and the lessons learned. His next product was a simulator for iPad and iPhone developers that sold thousands of downloads at $32 each. His third product was WeatherHD, with over 400,000 users paying $0.99 each in January 2011, nearly half of those outside of the Middle East. The next product in his pipeline, an ingenious take on personalized news, sounded equally promising.

I was unsurprised by what I found when I checked in a year and a half later. "We are approaching our seven millionth download," Amr told me, "half of which are coming from the U.S. We also released WeatherHD for the Mac, which stayed at the number two top-selling spot in the States during its week of launch." They had just released their most ambitious version via the iTunes App Store in the summer of 2012; it's visually stunning and offers new features like "Quickview," allowing users to see weather information from more than one weather provider over multiple cities. They have grown from three to 30 employees, all engineers from Amr's home town of Alexandria.

Navigating this period of historic uncertainty was not easy, Ramadan notes. "We tried to take it slow in terms of growth after the protests of January 25, expecting the dust would settle in a few weeks. It quickly became apparent it wouldn't settle down soon, and it wouldn't be clear fast enough where the politics or economy would go." Facing too many questions and possible scenarios, Amr did what great entrepreneurs do around the globe: hope for the best, plan for the globally competitive business they dreamed of, and execute. "Let me be clear," he smiles. "[Revolution] causes tremendous pressure on top of that of simply being a startup. One is always re-evaluating, guessing what could happen next, and building backup plans. But focus and execution is the only way; slow is not an option in the technology business."

And execute they have. With growth rates that would be coveted by many in Silicon Valley, Ramadan has pushed his team to constantly redefine what a great weather application can be. Proud of their unique, graphic visual interface, they immediately improved navigation between the many cities their average viewers monitor. "We just launched Quickview, which shows weather animations of several locations all at once in a simple, elegant way," he beams.

In the new release, Ramadan believes he is displaying his broader ambitions. "We are trying to set the standard on how a weather application—in fact, any useful consumer information app—should look like. WeatherHD is only the beginning, and will be the base of a series of consumer apps beyond weather that we hope will change a lot of things in the mobile space." They rebranded Clear Day in May 2013 and are now available in almost any language around the globe.

But can Egypt and the Middle East really keep up with the exciting innovation coming not only from the United States, but also from Europe, Israel, India, Asia, and Latin America? For Ramadan, the assumed precedent of innovation now coming from all corners of the globe, even places once ignored, only suggests things could move faster in the Middle East. "Technology here is at its infancy, but that means there are opportunities around every corner," he believes. "The reason why this huge market of over 350 million users has been underserved was that the young people were not encouraged to innovate, not from anyone around them, and they themselves had little hopes that a dream can come true." He believes that this way of thinking has been forever shattered in the last year. "The number one motivator of great engineers is having great problems for them to solve," he speaks as an engineer himself. "I have a world-class team at a fraction of the cost of what we could get in Silicon Valley— but we all love Alexandria, make great livings here, and are proud of building great products made in Egypt." Thousands of other startups, he notes, have concluded the same all over the Middle East.

Hind Hobeika is one of them. The winner of the 2012 MIT Middle East business plan competition is a Lebanese mechanical engineering grad from the American University of Beirut, Hind also happened to be a fiercely competitive swimmer. The daughter of academics, she once presumed she would become an executive in a large global company in the region like Proctor and Gamble. But she instead created a business around a product that she needed personally, and was deeply passionate about.

As a member of the AUB swim team, she found it frustrating that they only tracked their heart rates by counting them manually at the end of the race. And even as early heart-rate monitors came to market, she found most presented drawbacks for swimmers. "None of them," she told me, "were truly adapted to the biomechanics of swimming. Heart rate watches and other external chest belts were cumbersome and all but impossible to check while training." Then an idea hit her: what if she could create a small module that can be mounted onto any type of swimming goggles, that could read the heart rate and display it in real-time on the lens of the swimmer through a color code: blue if in the fat-burning zone, green if in the fitness zone and red if in the maximum performance zone? Her company, Butterfleye, became her answer.

Hind was invited to participate in a four-month "reality TV" competition out of Qatar, called *Stars of Science,* where she honed her prototype and her patience. "I was the only woman competitor among the five top contestants," she recalls. "Even so, some of the men refused to speak to me on camera as they didn't want to be seen working and interacting with women." She proved them wrong. Butterfleye came in third, and has captured awards and recognition, and investors, since. One of the leading seed investors in the region, Berytech Fund, took her first round. Ayah Bdeir, a top global interactive artist and engineer, who is active in the tech innovation ecosystem of the Middle East and a design mentor on *Stars of Science,* became a mentor. "Ayah provided me with a work space and moral support when I had no idea what to do next," Hind notes, "She and my mother were the two most important people in my journey."

"Clearly things were happening with tech entrepreneurs in the region," Hind told me. "But it was also clear from the start that Butterfleye was going to be a global product. Swimming is popular in the Middle East, but the U.S., Australia, and Europe—they are the nations with the biggest number of swimmers, health aware people, and tech freaks!" And she has built a global team. "As we are developing a technological tool for athletes to seamlessly monitor their trainings, we work extensively with electronic components, microcontrollers, but also with a lot of coding and web interface. My team is based in London, France, the Netherlands, and Dubai, so I spend 90 percent of my day on Skype." They branded their product to *Instabeat* at the end of 2012 and, with manufacturing up and running in China, formally announced their launch at the 140,000+ attendee 2013 Consumer Electronics Show (CES) in Las Vegas in January, taking hundreds of pre-orders with their first shipments in the fall.

If inspiration often comes from necessity, necessity is often inspired by tragedy. "My family history was notorious for high cholesterol and heart disease," Lebanese entrepreneur Ziad Sankari told me. "While there were many incidents leading up to that day, nothing could prepare me for hearing that I lost my Dad." Ziad was 17, his father barely 53. "It was this agonizing event that triggered my life's mission."

Sankari is a brilliant and intense twenty-something computer engineering graduate from the Lebanese American University. He later received two master's degrees—one in biomedical engineering and the other in electrical and computer engineering as well as a minor in entrepreneurship—as a Fulbright Scholar at Ohio State University in 2010. "I had thought at some point I'd be a university professor, like my father was in education," he told me, "But when I understood that his death could have been avoided with better and regular access to electrocardiogram data, as early as college I started thinking about how to solve this."

In college, Sankari had developed a prototype for a vest that could regularly monitor heart rhythms for at-risk heart patients, and it won the university's science competition. While studying in the United States, he focused his studies on improving this technology while also co-developing a nanotechnology biomedical company to help in the treatment of wounds care patients. But he remained most eager to return to his work in cardio monitoring, and to return to Lebanon. "Perhaps the most impactful work I did there was working on new computational models on physiological signals. For example, I studied how certain brain signals could offer detections for early onset of Alzheimer's. I began to think that this could work in detecting catastrophic events from electrocardiogram data as well."

He returned to Lebanon and took a job at the American University Medical Centers, among the most prestigious in the region, training doctors in the operating room on the latest computer-based biomedical tools. His goal was to learn more about how the health-care system worked in the Middle East. It helped him pay for his work on the side for what was to become his startup, Cardio Diagnostics, but it taught him about opportunity in the Middle East for health care. "There are significant challenges here," he explained to me, "Brands matter to both hospitals and consumers. Coming from the States was viewed as a plus. Say you're a startup from the Middle East and eyes glaze over. But the medical talent and resources here are excellent. The regulatory system is much easier to navigate, and I could hire medical talent at literally an eighth of what it would cost me in the States. I began to realize I could do something significant here, and it would allow me to use this success to go global."

A friend introduced him to a program that the Qatar Foundation had launched to provide grants for innovation in health and other areas of technology. He left the medical center to see how he could solve the challenges his father faced. "The world of technology had changed so much in the past decade. Not only was monitoring capability better than ever before, but mobile technology meant that really anyone could be monitored in real time by their medical professionals. I knew that if I could design a way for at-risk heart patients to have 24/7 electrocardiogram care on their person—the same quality one would get in their hospital room—I could create algorithms on that data in real time where medical professionals could be notified of a potential dangerous event." He spent a year in Qatar with engineers the foundation connected him to. He registered his company in the United States and began to file patents.

Cardio Diagnostics has designed a simple way for patients to apply adhesive monitoring tags on their chests to a lightweight vest with sensors that regularly send heart signals to a dedicated monitoring center. With proprietary algorithms he and his team have developed, they are able to analyze the data to detect possible warnings for a six-week period or longer, depending on when a doctor wants to observe an at-risk patient. They will partner at first with, and eventually build their own, cloud-based monitoring center in Beirut for their first tests. "Patient education will be a central part of this," he notes. "We don't want them to think necessarily that a call from a monitor means they are about to die—but it is an early warning to connect with their doctors to dig deeper into an irregularity, perhaps adjust their medication or go to a hospital."

There are currently cumbersome and wired devices in the United States, but usually only for one- or two-day monitoring, and they do not include the intelligence algorithms of Cardio Diagnostics. I saw an early version of their product in late 2011, and it could not be simpler to put on the electrodes and connect them with their vest. I told Sankari, though, that in preparing for a marathon I once had an electrocardiogram in a local Washington hospital. I was covered in wires and the devices kept falling off of me. He smiled at me. "This is the beauty of our design and of mobile technology. There are no wires, and you can remain active with the monitors easily held into place." Cardio Diagnostics' advisory board, a who's who of regional and global authorities in cardiovascular innovation, is enthusiastic.

Of course to go global, passing U.S.-grade FDA approval will be important. Ziad reminds me, "We are not a drug or an invasive medical device. We are a monitoring service that requires only lower level '510K clearance' from the FDA—an at most year-long process. Our goals now are to finalize the product, start testing in 2012, and build clinical data. We believe we can be in market in the Middle East, including FDA clearances, within 18 months and are about to finalize both choosing our device manufacturers. We have several of the leading hospitals in the region to help us in our clinical trials signed on."

It struck me that eventually they will be getting into the monitoring business—in my earlier life I looked at some investments in monitoring companies myself, like home alarms and life alerts ("I've fallen and I can't get up"). But 24/7 coverage is not an inexpensive proposition, and when life and death may be in the balance, expensive experts at the other end of that data will be necessary. Sankari answered, "There is no question, but technology is everything here. First and foremost, this is a unique, patent-pending series of capabilities that will save lives. This is a big idea. Second, by starting in the Middle East, we can launch and test faster and cheaper. The market opportunity here and in other emerging markets is enormous, but opens up the real gateway of entering the United States. Finally, to roll out, it must be done at the highest level of quality and I have no doubt we can raise the capital here and abroad to do so for the necessary scale. I also believe we will innovate out to build our monitoring. Our technology makes reaction times easy and understandable. Imagine a world where experts with iPads received easy-read data and alert medical professionals. The innovation that created this service can also create new ways to solve any monitoring service challenge we face."

There can be no debating the power of what the Improvisers, the Problem Solvers, and the Global Players are creating or the opportunity they represent. At the same time, they all—and the Global Players in particular—also lead to an additional and powerful question. The history of globally adopted technology innovation is often driven by entrepreneurs creatively addressing unique challenges and circumstances they face on the ground. As the Middle East is in the midst of historic change, are there opportunities to be found in its unique experiences and geographies that could make the region the next new cradle of world-class competitive innovation? In my travels, I became persuaded that there could be such opportunities in at least three areas: mobile technology, solar energy, and social networks.

Chapter 4

Leap Frog

The vibrancy and potential of Improvisers, Problem Solvers, *and Global Players* is clear. I have often wondered whether there will be a viable fourth category, where the unique experiences, cultures, geographies, and histories of the region inspire truly new, disruptive innovation as well. We in the startup community call this "leap frog" innovation.

After all, once upon a time, no one could imagine that Japan, Finland, or Korea would become leaders in hardware for home entertainment, mobile computing, or computer gaming. But now it seems almost strange that there hasn't been equivalent software innovation outside of the United States in years, arguably ever. Might the Middle East be the next hotbed? As long as the region continues to creatively overcome its challenges, and access to inexpensive technology continues to spread, might "made in the Middle East" become shorthand for global innovation?

Certainly wide-reaching innovation already happens regularly in emerging markets, spearheaded by enterprises that appreciate local market distinctions and seek to scale them to other growth markets. Dartmouth professors Vijay Govindarajan and Chris Trimble, in their book *Reverse Innovation,* remind us that these markets alone represent vast populations and spending capacity. The key to succeeding in emerging markets, they note, is in understanding the significant distinctions from the West. "They are night-and-day different," they caution. "In the rich world, there are a few people who each spend a lot; in the developing world, there are a lot of people who each spend a little."[1] Tailoring products or services to these realities now has a potential multiplier effect, because as access to modern technology increases, adoption in such markets moves that much more quickly.[2]

Nokia understood this. They grabbed nearly 60 percent of the India market in the last decade, for example, by both rethinking their business models and redesigning their offerings toward hyper-local needs. They offered fewer models, created cheaper software-based Hindi texting capabilities to replace hardware-based offerings, and added flashlight capabilities for significantly rural customers without regular access to electricity.[3] Similarly, in 2012, the largest mobile carrier in Kenya, Safaricom, re-thought the core purpose of its basic, low-end mobile phone. Kenya is a significantly under-banked country; less than a fifth of its citizens have bank accounts. It is a cash-based, widely dispersed society, where the majority of transactions are only a few dollars. Workers often walk miles to bring cash home or to their families, and robbery is a significant problem. Into this environment Safaricom launched M-Pesa, a simple, text-based mobile cash payments platform. Through a network that has grown to over 30,000 agents around the country, M-Pesa gives customers a unique PIN number and the ability to safely send and receive money anywhere in the country. In 2011, a whopping $10 billion passed through M-Pesa, representing almost half of the mobile transactions in the world. Over two-thirds of Kenya's 40 million people have signed up for the service. In fact, it's now far easier to send money person-to-person in Kenya than in the United States.[4] This remarkable innovation is now being rolled out across Africa and considered in the Middle East, with the potential to reach billions of users.

These local adaptations of existing technology are creating impressive new markets. But such experiences are still different from mass global consumer adoption of new consumer technologies. And few have started in the Middle East.

But as I considered which situations and experiences might foster this kind of innovation on a global scale in the Middle East, I identified three areas with interesting potential. First, with its near 100 percent average mobile penetration, and the rapidly growing adoption of smartphones that some experts believe could reach 50 percent within three years, what might this market have to teach the world about the future of mobile innovation? Second, the largest untapped resource of fresh water in the world lies beneath the Egyptian-Libyan desert, but there's no cost-efficient, reliable way to deliver the petroleum needed to power the pumps to get it out. What innovation in solar-powered pumping and agriculture could solve it? And third, what about the millions of people who communicated and coordinated on mobile devices and Twitter and Facebook during the Arab uprisings? They told stories. They toppled regimes. Might the next great global social network rise from their experiences?

I wanted to find out more.

The Mobile Revolution

William Hague is executive vice president, international of AT&T Mobility, formerly Cingular Wireless. AT&T's strategy has been to not focus on emerging markets much beyond roaming partnerships. They have generally been more focused on its domestic base where its business model and infrastructure are more responsive to higher-value markets like the United States. In more developed markets, consumer expectations for product sophistication, customer service and price are on the higher end, and the average revenue per user (ARPU) hovers around $60 per month—a sweet spot for AT&T. While ARPUs occasionally reach this high in the Gulf States, most Middle Eastern markets are well below $20—and in Africa, below $6.00. But William recognizes there is a mobile revolution afoot, with huge ramifications not only for telephony but for entire societies. That is one reason they stay connected to these markets through partnership.

His first "a-ha!" moment came 30 years ago as a Peace Corps volunteer in Togo, West Africa. "We so take instant connectivity for granted here in the States," he explains, "that we forget the incredible behavioral impact of *not* having it day to day." When he first arrived in Togo he quickly adjusted to dealing without accustomed comforts—cooking over an open fire instead of a stove, reading a book instead of watching a television, using kerosene lamps in absence of electricity, using buckets instead of showers. "But lack of immediate, daily communication stopped everything. Every day I watched people travel 30 miles to engage in some business dealing. The person they wanted to meet might be there or they might not. It was maddening. How can there be real progress?" He even tried to form intertown basketball leagues, and it was nearly impossible. "We had to arrange games weeks in advance, send physical notes driving there and back. I can't get over the money we spent in taxis alone sending messengers around," he says. "But think what happens when more people have mobile phones than have access to electricity?"

Hague is also AT&T's board member of the Groupe Speciale Mobile Association (GSMA), the London-based global trade association for the mobile industry. Representing over 800 carriers in 200 countries, they are, among other things, a clearinghouse for new market opportunities and innovation among their members. "In every meeting there is a new story of some innovation in an emerging market, not merely about increased access to mobility, but entire business environments that are springing up," he reports. To help me get a handle on mobile innovation potential in emerging worlds, he introduced me to Chris Locke, who, as managing director of GSMA Mobile for Development, is a sort of in-house futurist for the organization. He comes by his passion for technology and emerging markets the long way. Formerly an internet executive for AOL and the Virgin Group, he was also the Xerox Lecturer in Electronic Communication and Publishing at University College London, running the master's degree course in the same name. GSMA has proven a perfect marriage of his past and what he believes is coming.

"M-Pesa is the tip of the iceberg for mobile bringing banking for the unbanked," he tells me. "In almost every emerging market we see mobile phone penetration at 50 percent or greater. Banks in many of these same societies reach a fraction of that. Mobile can bridge this gap, but the real story is that they are creating new hubs of innovation for entire societies." He points out, as an example, that in Africa alone there are over 680,000 rural mobile base station towers off the electrical grid. Out of necessity they have their own generators for electricity—sometimes powered by wind and solar, but mostly diesel—which use only a fraction of their capacity. An entire cottage industry of entrepreneurs has emerged, re-selling this energy to power local villages, medical facilities, and, charging stations for people's mobile phones—in communities with little hope of seeing electricity otherwise. In India, companies like India Barefoot Power have built significant enterprises around renting and recharging batteries. In Nairobi, most rural lighting is provided by kerosene lamps, which are inefficient, unhealthy, and ecologically unsustainable. One entrepreneurial company, M-Kopa, has distributed thousands of small, battery-charged electrical lanterns for free. Each has a 2GB chip connected to M-Pesa, where, for a few cents, customers who never had access to electrical light and can't afford solar options can turn lights on and off with an SMS. "What is so underestimated," Chris tells me, "is that one can *never* predict any of this. It is innovation that comes from the ground up. Will mobile-paid lanterns take off in the United States? Of course not. But there are over one billion people without access to electricity. Think of what happens when they do, and what ideas will be created that will impact a billion others?"

Locke adds that the history of mobile is one wherein all parties—device manufacturers, service providers, governments—grossly underestimate consumer uptake. "If you look at almost any study by any government in emerging markets in the 1980s, almost all thought penetration would be to a few elite thousand users. They underestimated the hunger for communication, the innovation that would come with it, and the multiple impact of the speed of drop in pricing." He has no doubt that the adoption of smartphones in emerging markets will follow a similar pattern. "We have already seen it in developed countries who can afford multi–hundred dollar devices, but within a year or so we will see regular adoption of sub-$90 smartphones in Africa and the Middle East." Safaricom, in fact, tested one in 2011 in Nairobi and within months over 350,000 were sold. "These aren't iPhones; the feature sets are pretty simple. But they are real computing devices allowing calling, texting, and email and internet access. Penetration of higher-end smartphones alone in these regions already range 15 to 20 percent or more. Within three years that number could break 50 percent. Imagine the ramifications of that."

Kamal Shehadi, having spent the last 15 years advising or participating in the opening of the Middle East's telecom markets to competition, understands those ramifications better than most. He is the chief legal and regulatory officer for Etisalat, one of the largest mobile providers in the Middle East and Africa. Shehadi's thoughtful and analytic mind reflects his days at Harvard and Columbia, where he completed a doctorate in political economy in the mid-1990s. He combines a blunt, fact-based delivery with a warm and disarming smile, which has gained him a reputation, as one government official told me, "as the most incorruptible man I ever knew to serve in government." As a former consultant to the World Bank on telecom liberalization and privatization in the Middle East, and subsequently the head of the Lebanese authority for licensing and regulating telecommunications, Shehadi is a visionary with a pragmatic sense of political reality. Telecom found him by accident. During the mid-1990s, many Middle Eastern governments were considering a series of privatization initiatives to raise revenue in response to increased global competition. "I had a choice between telecom and finance," he recalls, "and telecom just seemed more interesting and attractive. The industry in the region was comprised mostly of state-backed monopolies, and I felt there was opportunity to make big change."

He found, however, that most governments at the time were also fairly comfortable with their state-backed telephony monopolies. They made money, they maintained control without taking the heat for any problems, and it was easy to manage an industry consisting of at most one or two players. Government officials in some countries had political and/or personal interests in these companies' success. But ultimately two things persuaded the political leadership to reconsider. First, they needed help introducing mobile technology to sclerotic and rigid monopolies, and the fastest way to "acquire" that expertise was to form public and private partnerships. Second, they saw an opportunity to generate new revenues without necessarily having to face head-on opposition, from those with a stake in the old way, to the reform of state-owned monopolies. In 1998, the Moroccan government held the region's first auction for mobile licenses. "This was the real watershed," Shehadi recalls. "The government, based on the analysis of consultants, thought consumer penetration might reach 50,000 from a few thousand—so a decent uptick in demand, but not a blow-out. They assumed that any auction bids for spectrum therefore might come in around $50 to $70 million. And they were not alone. Across the region, from Lebanon and Jordan to Saudi Arabia, the projections had been pretty timid." But when the auction was held, the winning bid by Meditel (a consortium of Telefonica and Portugal Telecom) came in at almost $1 billion. Clearly, the mobile companies saw far greater opportunity.

A few years later, Algeria garnered $800 million in a similar auction, also hundreds of millions of dollars more than they expected. By 2004, Saudi Arabia, Jordan, and Egypt followed suit. "There was resistance at first from the old guard, and you can imagine the previous monopolists were not happy," Shehadi shrugs. "But not only were the dollars compelling to countries under pressure to raise money, it became quickly clear abroad and in the region that competition was good for everyone. Politicians could boast that there *was* competition and that prices had dropped significantly—all politically desirable." The numbers speak for themselves. As Middle East countries raised billions of dollars in license fees, consumer prices dropped a hundredfold, sometimes more. Penetration went from near zero to a regional average over 80 percent in North Africa and the Levant, and over 150 percent in the Gulf countries by 2010.

And it had a profound effect on how governments thought about their role in these new competitive environments. To ensure the success of auctions and to attract regional players (like Etisalat, Orascom, Zain, and STC), and global players (like Vodafone and France Telecom), governments established the first independent regulatory authorities in order to convince regional and global bidders that they were serious and prepared for the long run. "The region underwent a process of 're-regulation,' clearing away old, bureaucratic, and rigid regulations and introducing contemporary, business-friendly, and flexible regulations," Shehadi explains. "This was crucial for the health of the telecom ecosystem." Comforted by these changes, investors were able to make the investments to build the networks and sell the services to millions of users.

Now the challenge is getting the level of regulation just right to move from the telecom revolution to the mobile computing revolution. This is no small feat when you consider the protections businesses and consumers will require for mobile transactions, cloud computing, and privacy guarantees. "Until recently, not *one* country in the Middle East and North Africa region would meet the standards required to safeguard the privacy and integrity of online transactions as in Europe or North America," Shehadi notes. "But this is changing—and it has already in some countries in the Gulf and will soon spread throughout the region. This sends a huge signal that the region is open for online and mobile business and wants to be competitive on a global scale."

By 2011, mobile providers were turning their attention to two unstoppable phenomena: increasing access to smartphones and data, and innovations coming from the startups pressing forward in mobile. For the carriers, building out greater capacity for data in these environments is very expensive. Some carriers have even partnered with competitors to share the costs, and governments have talked about greater investments in fiber backbones—but keeping up with demand is a challenge. Shehadi told me, "With the collapse of the global economy after 2008, most telecom investors became fairly risk-averse. But what many people miss, and we've seen this from Africa to the Philippines, is that the key over time to drive up revenue per user is simply education." Etisalat discovered that, regardless of the sophistication of the device or the user, the average person barely uses a fraction of the features on a given device.

The more features they use, the more of their bandwidth they use, and their per-user revenue increases. "I've seen repeatedly through my time in the region," Shehadi observes, "that as people have access to more mobile technology, they are willing to spend more on telecom or online. So in Nigeria our operation there set up shops with what we call 'The Geek Force'—young telecom consultants who tell you how to use different features on the phone. They were plugged into music, movies, fashion, and gave mini tutorials to walk-in customers. People got hooked on the services, and 'The Geek Force' became key to significant growth in our revenue per user. And this growth is central to our ability to invest and roll out more services faster." These efforts have not been as easy so far in the Middle East where customers are more reserved and more reluctant to seek help from a total stranger. "But it will happen."

Shehadi's colleague at Etisalat, Khalifa Alforah, holds what is becoming a common title at mobile companies in the region: director of digital services. Educated at the University of Kentucky and later in the UAE, Alforah has been at Etisalat for twenty years, and was a central figure in the rollout of their mobile efforts. "The other thing about mobile computing that people underestimate is that the cost of marketing with time decreases. User appetite, once they appreciate what they have, is unlike anything I've ever seen. They just like to jump in and use things." The key, he argues, is for organizations like his to be open to partner throughout the growing ecosystem. "No one enterprise has a monopoly on innovation; in fact the effort to try assures we can kill it. My goal is to constantly reach out to traditional partners (like telecom vendors), internet partners (like Google and Facebook), universities—but most of all the startup communities where amazing thinking is coming. There are things happening in the pipeline around commerce, mobile payments, social media, content (especially video), music, gaming—and we can not only support these but bring our footprint to bear to help innovation adoption at progressively faster times than ever before." Also key to success in the breadth of services will be complete interoperability among whatever payment methods customers they choose or bank they prefer.

The ramifications of these partnerships are enormous. When I was in Dubai in the fall of 2012, Etisalat had just launched "Etisalat Mobile Baby," a suite of mobile services for doctors, birth attendants, and midwives in Africa and the Middle East. Hundreds of thousands of women die each year in and around childbirth in these regions, a significantly higher rate than in more developed markets. Partnering with global wireless technology and services juggernaut Qualcomm and nongovernment organizations like the World Health Organization and D-Tree International, they have created the most comprehensive maternal mobile health-care program in the world. Mobile Baby is offering customers in Saudi Arabia, Tanzania, the UAE, and Nigeria ultrasound-based remote monitoring of pregnancy and clear protocols to identify and report any danger signs, as well as mobile connection to facilities where patients can be picked up in an emergency. The costs of such transportation are integrated into the first mobile payment capabilities right on the phone. As of this writing, over 500 birth attendants, 10,000 pregnant women, seven major hospitals, and 26 regional health facilities were participating. "This will save lives by the thousands over time," Alforah believes. "And it begins to make one question what problems can't be addressed at the scale of connection mobile offers."

Vodafone Egypt dives even more proactively into the local startup scene to keep their fingers on the pulse of what's coming. Vodafone Ventures in Egypt is headed by Mohammed Al-Ayouti, a Cairo University engineering grad and a pioneering internet entrepreneur in his own right. Having built a freelance web management operation in the late 1990s, he joined Vodafone as 3G was rolled out in Egypt. By 2007, he was asked to explore the potential of mobile internet, and launched the first "one [Egyptian] pound a day" plan, building one of the first mobile portals for their customers in the region. Al-Ayouti, like most of the players in the region, was stunned by the adoption rates of mobile telephony, so it was no surprise that data would follow suit. "We had to scramble at times to expand capacity and one-up increasing competition. We had the luxury of being able to tap into Vodafone's global resources. There is a reason we were the first to offer iPhones in Egypt," he notes. But it was the rise of the startup communities that he knew carriers had to engage with. "Look, we have to deliver numbers first and foremost today—but to ignore tomorrow is foolish," he told me over breakfast in Cairo. "There is so much we offer the ecosystem in terms of partnership, but the best innovation will come from the ground. We can accelerate their innovation by facilitating the ecosystem with our reach, experience, knowledge, and capital."

In 2012, Vodafone launched Xone Egypt, which will commit roughly $3 million at launch to invest in at least ten seed-stage startups. "We have three criteria," Al-Ayouti explains. "Is the innovation a strategic fit with us? Is it truly commercially viable and scalable? Do they have outstanding management?" In exchange, Xone will help incubate early stage companies with space, resources, and hands-on support, as well as integrating them with Vodafone's own next-generation labs to ideate, test, and outreach to developers around Egypt. "We are helping to create a sense of speed and urgency with the efficiency we are creating here," Al-Ayouti enthuses, "but I hope we will make Vodafone easier to work with and also re-engage in our own roots in entrepreneurial innovation." They also offer connection and mentorship opportunities with Vodafone Xone's global headquarters in Silicon Valley.

In October of 2012, they announced their first three investments. To engage in mobile e-commerce, they backed Eshtery, a mobile virtual supermarket that leverages quick response (QR) bar codes to help shoppers buy everyday items online. Excited by their earlier success backing and supporting one *Problem Solver*, the Cairo traffic navigation mobile startup Bey2ollak, they jumped on another, Ogra, the taxi booking service for Cairo. Hoping to expand their presence in video, they also invested in GyroLabs, which connects existing television broadcasting to more interactive applications online and on mobile devices. "Any one of these companies could be game changers for Egypt and the entire Middle East," Ayouti notes. "Some globally. These are early days. But the ramifications on Middle East society, on major players like us, for a new generation building scalable businesses in technology—all in a still relatively upswing in mobile and smartphone adoption—who knows where this can all lead?" The next wave of investments will be completed by the time this book is published.

"You know, we have a lot of sun . . ."

One need only fly in to Cairo to see the potential in solar energy in Egypt, and the rest of the Middle East. According to the 2011 Global Market Outlook by the European Voltaic Industry Association, a leading trade association for solar-powered electricity, Egypt and the Middle East overall is uniquely suited to be a juggernaut in solar. With its clear skies and flat deserts, it has the potential to double the kilowatt per square kilometer ratio of southern Spain. The EVIC further estimates that one square kilometer of land in the Middle East has the power to yield in energy the equivalent of 1.5 million barrels of crude oil.[5] The European Union's Solar Radiation Atlas and the German Aerospace Center estimate that Egypt's economically viable solar potential is many times its current electricity production.[6] Historically, solar has remained at a disadvantage to heavily subsidized conventional sources of energy. KarmSolar believes that the drop in technological costs worldwide and a phasing out of subsidies offer opportunity now.

"One of the challenges," KarmSolar founder Ahmed Zahran told me in his modest one-floor office in the leafy area of Cairo, Zamalek, "is that the opportunities offered by alternative energy are so large it plays to a feeling that the only way to go at it is as governments went after oil. That it will take enormous government infrastructure and large business investment to crack it. In some cases that may be true. But how many digestible, smaller opportunities are out there that smart, flexible innovation in solar could solve instantly? And in fact that they are digestible doesn't mean they can't, with time, become very big." It is a little known fact that by far the largest collection of fresh water resides deeply in the aquifers below hundreds of miles of desert under Egypt, Libya, Sudan, and Chad. Zahran and his team of ten, in partnership with Worldwater & Solar Technologies, a leading water and energy technology company in Princeton, New Jersey, believe they can leverage solar power affordably to help pump water to farms bordering on the desert throughout Egypt.

Zahran is the intense, thirty-two-year-old son of an air force engineer who later founded an operations and maintenance company that serviced some of Egypt's largest prisons. "His first business actually failed; his second was quite successful," he recalls. "I saw how people ignored him when he was down, sucked up to him when he thrived. It made an impression on me—it taught me you could fail and come back. And it taught me that you really only know people when things are tough." The rest of Zahran's family is equally established. His uncle was head of security and then governor of a large area, before being dismissed as Minister of Domestic Development after a political clash with some figures in the Mubarak regime. His mother was a prominent news anchor and political analyst. He wanted nothing to do with any of it. At the American University of Cairo, he was active in the Philosophy Club, the leading group for political debate and activism, where he was known as both a do-gooder and a rebel.

It was with some irony that when he graduated during the recession of 2002 he took a job with Shell in their financial group, and spent time at their headquarters in Tunisia and London. "It was an amazing five years," he recalls. "Finance, energy trading, all that they did didn't move me, but it was all interesting and got me thinking about who I was in college, about impact, about the potential and scale in alternative energies." He formed a mentorship with a Shell executive, an Egyptian, who had broken off in 2008 to start his own oil company in Egypt, and created a subsidiary to decrease product emissions through carbon trading. "It was a good idea, and I worked with him for three years. But the whole idea of carbon trading, we found, was not well designed by the UN and wasn't making any impact in lessening the carbon footprint." As a young employee with access to significant data, he became interested in the potential of solar. When he started making connections in his own mind between the potential of water access and affordable energy to drive it, his idea for a company, KarmSolar, was born. During the Arab uprising, business came to a dead stop and he joined his college classmates in Tahrir Square. He knew throughout it, however, that he wanted to re-dedicate himself to impact through entrepreneurship. In October 2011 he and three colleagues left to start it full time. "We knew that the company would continue the revolution in our own way. We knew a lot about alternative energy, and we knew the kind of change it could create."

When one flies across Egypt, the importance of water is palpable. For miles around the Nile River the land runs green and lush, full of agriculture. And then it cuts abruptly to white, unrelenting desert. "It is hard to fathom with what you saw, that the soil is rich and it lays hundreds of feet above more water than will pass through the Nile for nearly 3,000 years. There is more water than in all of California. And less than 1 percent of it is currently accessed." Less than one-fifth of the potentially arable land in Egypt is in use right now, and the water that is pumped is powered by unreliable shipments of diesel fuel. "You've seen these spaces," Ahmed tells me. "One has to allow long distances to move fuel for farms to pump water. It is unreliable, it is difficult to store at any quantity, and even with government subsidies of as much as 80 percent—which are about to decrease and may even go away—it is expensive. What farmer could risk cultivating the remainder of his land with that kind of uncertainty of water access?"

I asked him why solar hadn't yet been used to address this opportunity, and he looked disgusted. "The hardest thing for outsiders to appreciate when considering Egypt, the biggest change that has to happen here and I think *is* changing, has been our absence of imagination. *This* was the greatest legacy of the Mubarak regime. One understands petroleum, one knows that with limited access to it, he can perform in limited but sort-of adequate ways—but farmers can't think beyond it, they can't think big." There really was no past experience in alternative resources for people to call upon. There were some small government projects, some billboards and streetlights powered by solar or wind but few successes at scale. And in fact, as Ahmed soon learned, most of the lessons were negative. "People don't think it even works. Panels blow away. Farmers who were willing to try it were asked to install things themselves and it wasn't easy. Finally, they are suspect of ideas that don't come from the government. It is an education task. But it is changing. And we're in a three-fold sweet spot: we are in the best location on earth for this in the solar belt; we're sitting on all the water that is needed; and despite the issue of diesel, we're in one of the largest markets for water pumps in the world."

Ahmed's chief technologist, Xavier Auclair, is a French engineer and a true believer. He notes that solar technology is not without its challenges. The main one is matching the specific farmer's water needs along the year with the varying flow rate of the pump under solar energy—i.e., a maximum at noon, nothing at night, and intermediate in between. Energy storage through batteries for night use is too expensive and inefficient to be realistic for large capacities for the time being. Thus KarmSolar optimizes the sizing of each component, including water storage, to ensure reliability of water throughout the year at a relatively cheap cost. "Our technology that can connect existing pumping to solar capabilities will simply ensure steady access to water and great reliability to expand farmable land," he told me after joining my meeting with Ahmed. "Farmers should worry about crop production. We can worry about their energy needs."

KarmSolar plans to be the "solar management interface" of Egypt. They work with farmers to plan and design their water and expansion plans, install basic solar capabilities for pumping, and monitor their systems entirely online. They will also connect to weather information to help manage expectations should conditions interfere with solar use. "Every tool farmers will need to understand the potential of solar, how to integrate it in their existing pumping systems, how to plan for best crop optimization and alternate crops, what water storage if any they will need, monitoring the efficacy of the performance of their systems—all can be at our and their fingertips," Ahmed explains. KarmSolar will effectively be both a technology creator and general contractor to the whole process. "Once the needs assessment is made, we will connect with our subcontracting partner for implementation." For smaller farmers dedicated to food production for their local markets, but who may still not yet be able to afford these less costly solutions, KarmSolar is working to decrease costs further and develop financing solutions.

David York, senior vice president at KarmSolar's U.S. partner in Princeton, Worldwater and Solar Technologies, told me that his company saw the opportunity immediately. To them, KarmSolar was seeking to essentially turn the desert green by solving the significant cost and reliability issues of supplying diesel fuels to very remote locations. He told me, "Their approach is unique because there are no other companies, to our knowledge, that are able to leverage solar energy to directly drive these very large water pumps for irrigation in remote parts of the world. Typically, these very large pumps and motors require a reliable, sustainable source of electricity like the electricity grid. Due to the variable nature of solar energy, there are several programmable interconnection capabilities required to stabilize the supply of electricity to these pumps and motors. Their ideas and our patents are capable of stabilizing and matching the appropriate amount of electricity to the pumps and motors through its interconnection technology." York believes that the largest agriculture and water services companies (such as Suez, Veolia, John Deere, Grundfos, and Culligan) should partner and pool their technology to utilize the 75 percent of the earth's unused arable land to grow crops and provide food security all over the world.

The business opportunity here, of course, could be significant. But for Ahmed, what he is building is part of a broader trend he calls "Disconnected Development." Remember how mobile providers, having built independent sources of electricity for their rural cell towers also empowered entrepreneurs to build businesses around them? Those efforts were not part of any grid, they didn't rely on any central planning. They became access points to individual communities, who then created the innovation. In the aggregate, the individual impacts become big. And they facilitate connections among communities that were all but geographically impossible before. "This is exactly what KarmSolar is as well," Ahmed notes. "My generation's experience is suspect of central planning. It is not as often as effective as what communities understand of their own needs or what they can do for themselves. And now technology and renewable energies allow for incredible localized innovation that still scales. Imagine cities one day without central water, sewage, or energy grids, but facilitated in smaller communities, even individually. Take KarmSolar to its logical conclusion—businesses having access to near limitless energy and water. This means farms and communities rising in the middle of deserts in Egypt and around the world. Imagine Egypt and places like it going from 6 to 8 percent of land use to 25 percent. What will that mean in alleviating overcrowded cities like Cairo? Our part of the world can and should focus on these kinds of capabilities because the opportunities are huge, not only for innovation here, but also for anywhere in the world."

The Next Facebook?

The concept of Disconnected Development and unique local experiences has implications for the consumer internet as well. It's pretty hard to think of a great consumer-facing platform that isn't, by its nature, social. Should it be surprising, then, that fresh off the Arab uprisings, so often coordinated and communicated through Facebook and Twitter, entrepreneurs in the Middle East have a special perspective on consumer-facing platforms and social networking?

Yasmin Elayat certainly does. Born and raised in Silicon Valley as the daughter of a successful tech entrepreneur, she visited Egypt each year for three months throughout her childhood. In 1997, when her grandfather in Cairo passed away, she and her family decided to move there. In 2001, while studying computer engineering at Santa Clara University, she transferred to the American University of Cairo. Her ambition—to marry computer technology with storytelling and interactive design—took her later to NYU for a master's degree. But the protests in Tahrir Square convinced her to return to Egypt for good.

"In February 2011, I took a huge leap of faith," says Elayat. "I quit a great job in New York, and moved to Cairo to live off my savings and work full-time on what was essentially an art project that I really believed in."

"Millions of Egyptians were capturing moments of the uprisings on their mobile devices and social networks in real time, allowing the world to witness the frontlines of history in the making. We believed a collaborative storytelling platform to create the first crowdsourced web documentary would be the best way to capture it all. We could empower the source as the storyteller—essentially having a country write its own history."

Their site, 18 Days in Egypt, offered an innovative visual technology platform for collaborative storytelling. A grant from the Tribeca Film Institute's New Media Fund, the Ford Foundation, and a successful Kickstarter campaign all helped her and her co-founders document changes in Egypt in remarkable and unusual ways. People posted their stories, photos, tweets, and videos by the thousands.

The experience inspired Elayat and her team to think about broader ramifications of collaboration from these experiences, and what the platform that powered 18 Days could become. "We all create millions of media fragments of important moments and experiences in our lives on Facebook, Twitter, YouTube, and other services," Yasmin told me. "However, today those important moments from our lives are fragmented and scattered across different social media services, out of context, and buried under the avalanche of always-newer events."

Path, Instagram, and other social platforms capture daily experiences as one narrative. But, she argues, we all have many different shared experiences each day. There are no easy solutions to take all our important moments, curate them, and create a visual story to share with our friends or the public at large.

"Storify, Storination, Kaptur, and others are exploring this," she notes. "But what we learned form 18 Days in Egypt is that the best stories are those that are told together. Our next iteration is a mobile-first, web-second storytelling experience for groups to easily tell stories of small, personal events (like road trips, weddings) or [about] large public events (like the campaign trail, Olympics, conferences) in an easy, visual way."

Ahmed Soliman similarly thinks the time is right for global adoption of any great product—as long as it is, well, great. "I suspect there may be some resistance, at least in the West, to sharing personal data and experiences if they perceive the platform is not secure in places like the Middle East. But good infrastructure is a requirement anywhere. It just means building a product that says 'this is so awesome I don't care where it's from, I'm just going to use it.'" Soliman is CEO of CircleTie, an Egyptian-launched mobile geolocation social network he believes will leapfrog popular but aging U.S.-created services like Foursquare. "They, Google and Facebook, focus on your search patterns and your given location as a proxy to who you are or what you want in a given moment. But who we are also has a context—as simple as what is the time of day, what is the weather, what were you just doing—that is a much fuller picture of who and what you may wish to connect with."

Soliman is a Cairo-based computer engineer and a self-described tech geek. But as interesting to him as the technology itself is the psychology behind why people do what they do with it. "I loved puzzles and problem solving, which made me an effective coder," he explained. "But it was my experiences in virtual worlds like gaming that helped me see how raw emotion and interactions would manifest themselves among players who didn't really 'know each other.' It was fun, which means it is engaging and you learn more in a way than one does in boring school classes." But it was also instructive to his perceptions of people, what they might do, what context might make them act in surprising ways, and what problems they could solve together—all of which inspired his entrepreneurial thinking.

His first job out of college was as a programmer at IBM, and while he never intended to stay in a big company forever, he made some money, built some connections, and learned what worked and what didn't in programming. He also learned management skills—how to plan a project, meet deadlines, communicate with customers who often didn't know what they wanted technologically but allowed him to lead in creating elegant solutions for them. When friends offered him a job in 2008 in an e-learning platform for the region, he jumped at it. "We had an investor, but no product, no concrete vision," he recalls with amazement, "I knew it would be fun, but had no idea really how hard it would be on our own."

While the company failed by 2010, he was now only interested in start-ups and joined as the first tech hire for a new computer security company. He and some buddies, however, were also plotting a side project.

"We actually started getting together to brainstorm a host of ideas," he told me, "But we kept coming back to our mobile devices, how we all used the Western services like Google, Facebook, but there was nothing really for local markets and entertainment—no Yelp, no Foursquare. It seemed like a gaping opportunity." Initially, therefore, CircleTie was something of an Improviser—a localization of mobile social networks in the United States. "We were a city discovery tool. Not merely a directory, though getting a lot of local entertainment data was central to our launch. We were first and foremost a discovery tool focused on your friends—what are they up to, what do they like, what are they saying about places. And we even had movies, which most social networks then did not."

Ironically, the Arab uprising had first a negative, then a very positive impact on the company. "We released right before the Revolution and had circled a serious 'Series A' round with a local VC. We had gathered over 40,000 users before we were saying much publicly," he pauses for emphasis. "The Revolution came and everything simply died. Nobody was looking to 'go out,' they were looking to change our society. It took months to bring back even 20,000 users." This, however, led to something very positive. In between their own political activity, they turned all their attention to what they were learning on the streets and what might make for a unique product. What, they asked, could happen if, in addition to search, intent, and location, they built an algorithm to build in context?

"What good is a restaurant result for dinner if it's 8:00 AM," Soliman and the team posited, "or planning to connect with friends at an outdoor place if it's about to rain? We began to think context is as or more important than location." Soliman, in fact, had started a master's degree at the American University of Cairo in context-sensitive mobile search. "It is a hard problem to solve," he notes, "But solve it we have." CircleTie's recently released check-in process combines the elements of other social networks, but builds in context. Its user experience also makes it easy to visually ascertain if a location is open and leave an instant review in one click. In addition, the user controls which people they wish to notify, rather than broadcasting to their entire social network and, again, the relevant context to help them connect. Their new beta popped in October to 60,000 in Cairo, and they are populating data for Beirut, Amman, Dubai, Alexandria, and Riyadh. "Having basic city data and content is a cost of entrée to make the app appealing in any city, but it is the ongoing learning and data we acquire in our contextual engine that makes the experience most unique." CircleTie is in rich conversations with the major mobile players, like Vodafone, to combine their reach with their targeted expertise and innovation.

Is this ready for the West? Soliman doesn't skip a beat. "This product is also English-based, because we think eventually that will make it easiest for global adoption. Other languages will come to." In many ways, he speaks for everyone pursuing "leap frog" innovation in the region. "Obviously it would be great to make it in the United States. There is no market like it and we're having partnership discussions with the obvious players there. But what so many people miss is that it is a *very* big world out there. The Middle East will be significant, but 'going global' for us is taking our unique technology to other underserved growth markets and helping *them* leapfrog their engagements can be a path to reaching billions."

So what is next? "Eastern Europe," he says immediately. "They have outstanding penetration of smartphones, love social engagements, and are not well catered to by the big players. From there the rest of Europe, and who knows."

∾

*Ramez Shehadi is a distant cousin of Kamal at Etisalat. A Lebanese-*born engineering grad from Rutgers and the University of Toronto, Ramez has spent the last decade in management consulting, first with A. T. Kearney and then building and heading the technology practice for Booz in Dubai. Aside from advising top global technology companies across the spectrum of social media, applications, security, cloud, and mobile strategies, Booz has become a leading go-to source for data on what is happening in the tech sector in the Middle East. "Our reports have made clear the trends of adoption and rise of startups in the region," he told me and, in fact, I have used their data extensively in this writing. "But I see all the details, carve it 100 different ways. Until we had the explosion in the mobile space that in turn helped barriers to come down for internet accessibility, it was hard, frankly, to really dream. In the last three years, I think pushed over the line by the Arab uprisings, there is an entirely different dynamic. Study the ecosystem builders—the incubators, the investors, the conferences, the meet-ups, the caliber of information sharing all enabled by technology and betting on these startups. That will give you a sense how the society, the cultures are evolving as well."

I asked him if he had an "a-ha!" moment—that piece of data, that case study, that experience where he felt it all had come together, marked a tipping point. He didn't skip a beat: "We are in the middle of the "a-ha!" moment right now—the start of the hockey stick."

Chapter 5

The Ecosystem Builders

In the blurry, uncertain weeks after Mubarak fell, a small story came over Twitter that I had to read twice to believe. The word "exit" at the time was used solely in connection with the departure of a politician or business executive caught on the wrong side of historic, popular forces. It was pretty shocking, then, to hear it in a different context—the "exit" investors describe when a company is sold. Cairo-based SySDSoft, a leading 4G wireless software developer, was acquired by Intel.

I had met Khaled Ismail, the company's founder and CEO, in Cairo a week before Tahrir Square. His was a classic startup success. Having received his PhD from MIT, Ismail founded his company out of both passion and necessity. He was building operations in Cairo for a U.S. company that failed to survive the bubble burst of 2001, and he saw significant talent and market opportunity in region. He started with just two employees. "It was not very difficult," he reflects of those early days, "as I was blessed with a great team. My main challenge was always to find new customers abroad who were willing to trust an Egyptian company to deliver top-notch technical work for them." But find them he did, and

SySDSoft quickly grew to nearly 100 engineers, moving from offering engineering design services to developing its own intellectual property in the 4G telecom world. Intel, who doesn't take outstanding engineering talent lightly, was clearly betting on that team and market even in a time of turbulence.

In his early fifties and scholarly, with eyeglasses and an analytic approach to problem solving, Khaled is a bridge between the early Middle East tech entrepreneurs and the new generation. "It is truly a hundred times now what we had even two years ago." He paused to reflect. "But of course, a large number of these startups will fail, and it could bring us back to square one, where people are afraid to take risk. It is more important than ever that we mentor such startups to ensure the greatest success, or we will be regretting the failure to build the proper ecosystem."

"Ecosystem" is one of those great, elusive techno terms that means something slightly different to everyone, much as the U.S. Supreme Court famously described pornography: "You know it when you see it." People may differ on what variable creates the best environment for startups, but there is little argument over the core ingredients. "It is about access to an extended community of talent and resources at scale across the spectrum of what it takes to build world-class product," Ben Horowitz told me at his favorite diner off the beaten track of more hip Silicon Valley hotspots. "A great ecosystem is about how one can easily connect the best, smartest, experienced ideas and talent; the smartest fellow entrepreneurs, investors, and mentors; access the best lawyers, marketing, accounting, and human resources. They are communities of support but also create incredible competition to breed a culture of excellence."

Great ecosystems require many different kinds of support, but in my experience, three core categories stand out. The first I call the *Investors*—women and men who not only provide the necessary financing to support an idea from birth through scale, but the mentorship, business relationships, and access to services like accounting, legal, and HR that young companies so desperately need. The *Conveners* are the individuals and platforms that help entrepreneurs connect with each other, and network to expand their horizons, learning, and opportunity. And the

Recognizers, those who organize competitions and shine light on the best ideas in an ecosystem, offer not only a sense of accomplishment to entrepreneurs, but also confidence, even an imprimatur, for investors.

These three groups face distinct challenges in building startup ecosystems in the Middle East, which are nascent by developed-market standards. Prod entrepreneurs and investors there, even gently, and you'll get an earful on the challenges. Regulatory weight and uncertainty, which varies by country, is often top of mind. Egyptian-American Ahmed Alfi has invested in technology and media from Los Angeles for nearly two decades. He returned to Cairo in 2006 to embrace the growing technology opportunities and founded one of the earliest venture capital funds there, Sawari Ventures. He believes the uneven and inconsistent application of the law in the region is the greatest threat to the startup ecosystem. It can keep investors on the sidelines in taking minority stakes in a company—a common way startups are funded—if their path to legal redress is unclear when wronged. In addition, sustained ineffective regulation and bureaucracy are an outgrowth of a lack of legal recourse. Even in the post-Mubarak era, he argues, the government in Egypt believes it is there to protect investors from themselves. "Most of the regulation is pre-emptive, solving problems before they occur, because they can't be solved in court and there is little incentive to protect minority investor rights," he explains. For instance, any new company has to appear physically before the Ministry of Investment, lawyer in tow, not only to receive approval but to set valuation. In Egypt it take weeks, even months, to then issue new stock; founders can't sell shares for two years and there is no provision for convertible notes that have become common early financing mechanisms in the United States or an easy way to grant stock options to key employees.

Intel's director of global business development, Karim Fahmy, argues that broader cultural challenges around work ethic are more significant challenges than regulatory ones. Born in Cairo, he was educated in the United States and worked in Intel's manufacturing operations there before returning to Egypt in 2003 to head up their operations. He recalls with a laugh, "On my first day, in the heart of summer, I arrived at our relatively new operation at 7:30 A.M. to find everything completely shut. A security guard told me people don't show up until 8:45, that the air conditioning doesn't even go on until 9:00. By 10:00 our sales guy strolled in." At the same time, he was floored by strengths he believes build a foundation for a strong ecosystem. Local technology assembly capabilities were excellent. The regulatory worlds were easier to navigate than he had thought and he never experienced any corruption. In fact, the technical skills of his government customers were better than their counterparts in India. Every major technology juggernaut—Microsoft, IBM, HP, Dell—had been established there for years, if not decades. "We had a way to go, especially on the startup side, then," he told me, "but the foundation stones are there, and now the new generation is building the ecosystem on its strengths and simply bypassing its weaknesses."

Alfi concedes that it is easy to think only about dysfunction in the Middle East, but he is intrigued by what Egyptians do despite it. "Stop and think about it. For a year since the uprisings we functioned pretty well without any real government. Eventually government will have to make systems work, but in the meantime entrepreneurs have been building their own companies, solving problems, building their own ecosystem regardless." One Saudi early-stage investor captured what is perhaps the most repeated theme I have heard throughout my travels in the region: "All we need is a few success stories and success will breed success. Better regulation, more incubators, and stronger legal structures—all fine. But I will tell you that there is a pent-up demand here. Successful companies build a successful ecosystem, and vice versa. There is abundance of cash here and among the wealthy expatriates. The successes are starting; we need to show and celebrate them."

Things are moving so quickly in established markets and the network effect of those ecosystems is so strong that it's hard to attract the best talent to emerging markets, Horowitz believes. "Even in the States, while exciting things are happening in places like New York and other cities, they are still relatively small." He pauses. "I will say, however, that one of the greatest challenges of the ecosystems in the West is their echo chambers—the same people rallying around the same ideas, and trends can become a lot of noise. Fresh ideas, fresh thinking will absolutely come from places unencumbered by this."

The *Investors, Conveners,* and *Recognizers* I have met could not agree more. Comprised of local and regional entrepreneurs, experienced global expatriates and leaders from ecosystems around the world, their size and growing influence are startling. It's crucial to understand their role when assessing new opportunity in the Middle East.

The Investors

During my trip to Cairo in January 2011, I was asked to sit on a panel hosted by the American Chamber of Commerce. Their membership includes the most successful business leaders in the region, and it was an austere, suited, and serious crowd. I addressed some 300 of them in the ballroom of the Four Seasons. As I was watching their eyes glaze over while I described the potential in the startups I had seen, an epiphany hit me. The executives in this room could fund an entire ecosystem of startups in these early days without breaking a sweat, but none of them had put up a dime. This hesitancy persists to this day. When Saudi Prince Al-Waleed bin Talal, reputed to be worth over $18 billion, placed a $300 million bet on Twitter, Twitter itself lit up with tweets from young entrepreneurs in the region, all variations on the same sentiment: "Great, how about 10 percent of that for *our* startups!" It's understandable that investors remain on the sidelines, given the history of political unrest, poverty and corruption. But this doesn't explain why the great wealth that does exist in the region continues to fund enormous real estate and energy projects and create a Dubai out of a desert. "The good news is we have the money," one regional government official told me with an ironic laugh. "The bad news is it's in our pockets."

"You hit the nail on the head," Hany Sonbaty agreed, dropping the mouthpiece of his hookah pipe late into one lovely evening in a restaurant on the Nile. Sonbaty is a young Egyptian, a London-trained investment banker who joined Alfi in launching Sawari Ventures. "It is rooted deeply in our culture to want to invest conservatively, and in hard

assets—things like property that 'feels' real, that even in times of political uncertainty is something one can touch even live in." He smiles,
"And we like to show each other how successful we are by pointing to our
latest apartment building, or hotel, or manufacturing plant. It's hard here
to say, "Look how important I am, click on that website." Alfi later laughs
when I asked him about this. "The whole idea in venture capital is that
you hope to pick some real winners, but some companies absolutely will
go to zero. We Arabs don't like 'go to zero.' Failure is frowned upon, let
alone embraced anywhere in the region."

Alfi has a unique vantage point. Nearly four decades living in the
United States allows him to effectively bridge the American and Middle
Eastern mentalities. He and Sonbaty could see that something different
was happening among a new generation of entrepreneurs well before the
Arab uprisings, but Tahrir Square electrified their country with hopeful
patriotism. "Egyptians have always loved Egypt, but they haven't always
felt that Egypt belonged to them," he says. "People are feeling empowered now; they have demonstrated together for their rights and have
stood guard together over their homes and families. They are responsible
for Egypt now." Sonbaty adds that the new generations are already moving at internet speeds, refusing to wait for fixes to the obvious political,
structural, and economic challenges of the region. "The new generation
is educating themselves and bypassing failed systems. They are seeing
online what can be done and no longer being told what can't be done.
They are hungry for success and recognition." They believe that a rising
venture community feeds the ecosystem not only by bringing in capital,
but also by providing the kind of broader infrastructure that allows for
scalable success.

With this in mind, Sawari Ventures launched Flat6Labs in 2011, the
first of a crop of tech startup "accelerators" now popping up in Cairo, Alexandria, and around the Middle East. Like YCombinator, 500 Startups,
or Dog Patch Labs in the United States, Flat6Labs is a beautiful, open
office space where up to seven tech startups can be housed and supported for three months at a time. Flat6Labs provides early seed funding, computers, internet access, and training and access to basic HR,

accounting, and legal services. Each week, entrepreneurs and business school professors from Egypt and around the world mentor these start-ups, offering sessions on topics like marketing, user experience, digital advertising, project management, and more.

Sawari was more than happy to donate a floor of its renovated, turn-of-the-century building in the leafy Giza neighborhood right off of the Nile to help launch Flat6Labs. The American University of Cairo signed on as their partner eleven days before Tahrir Square, and their first entrepreneurs were "birthed" nine months later.

Sawari's next task was to find someone to lead Flat6Labs. Appropriately, they found the answer on Twitter. In April of 2011, 27-year-old Alexandria University computer science alum Ramez Mohamed was enjoying a successful career in website design for businesses, and later in mobile applications for one of the largest content and e-commerce portals in Egypt. Though he had never heard of a "tech accelerator" until he began to follow Sonbaty's tweets about Tahrir Square and entrepreneurship, he tweeted back his reactions, and eventually they agreed to meet. In preparation, Mohamed studied all the accelerator models in the United States and came loaded with ideas for Egypt. It was he who proposed the three-month cycles Flat6Labs would eventually adopt, and the rigorous vetting of online applications followed by the around-the-clock boot camps to coax out the best entrepreneurs of the generation. He wanted his companies hyper-focused on their businesses, and so established a central tenet: "no religion, no politics" in any discussions in their offices.

The process Mohamed created is simple and Darwinian. Each quarter, a new "cycle" commences, wherein Mohamed and his team select up to seven startup concepts from hundreds of candidates that apply online. Flat6Labs seeds each investment with the Egyptian pound equivalent of $10,000 to $15,000, in exchange for 10 to 15 percent ownership of the company. The selected teams are hosted in Flat6Labs headquarters. Each week they present their progress internally and to advisors and guests, and at the end of the cycle, on "Demo Days," they present to outside investors, mentors, media, and the business community. After each three-month cycle, Sawari invites other investors to fund the companies

(Sawari stays on as a passive investor or chooses to co-invest.) Once a company completes its cycle, it has to move out of the space—with or without backing.

Flat6Lab's first companies cover a wide range of concepts including online collaboration tools for businesses and their clients, online video services to offer greater access to on-demand programming, consumer-facing social recommendation engines for restaurants and other local entertainment and needs, and lots more. In a city and country suffering from significant infrastructure challenges, many entrepreneurs see digital paths as the way around them.

As the local angel investor community continues to develop and expand, Alfi, Sonbaty, and Mohamed plan to launch 100 startups or more through Flat6Labs by 2014, and believe other accelerators will expand as well. Since its inception, Flat6Labs has added some of the most distinguished cross-sector entrepreneurs in Egypt to its mentor and speaker network. They have operated four cycles and invested in twenty-four companies, most of which have gone on to raise further rounds. They have brought several of those companies to tour the United States, and in a whirlwind tour of Egypt in the fall of 2012, Secretary of State Hillary Clinton surprised them with a visit.

And there is more to come. When the American University of Cairo moved to its spacious new campus outside of Cairo in 2008, they planned to sell some of their old facilities. One particularly desirable part, known as "The Greek Campus," covers almost a full city block and one third of the old downtown campus. It's large, historic expanse—combining wonderful, classic nineteenth century buildings and more modern facilities—would be perfect for offices, restaurants and large gatherings. Located a quick walk from the Nile and National Museum and one of the business hubs of the city, it could not be more central or convenient.

It is, however, also a baseball's throw from Tahrir Square. And since the January 25, 2011 uprisings, it has sat untouched and untouchable. On the second anniversary of the uprisings, kitty corner from one end of it, thousands of protestors threw Molotov cocktails, set fires, and broke windows.

"I saw opportunity," Ahmed Alfi told me in a cushy law office in New York City in late January 2013, just as the violence had, for the moment, settled. He was there negotiating final documents with the American University of Cairo to turn the Greek Campus into the largest, most modern, most tech-friendly open work space, data center, auditorium, incubator, and tech offices in the Middle East. "If I'm wrong, I'll lose everything," he says bluntly, "But I just don't think betting against Egypt is the right bet."

Alfi has signed a 25 year lease to develop and manage the 250,000-square foot campus, today comprised of stately old classrooms, more modern library and auditorium facilities, a former restaurant and spacious court, open and airy courtyard. Google intends to sponsor the wifi-ed open work space that will allow techies to come to meet, brain storm, and create new ideas. He will move Flat6Labs here, as well as several portfolio companies, and other venture firms and global tech players are planning to move or open offices. Ghandour's Aramex plans to open a shipping and service center to help entrepreneurs and rising e-commerce players easily transact business. The American University of Cairo is exploring new activities, such as a potential children's science museum.

The partnership, announced in February of 2013, will break ground in the spring, and Alfi hopes space will begin to welcome entrepreneurs and ideators before the end of 2013. "It is a fantastic historical complex," he enthuses as he shows me dozens of photographs he's taken of almost every yard of the existing campus, "and it will help revive the entire downtown area and create a center of gravity geographically which is important for any ecosystem."

Usama Fayyad has a similar vision for Jordan. Fayyad is a bull of man, built like a linebacker, completely bald with the intense methodical and investigative mind of the great professor of data and analytics that he was. His intensity is offset by his warm smile and passion for his country, Islamic history, and poetry. Like Alfi, he also returned to the region after several years in the United States, in Usama's case in Silicon Valley, where he created and sold several successful technology and data companies. Yahoo!, in fact, acquired his last company and he spent over four years at the internet giant as executive vice president and chief data officer. He heads Oasis500, one of the first tech startup accelerators. Oasis500 is a privately held company backed by King Abdullah II, who challenged the private sector to address the gaps in the ecosystem that were preventing the numerous Jordanian IT graduates from forming tech startups. Founded in 2010, Oasis500's goal is to mentor, accelerate, and invest in 500 regional startups, and train, through "Boot Camp" sessions, 45,000 more within six years. Fayyad notes, "We are among the largest training, selection, earliest-stage angel investors, and next-stage investment facilitators in the region. Gatherings, meetups, competitions, mentorship—these are all essential. But where the rubber hits the road, where startups succeed or fail, is in successfully offering real funding and building paths to both a fast-growth mentality and culture of hard work."

Fayyad has put his stake in Amman, leveraging its well-trained IT population and a relatively low cost of doing business. Located geographically in the heart of this rapidly growing region, he notes Jordan is "an amazing place to do startups that benefit from local strengths, political and legal stabilities, and its capitalist orientation—it is a great environment to operate and grow companies." Oasis500's numbers are impressive. As of October 2012, they invested in 54 companies (well above the 32 they had expected) in 17 classes or "waves" of five weeks each. Twenty of these have received follow-on investments within four to five months of their launch at valuations ranging from three to ten times their initial investment. Startups have been mostly in digital and mobile content and e-commerce. Over 700 additional entrepreneurs have been trained (they expected 150), and they have held additional sessions for entrepreneurs in Ramallah, Palestine. "What can't be underestimated is culture," Usama emphasizes. "In Silicon Valley, successful entrepreneurs take for granted instilling a strong work ethic, put enormous value on speed and iteration and the need to fail fast and move on with what you learned. This is not endemic in our region at all." He pauses and smiles his enormous grin: "It is endemic in Oasis500 companies, and creates a good example for a broader ecosystem in Jordan and throughout the Middle East."

One of Fayyad's key insights is that while the talent in Jordan and elsewhere is strong, and the eagerness to learn even stronger, "plug and play" courses from the United States were not terribly effective locally. He first realized this when two Palestinian entrepreneurs showed up offering to run a seminar on "crossing the chasm," based on Geoffrey Moore's book of the same name. Moore discusses the strategy of releasing new tech product initially to early adopters rather than the larger majority of users, but then figuring out how to cross the chasm to the "early majority." Fayyad was very familiar with the book, used the methodology in his startups and, in fact, had Geoff Moore as an adviser who helped train the sales force of one of his companies. Since he agreed with its lessons for market segmentation and focus in product development, Usama figured, why not have them in?

He sat through their entire session, and at several points nearly fell out of his chair. For four hours he listened to localized versions of Moore's ideas. Case studies were all from business situations the entrepreneurs saw in daily life, with cultural nuances and local, colloquially spoken Arabic. "I realized that these kids were getting more in a few hours than I was going to offer them in five days of a seminar. I spent years in Silicon Valley, but learned that day that empowering this ecosystem will not be about importing material and teaching it, it's all about ways to make it reach them in the right context." Oasis500 began to create more and more of their own teaching materials. "Our investment money is important to these startups," Fayyad told me, "but relevant mentorship and acceleration is where the ecosystems take off."

He believes most of the opportunity for tech startups in the region at first lies in the Improvisers—those leveraging the opportunities that were already proven in the West—and invests accordingly. He too agrees that there is a great tailwind behind e-commerce. "In 2011, e-commerce was a $7 trillion industry globally," he throws up his hands. "Do you know what it was in the Arab market of 350+ million Arabic speakers? Less than $300 million!" For Fayyad this significant gap means only opportunity. As an example he cites their investment in a Souq.com e-commerce portal competitor, MarkaVIP. He knew and liked the founder

Ahmed Alkhatib from his days as the fourth employee at the Silicon Valley personalized gift site, Zazzle.com. Alkhatib came back to his home country of Jordan determined to build a startup and grow it fast with major funding. Starting with seven employees and seed funding, within a year he raised more than $15 million and now has over 350 employees. "Raising this amount of money so quickly was unheard of in the region," Usama notes, "but Ahmed showed real growth, doubling revenues every month. This opened up the eyes of many local and U.S./E.U. investors who clamored to participate in oversubscribed funding rounds. It is a great example of how big the untapped opportunity for IT in the Middle East really is."

Ecosystem building is happening even in Saudi Arabia, a country recently known for preventing half of its population from even driving. The numbers on the ground there are remarkable. Internet penetration was approaching 50 percent by 2012; mobile penetration surpassed 200 percent; and smartphone adoption, at nearly 30 percent, dwarfs any part of the region outside of the Gulf. There are over four million Facebook users, and the Saudi-based sports portal Kooora.com is one of the most trafficked sites in the world, with over one billion page views per month in the Middle East alone. The country has the highest YouTube per capita usage in the world with over 180 million video playbacks per month and, of all things, boasts the region's largest woman's portal, HawaaWorld .com, with over 100 million monthly page views. With per capita income of $24,000 per year, and a potential e-commerce market of $16 billion in the coming decade, I have yet to meet a startup or venture capitalist in the region who isn't trying to find a way to capitalize on opportunity there.

One of the most important ecosystem builders is Riyadh-based, Saudi-founded N2V, which started as part of the National Technology Group (NTC), the largest IT holding company in the region. N2V is comprised of 25 independent companies and over $700 million in annual revenue. The family business started in 1985 as an exclusive distribution partner for global tech players like HP, Dell, and Microsoft around the Arab world. In 2003, they began investing in the internet space and in 2009 formally created N2V to hold and expand these companies in consumer web, e-commerce, and mobile ventures. N2V is not so much a venture capital firm as an owner and operator of startups. Like Maktoob founder Samih Toukan's Jabbar, N2V finds or launches companies by providing talent and ideas, takes a majority stake after giving management equity, and furnishes the enterprises with shared services like technology, legal, and accounting. Aside from Riyadh, they now have offices in Dubai, Amman, Cairo, Beirut, Manama, and Silicon Valley.

Founder Rashid AlBalla is a hard-nosed, data-driven executive, but he is open to following whatever direction the new generation takes with technology in the Middle East. AlBalla has navigated N2V through many experimental fits and starts since its founding in 2003. "We had our share of trial and error navigating MENA's online industry," he recalls. But they also had significant successes, including the creation of one of the region's largest online advertising and analytics networks, Net Advantage, the online payment tool OneCard, and the leading Bloomberg-like terminal screen business and online brokerage firm, Mubashar, which is now one of the largest brokerages in the UAE. Acquisitions of web experiences in other categories, like the women's website HawaaWorld, followed. "I usually explain to entrepreneurs in Saudi and in the region that entrepreneurship is not as risky as they think," he told me. "What do you really have to lose? So a startup doesn't work, so you spent two years of your life learning at a lower salary. You're not likely going to jail, you're not going to lose your house and you will easily find a job with a great salary because of the demand in the market." AlBalla nods knowingly: "You can't, however, afford to miss the opportunities in not trying."

Jabbar, Sawari Ventures, Oasis500, and N2V now represent a vanguard of the growing investment activity. According to another leader of the Jordan and Middle East venture ecosystem, Emile Cubeisy of Accelerator Technology Holdings, nearly two dozen outstanding local and regional firms are deep in the fray. Accelerator Technology Holdings, founded by Fawaz Zu'bi, the former ICT Minister of Jordan in 2005, has 28 investments across the stages of startups and through a partnership in the United States, Silicon Badia, is looking to help their investments compete globally. He told me, "We will see more deals done in the range of \$2 to \$10 million in the coming year or two, driven at least in part by more external investors looking into the region." In fact, global investors like Tiger Global Management, J. P. Morgan and General Atlantic, Summit Partners have laid down tens of millions in bets through January 2013. Even the legendary Palo Alto venture capital firm Kleiner Perkins has turned to Istanbul as a perch to view the entire Middle East, and massive regional sovereign wealth funds, like the Abu Dhabi Investment Administration, have opened a venture arm.

If success breeds success, it can also spawn new challenges. I shared with Fayyad my observations of a barbell effect, where there was increasingly capital at both the very early and very late stages, but little in between. Fitting to his personality, he put it more bluntly: "It is simply financial constipation," he says unsmilingly. "An amazing amount of creative cool ideas, energy, and talent can't pass to the later stage without the interim capital—what they call in the States the 'Series A, B or C round'; so the later-stage capital sits there not finding suitable deals to be deployed in." But this, too, is changing for interesting reasons. As real estate and the regional stock markets remain weak, and young companies succeed, he is encouraged. "It's a perfect storm of investors saying no land, no stock market, maybe it's time to back these kids who are exploring the future of technology—who have, by the way, extraordinary growth rates as they raise one round of financing to the next quickly."

Arif Naqvi, co-creator and funder of the Celebration of Entrepreneurship whose Abraaj Group mostly invests in mid- to large-sized enterprises across emerging growth markets, has clearly dedicated significant time and resources to building bridges from the early to later stages. For him, it is about this time in history. "These young populations have strong aspirations for a better life and are better educated, better connected, more politically aware, and have a stronger sense of national pride and dignity than many give them credit for," he says. "As such, they want to have a voice in deciding their own futures. Unleash them, support them, on their terms and with time, the structural impediments will be issues of the past."

The Conveners

One of the most exciting, if not moving, moments in the Celebration of Entrepreneurship that started my journey came toward its end. The gathering was, for the most part, an "un-conference" with few central sessions and no keynote address. Most of the action took place in break-out sessions, with subjects ranging from "how to start a company" to "top ten mistakes" to "latest tech breakthroughs." But as the gathering ended, host Arif Naqvi wasn't satisfied.

He wrapped the gathering enthusiastically, but cautiously—warning that momentum mattered. He argued that concrete actions to build the region's ecosystem would be a joint effort, that it needed the help of everyone in the room. And he tossed out an idea he called *"Wamda"*—Arabic for "spark." The region needed a resource, he argued, one part think tank on entrepreneurial learning and trends for the Middle East, one part portal of the best news and information about regional startups and funding. He asked the crowd to come forward and pledge to support Wamda.

His friend Fadi Ghandour, unsurprisingly, was the first to do so. But slowly, by the dozens, entrepreneurs, corporations, investors stepped forward in front of the crowd of over 2,000 to add their support. Wamda .com was now a reality. They asked me to become an advisor, and after a year of successful experimentation, they brought in a young star to lead it: Habib Haddad.

I had heard plenty about Haddad. A thirty-ish, Lebanese-born, Boston-based entrepreneur, he had recently created the leading online Arabic transliteration engine, Yamli, and was a popular blogger during the Arab uprisings. I first met him at Peet's Coffee off of Harvard Square on a stunningly cold Boston day, his tall, lean figure and shaved head bearing neither a coat nor hat. He has the tenacity and speed of mind that I've come to admire in many young Lebanese entrepreneurs who saw war as children. He is constantly processing great reams of information, weeding through what matters most, and betting accordingly.

He told me later that because his father was in the army, he spent his youth going where the bombs were. "It sucks," he shrugged, "but you can't do anything about it. In the short run it meant no school the next day, but it never struck me that it all would cripple the future." I watched one of his most fascinating exchanges at a warm restaurant in downtown Beirut, when he chastised a friend for complaining about the challenges of starting a company in Lebanon: "So the internet goes down for a short while, it comes back. Are you kidding about complaining about electrical outages? Don't you have a generator like everyone else? What's the matter with you? Entrepreneurship is about working around bullshit."

A restless but successful math geek in high school, he studied computer and communications engineering at the American University of Beirut. Haddad subsequently received a master's degree in electrical engineering with a specialization in multimedia and graphics from the University of Southern California. While at USC, he connected with software developers from MIT. They were experimenting with a capability to transfer photographs to 3D, and Haddad had his first vision for a startup. "Everything in school was pretty, well, academic," he recalls. "But in a startup, if you see things, you can build them and make them work." He packed up and moved to Boston to join the effort, never negotiating hard for compensation or equity. But he loved the ride as they grew to 40 employees. Then, out of the blue, the CEO gathered everyone together to tell them they had run out of money. "This was a huge learning experience," he says, philosophically. "I was heads down, but if I had really considered it, we never had a clear vision as a business. We hired quickly, but not always the best. We fired slowly. Leaders weren't transparent with us. We never should have been surprised." But, in the end, none of this mattered to Habib. Entrepreneurship, in whatever form, would be the essence of the rest of his life.

After a brief vacation, Habib was actually hired back to what remained of the company to do hardcore computer engineering work, programming, problem solving, and debugging. In Boston he met other young Lebanese expats, who, like him, wanted to reconnect with their home country and see if their skills could have impact there. They founded the International Network of Lebanese Entrepreneurs and technologists (INLET), with over 500 members, just before Israel invaded Lebanon in 2006. "All work stopped for me. I remembered, as a kid, always feeling that when war came I couldn't do anything about it. Now, I thought I could." He founded Relief Lebanon, an organization to channel expat dollars back home. It would turn out to be one of the great learning experiences of his life. He slapped up a website and cold-called all the relief organizations he could find. The Red Cross returned his call, and set up a bank account where he could to process funds instantly. Haddad and a small team compiled a list of every church and mosque in the United States with any ties to Lebanon. In two months, to their shock, their little website raised $2 million. "I learned there people want to give back, and the best to engage them is to move quickly. My favorite word is *'yalla'*—just do it. If they knew I was 26 at the time without any backing they wouldn't have returned my email. By being in motion, just getting stuff done without a ton of strategizing, it all worked." And he was fearless. When he decided to start Yamli, he had $100 left in his bank account, maxed-out credit cards and had sold every piece of furniture in his apartment but for his bed.

After his success with Yamli, he and other successful expats from the Arab world decided to turn their attention back to the region full time. They created one of the first gatherings of local startups, which they called "Yalla Startup," in 2010, shortly after the Celebration of Entrepreneurship gathering in Dubai. "We held it in Beirut, but got buses to bring in programmers and entrepreneurs from Syria and Jordan," he recalls. "On the buses, entrepreneurs would give TED-like talks about what inspired them and their ideas. Kids came with sleeping bags, and 34 specific ideas were pitched at the main event."

The Arab uprisings didn't so much change Habib as confirm what he saw happening on the ground. "I and so many of my friends were not naturally politically inclined. But like my experience in Relief Lebanon, you don't have time to meditate on how it will affect you. Everything we were doing in startups, like the uprisings, was about fighting the status quo." He still had a part-time hand in Yamli, and separately created an enterprise that transcribed thousands of vocal tweets to text during the uprising. "Most entrepreneurs I knew were engaged; no one was on the side, it was a spirit of power of Yalla."

When Arif and Fadi recruited Habib to lead Wamda.com, their timing could not have been better. He brought on American journalist Nina Curley, who built a staff of full-time writers and over 40 outside contributors, creating a level of quality control and scale unprecedented in the region. There, every breaking story, every piece of research on Middle East startups, any of the growing number of conferences, hackathons, and meetups were covered and shared with the broader community. Wamda.com became the must-read-and-share web experience for the region, reaching now hundreds of thousands of viewers a month and growing rapidly. Entrepreneurs love the coverage, and investors take note of what is happening. Nina told me, "In an environment where tech news often consists of simply publishing press releases, we fight for transparency and honest dialogue. We point out things that should change, examine successes and failures and open conversations in the community." Habib agrees that Wamda educates the market. "We see the trends and report them. But we also drive influence. Before, information was pretty spread out. Last fall we reported on a regional startup a bit like Angry Birds, and after our analysis, they received 500,000 downloads in two weeks."

Content, however, is one of three legs on the Wamda.com stool. In part to address the "barbell" challenge of follow-on investments, Wamda launched a fund to put their money where their beliefs are. "Some people think this is a conflict of interest, but we run our investments utterly independently from our content," Habib notes. "The reality is in the early days of all this there is plenty of capital out there, but it is still looking for reassurance that investments can succeed. Our entrepreneurs aren't going to build the next Twitter right off the bat, but success will build success." He believes their investing helps to build these early successes and will help fund greater outreach and projects for Wamda. As of Fall 2012, they had successfully bet on their tenth startup, and launched "MixNMentor" gatherings to bring successful entrepreneurs together with the new upstarts. Their global network of mentors also ensures broader market introduction for their companies. As a final leg of the stool, they have also worked with regional corporate partners to offer entrepreneurs benefits, like their recently launched "Wamda Card," which gives discounts on basic services, from office supplies to travel.

Omar Christidis has stepped up into a different part of the ecosystem, connecting and improving the talent pool. He created ArabNet, now the largest must-attend summit for technologists and startups in the region. It regularly attracts over a thousand young entrepreneurs and investors from every country in the Middle East, and all the top global tech players are there to see what they can see. The twentysomething Yale grad has the polite, almost gentlemanly demeanor one would expect, given his membership in its centuries-old a capella group, the Whiffenpoofs, as an undergrad. He laughs, describing the mix at the conference: "Sponsors may not show up easily yet, but the entrepreneurs do."

Held in a modern Beirut conference hotel, ArabNet covers all the themes one would imagine—the future of mobile, cloud computing, e-commerce; tactical entrepreneurial concerns like how to raise money, build a board, hire the best talent. Participants tweet their learning, complaints, and commentary furiously throughout the sessions. I had to keep from laughing out loud during a panel of large telecom companies trying to justify what the crowd, to a person, saw as their high monthly bills and mediocre customer service. All the tweets were followed by the hash tag: #gladwehaveskype. The gatherings are packed, the energy electric, though as I've found typical of such gatherings in the United States but with a particular panache in the Middle East, everything eventually and inevitably runs late. "It's to be expected not only because we Arabs run late," one e-commerce entrepreneur told me, "but also because we love seeing each other here. All year we are heads down in our cities, connected to friends, partners, and employees interactively. At ArabNet we can connect physically and that is important."

Omar was born in Damascus. His father's family is Greek Armenian Christian and mother is Syrian Muslim; his parents had to elope in order to marry. Like Habib, Omar came of age in the midst of ongoing war, and his time at the prestigious American Community School, which served Americans, foreign nationals, and students from the Arab world, broadened his worldview. "In our household we were very much Arab first and foremost, so what happened in different countries in the region meant something. We were not overly nationalistic. It has made me better at my job. I go to these countries and I feel at home wherever I go. I don't feel limited." He considered Yale the number-one most formative experience of his life because he was surrounded by a community of peers committed to find ways to "contribute." "We Lebanese are known to not be very good planners, because we've been raised not knowing what might happen next. Our lives have been a series of force majeure events," he laughs. "But I believed that whatever I did needed to have impact and make a difference."

After starting and delaying an MBA and a stint at a consulting firm, Christidis was fed up with the pace and hierarchy of working for others and returned to Beirut in the summer of 2006 to work at his mother's events company. Beirut was in its ascendency, people were hopeful, and tourists were flooding the thriving, hip metropolis. And, then, as if on cue, the war with Israel commenced. He decided to return for his MBA and tried several ventures in the United States, but when the 2008 global crisis came he would return to the Middle East for good. "I saw the most intelligent graduates without jobs in New York City, I figured why not?" he recalled.

While at Yale he had co-founded the Yale Arab Alumni Association and helped build a strong network of like-minded and development-oriented people through networking and business events. Between his brief time with his mother's events business and this experience, he found his bliss in bringing people together. "I am of the generation where great tech events and coder competitions in the States were common. No one was doing this in the Middle East and I knew the talent was there desperate for it. ArabNet just made sense."

For Omar, the fundamental challenge in the Middle East is human resources. "There is amazing talent here," he notes, "But very little experience." He calls it the "challenge of collective experience"—a sort of catch-22 wherein established companies and startups alike are hungry for talent but have trouble finding it, and the best talent often lacks significant experience.

As has already happened in the West, local technology startups are taking it upon themselves to match talent to recruitment needs. Companies like Ahtaboot, Bayt, Laimoon, Wuzzuf, and TasmeemME are just a few of the regional leaders offering sophisticated job boards, matching capabilities, career services, and social connections. Nabbesh.com, launched in 2012, created the first social network allowing people to post their skills and talents in the context of their specific lifestyle needs—i.e., seeking jobs, or even part-time projects, near their homes.

And then, in 2012, a Western juggernaut arrived. Before the career management social platform LinkedIn even officially opened operations in the Middle East, they discovered that five million of their 175 million members were based there. LinkedIn's regional lead, Ali Matar, understands the Middle East's talent opportunities and challenges better than most, having worked for Oracle, Procter and Gamble, and SAP throughout the region. "The single most important thing people miss is that there is no *wasta* on *any* of these platforms," he told me, reminding me of the comment Fadi Ghandour had made about the internet overall. "They are all about talent rising to the top, less and less about "who do you know," which makes everyone want to up their game. There really are no categories or hierarchies here. CEOs, mid-level execs, and aspiring employees can all be on LinkedIn and these others platforms." He adds that, with 60 percent of the region's population under 30, and "more mobile devices than toothbrushes," social networks are where both recruiters and the recruited go first. Hiring can be as close to borderless as ever in history, if talent is willing to move.

At the same time, Matar also feels that many of the most talented prospects do feel some connection to home, and that matching talent is only as useful as the quality of talent that is being built locally. "Building local talent is so central that, in many ways, this is why we opened a physical presence in the region," Matar explained to me. "As a global company we have to find ways to be attuned to local uniqueness. Something very powerful is happening in the Middle East where talent is teaching talent, people are gathering and connecting to better themselves on and offline. Companies are partaking in this engagement as well, understanding that it enhances their brands and the desire for the best talent to join them. It is true everywhere, but particularly sensitive in the Middle East, that it takes ages for companies to build brands here, and seconds to destroy them. We are transforming ourselves in the region today." He notes that these tools are not merely meant for the tech and startup communities, but to be adopted at scale in oil, health care, and finance. "The internet overall was something of a social utility for people to find things, say, in 2010. In 2011 everyone realized the internet and social networks could be significant political instruments. In 2012 employers and employees understand it is a vehicle of both job training and job growth across all sectors."

Accordingly, Christidis is expanding ArabNet toward talent training for the startup communities. "Go to Silicon Valley," he laments, "and the highest-paid person is likely the software engineer. This is not the case in the Middle East, where they are cheap." Obviously, at one level, less expensive labor is a competitive advantage, and he sees demand rising, especially in Egypt and Jordan. But if one needs programmers comfortable in cutting-edge coding languages—like Django, Python, and Ruby on Rails—they are fewer and farther between.

"There are plenty of startup competitions all over the Middle East today, which is great," he says. "But no one is doing real hacking competitions at scale." To help correct this imbalance, ArabNet is hosting a series of developer competitions in Beirut, Amman, Riyadh, Cairo, and Dubai in 2012 and 2013. Open to everyone, they will aim to find the best contestants over four rounds. Participants will have to concurrently display their skills in speed and creativity, as they're first tested for basic skills, then moved through increasingly complex solutions for coding, app development, social network, and data mining. Top engineers from Nokia, Google, and Microsoft and the like will judge each gathering, awarding different levels of finalists anywhere from $500 to $2,500. Over 400 hopefuls showed up in Beirut alone. What will be invaluable to the ecosystem, Omar believes however, will be determining the caliber of contestants each competition, in addition to choosing a region-wide winner. "We tend to know the A and B guys in the Middle East," he told me, "but this will get so many in the middle to step up their game. Examples of success across the board here—whether a new company that gathers a huge audience, a startup that exits big, a programmer who makes globally competitive code—it just makes others do the same."

The Recognizers

There's nothing new about ambitious startups duking it out for the recognition and money that comes with winning a prestigious startup competition. What might be surprising is that two of the largest competitions in 2012 were hosted in the Middle East, open solely to Middle Eastern entrepreneurs. And that their sponsors, MIT and Google, are among the most vaulted names in global technology.

"In fact, the time is ripe now," notes Wael Fakharany, Google's Regional Manager for Egypt and North Africa, and founder of Ebda2 (Arabic for "beginning"), Google's first regional competition focused on Egyptian entrepreneurs. "There are many unsettled places in the world showing remarkable innovation today." He points to the basic demographics of Egypt: More than 17 million enrolled students; over 2.3 million Egyptians working in the technology sector; over 35 million people actively using the internet and over 90 million mobile users. "We believe that one of the next waves of impact and growth will emerge from this part of the world," he says.

This confirms the momentum that Hala Fadel, a Paris- and Beirut-based global investor and founder of the MIT Enterprise Forum of the Pan-Arab Region, has seen there recently. This year's MIT Business Plan Competition, done in partnership with the Saudi corporate social responsibility effort Abdul Latif al Jameel Community Initiative and covering all of the Middle East, is her fifth. "During 2006, our first year, we expected 200 applications from around the Middle East, but received over 1,500," she says. "This year, over 4,500 teams of three people or more competed—that means over 13,000 potential entrepreneurs." She added that nearly half of the teams this year included women. "We even received over 100 applications—get this—from Syria!"

MIT pitches ranged from addressing local and regional needs to aspirants looking to compete with world-class global technology startups. First place, along with a $50,000 prize, went to Butterfleye, the smart goggle for swimmers that monitors their heart rate and tracks their fitness I described as one of the global players among the *New Breed.*

The winner of the $10,000 second-place prize, Qabila Media Productions, took off when its crowdsourced video services went viral during the Egyptian uprising. Third place finishers Silgenix, also from Egypt, created an integrated circuit design company specializing in increasing the battery lifetime of portable electronic devices. Other finalists created regional social networks, e-commerce platforms, online education courses, and capabilities to increase internet connection speed and reliability. Competitors hailed from every corner of the region, from Saudi Arabia to Palestine.

Google was among the many global tech companies in the region connecting entrepreneurs long before its executive, Wael Ghonim, became a leader among the protesters. It held a conference last December with the goal "to invest in the Egyptian talent pool and increase online penetration by giving developers, academia, and businesses the tools to grow local content in order to make information more relevant and more accessible," says regional director Wael Fakharany. More than 2,000 people attended over the course of three days. Similarly sized gatherings are happening regularly from Beirut to Morocco every month.

More than 4,200 entrepreneurs competed in Google's Egypt-focused Ebda2, culled down to 20 finalists over nine months of training, mentoring and judging. To create awareness, Ebda2 and Google staff chartered a bus and traveled across the country to gather participants and offer training. Visiting twelve universities in twelve cities, from the large urban centers of Cairo and Alexandria to the smaller cities such as Tanta, Fayoum, and Port Said, they met more than 1,500 entrepreneurs with ideas for everything from consumer internet to health care.

The winner of $200,000 was Bey2ollak the six-person team taking on one of the most vexing problems in Egypt—traffic. "I could not believe my eyes as I spent a day meeting with the finalists," says Mohammed

Gawdat, Vice President of Google in Southern and Eastern Europe, Middle East, and Africa. "The passion, the energy, freedom of expression, thought leadership and the healthy disregard for the impossible blew me away. I felt as if I were spending the day with Googlers."

Do these competitions matter? "We believe that the internet is a net contributor to the economy in the region and in Egypt," notes Fakharany, "but it is also the best-kept secret. We spent $200,000 in this one, but we are committed to spend another $2.3 million over the next couple of years. The face of Egypt can be changed through technology."

Fadel believes that the connectedness created in gatherings like these help foster further innovation, just as it does in the United States. "Being an entrepreneur is, by definition a lonely thing," she says. "The odds of failure are great. One cannot underestimate the importance of mental support to startups when participating because they realize that they are not the only ones working hard in this region when they see others like them doing the same and succeeding."

Both Fadel and Fakharany believe we are in the earliest days of this startup boom in the Middle East. Global and local institutions, in fact, have been hosting hundreds of competitions throughout the region, and more will come. "Success breeds success," says Fadel, echoing so many of his contemporaries. "It's just basic math."

Name a country in the Middle East, and I'll name you dozens of women and men like these.

∽

No one can put the rising ecosystems in the Middle East in better context than Linda Rottenberg. Endeavor Global, which she co-founded in New York City, supports 726 (and counting) high-impact entrepreneurs who are leading 455 game-changing companies in 16 growth markets around the world, including Egypt, Greece, Mexico, and Indonesia. These entrepreneurs have created over 200,000 high-quality jobs, and last year generated in aggregate over $5 billion in revenue in their markets. In 2012 they launched the first self-sustaining business model for a nonprofit through the Endeavor Catalyst fund, which enables Endeavor to co-invest in its entrepreneurs raising professional rounds of equity capital. Endeavor has local chapters headed by top business leaders in each of their markets around the globe.

Rottenberg is a force of nature, one of the great champions of "high-impact entrepreneurship," a term she coined some years ago. It means finding, backing, mentoring, and connecting the people with the biggest ideas, the ones with the greatest potential for revenue and job growth, both in high and low tech. Some years ago when she willed Endeavor into Brazil she literally created the Portuguese word for "entrepreneur" and got it published in the local official dictionary. In so doing, she received the nickname "Chica Loca." For her, opportunity knocks where the chips are down. In 2012, Endeavor opened operations in Greece during the height of the austerity protests. "Chaos is the catalyst of innovation," she declares when we meet in her airy loft office in lower Manhattan. "When economies are down, entrepreneurs look up. Stability is the friend of the status quo."

At Yale Law School in the 1990s, Rottenberg worked with a professor on a project building law and business programs in South America. The palpable frustration she felt coming off the young and talented people there put her on the path that became Endeavor. "No one, whether student or taxi driver, felt there were paths available beyond what they did or some government job. This was the era of Apple and garage startups in the United States, but no one there even had garages." She understood that local context meant everything, and that role models change how people look at themselves. "Small numbers move the needle. Endeavor participated with Stanford Business School and the World Economic Forum in a study of 380,000 companies around the world, and found that five percent of the business builders ended up creating almost two-thirds of the jobs." And, she would soon learn, it wasn't only about the direct jobs and profits, but ecosystems those companies created. She calls it the "PayPal Mafia Effect," after the extremely successful e-payments company whose employees subsequently spawned many new startups.

"Don't underestimate the power of hope," she says, sounding almost like Bill Clinton. "I'm a big believer that when someone succeeds, and even when others fail, they want to raise the bar." She has learned from her experience and in any part of the world that there are countless committed, talented, and dedicated people who know their region, know its issues, and understand its opportunity. They are willing to roll up their sleeves, take on their scars, build, and mentor others. "An ecosystem comes from this. Big things happen."

But it takes time, and a willingness to weather bumps. She recalls companies like Mercado Libre, a tiny e-commerce startup that launched a decade ago in Argentina's then-nascent tech community, went public on the NASDAQ in 2007 and is now worth well over $4 billion. "Argentina and Brazil are the hubs of e-commerce in Latin America today. High-impact entrepreneurs like Marcos Galperin, Mercado Libre's co-founder and CEO, and other tech innovators he has helped spawn either through direct investment or through his inspirational role-model effect, are the reason why." There will be booms, and there will be crashes. Irrational exuberance can quickly become irrational depression. "When the busts come, people will leave, people will say 'I told you so,'" she smiles. "And then things happen."

The Middle East ecosystem has gone from engaging and connecting with technology, wondering "Can it happen here?" to confidently proclaiming, "It *is* happening here." Rottenberg recalls, "Back in 2007 I attended a global gathering of business executives, the World Economic Forum, which they held at the Dead Sea in Jordan. The fear of failure was palpable; speaker after speaker said, in effect, that they from the Middle East would never catch up in the entrepreneurial space, the Middle East had no culture of tolerating failure or supporting young innovators." But she will never forget one young woman. After all the discussion of what technology was already doing in other corners of the world, she turned to Rottenberg and said, "I'm leaving my job at Cisco tomorrow. I need to start something."

Today, Endeavor and many other entrepreneur support organizations operate throughout the region with new incubators, accelerators, and venture capital firms cropping up regularly. And as Rottenberg witnessed in Latin America, the entrepreneur role-model effect is beginning to multiply throughout the region. Whether it's young techies aspiring to be the "next Maktoob" or young Lebanese designers imagining themselves the next legendary artist/entrepreneur Nada Debs, the innovation and entrepreneurial spirit spreading across the Middle East is palpable. "This is the real Arab uprising," Rottenberg smiled.

Arif Naqvi (left) is the Pakistani-born founder of the Abraaj Group, one of the largest global growth market private equity firms in the world, with over $8 billion under management. He held the Celebration of Entrepreneurship 2010 in Dubai with Aramex CEO Fadi Ghandour (right), where over 2,400 young entrepreneurs and investors from around the region gathered to network and connect. A few months later many of these young entrepreneurs were in Tahrir Square or in other protests that became the Arab uprisings.
CREDIT: Courtesy of the author.

The Dubai hub, one of many around the world, for the logistics juggernaut in the Middle East and Africa, Aramex. This is one of countless aisles managing regional e-commerce inventory. Their "Shop and Ship" program takes on the logistics challenge for any company trying to ship from the United States, Asia, Europe, and the Middle East. Their new eHouse initiative will be the inventory management and back-end for e-commerce startups in the region.
Credit: Aramex

The highest-selling paid weather app in the world is WeatherHD, with over five million downloads, built by founder Amr Ramadan and the Vimov team in Alexandria, Egypt.
CREDIT: Vimov, LLC

Kuwaiti-born media entrepreneur Naif al Mutawa created the comic book and animated superhero series The 99, the first in the Middle East, now reaching a global audience of nearly 750 million. Here at one of his many book signings, he autographs comic books for the series' young fans.
CREDIT: Teshkeel Media Group, Inc.

Habib Haddad is a serial entrepreneur and CEO of Wamda.com, the largest online resource platform for entrepreneurs in the region. Here he asks a crowd at an e-commerce gathering in Amman Jordan, "How many have recently purchased or soon intend to buy online?"
CREDIT: Habib Haddad and Wamda.com

More than 4,200 entrepreneurs competed in Google's first Egypt-focused Ebda2 in 2012. They culled down to twenty finalists over nine months of multiple rounds of training, mentoring, and judging. To create awareness, Ebda2 and Google staff chartered a bus and traveled throughout the country on a road show to gather participants and to offer training, visiting twelve universities in twelve cities. The winner, crowd-sourced traffic app Bey2ollak, won $200,000.
CREDIT: Maha Abouelenein, Google Egypt

MIT Enterprise Forum of the Pan-Arab Region, co-founded by Hala Fadel, held its sixth annual region-wide startup competition. Over 4,000 companies submitted proposals, representing over 12,000 entrepreneurs.
CREDIT: Hala Fadel, MIT Enterprise Forum of the Pan-Arab Region

When these Yemeni high school women learned that fire was a risk with kerosene lanterns in tents near their homes, they went online to learn how to develop solar-charging stations to power electric lanterns. They won the region-wide INJAZ startup competition in 2012, and wore their finest traditional clothes when honored.
CREDIT: INJAZ AL-ARAB

ArabNet, founded by Lebanese Yale grad Omar Christidis, is the largest must-attend gathering of startups in the region. Each year over 1,000 entrepreneurs and investors plot their futures in Beirut and now Dubai. In 2012 they expanded their activities to include programming sessions around the region (this one is in Beirut) to help find and train the best engineering talent for entrepreneurial careers.
CREDIT: ArabNet

Lebanese-born university swimmer Hind Hobeika dreamed of having the ability to monitor her heart rate while training. She has developed Instabeat goggles, which will launch globally in 2013.
CREDIT: *Hind Hobeika*

Lebanese-Jordanian entrepreneur Fadi Ghandour is the creator of Ruwwad, a remarkable youth center in one of the major refugee camps in Amman, Jordan. Part school, library, arts class, computer center, and after-school program, Ruwwad is run by the community to help youth and families take ownership of their own challenges and opportunities. Dardashat is a foundation of Ruwwad, weekly sessions where young people are encouraged to explore their notion of self, relationships, rights and citizenship, and career and life goals. Thousands are benefiting, and the model is being expanded elsewhere in Jordan, Lebanon, Egypt, and Palestine.
CREDIT: *The Arab Foundation for Sustainable Development*

During her visit to Cairo in 2012, Secretary of State Hillary Clinton met the entrepreneurs at Flat6Labs, one of the leading startup incubators in Egypt and around the Middle East.
CREDIT: Photo by Karim Mansour and Flat6Labs.

Ahmed Alfi, fourth from the left in a Flat6Labs t-shirt, is the founder of Sawari Ventures and Flat6Labs, returning to Cairo after two decades of investing in Los Angeles. Ramez Mohamed, standing at left, runs Flat6Labs, and Sawari partner Hany Sonbaty, kneeling in a Flat6Labs t-shirt, third from the right, is active in all.
CREDIT: Photo by Karim Mansour, Flat6Labs.

The new campus of the American University in Cairo is a gorgeous expanse outside of old Cairo, and its business school, under Dean Sherif Kamel, is leading in curriculum focused on entrepreneurship.
CREDIT: The American University in Cairo

Incubator/Accelerator in Jordan, Oasis500, funded by the leadership of the King of Jordan and the private sector, is headed by Jordanian/Silicon Valley serial success Usama Fayyad. They are committed to fund and launch 500 startups in Jordan alone, but have had entrepreneurs from Syria to Palestine knock down their doors. This is one of their classes of new companies.
Credit: Oasis500

Chapter 6

Startup/ Turn-Around

THE EDUCATION OF A NEW GENERATION

The ten-year-old boy, nervous and shy, sat at the front of his class-
room of 70 children. The instructor turned to him and asked, "Why are
you here?"

He pushed his dark, oversized glasses back on his nose and whis-
pered, "To be confident."

The instructor smiled: "What? Louder."

The boy's voice rose to a conversational pitch. "To be confident."

The instructor walked over to him: "Shout it out, please!"

The little boy shuddered a moment, but he was smiling. "To be confident!" he called out.

"Stand on your desk and shout even louder!" cajoled the instructor.

The class laughed as the boy climbed up on his desk and shouted,
"TO BE CONFIDENT!"

"There!" said the instructor, satisfied. "*Now* I know why you are here." And the class cheered.

Soraya Salti saw herself in this moment in the Jordanian public school classroom she visited that day. The daughter of a Jordanian father and American mother, she also attended local schools. "I was a very shy person in class," she remembered. "I never spoke out. No one ever pulled me out of my shell." What, after all, would have been the point? While Jordan, like so many countries in the Middle East, has invested significantly in guaranteeing children access to schooling, the outcomes are mixed and confusing. The curriculum consists largely of rote memorization and preparation for standardized tests that are necessary to get into college or a government job. She shrugs, thinking about it: "But there is little emphasis on critical thinking, no connection to the issues of our communities, country, and region. Books are outdated and there is little interaction between teachers and kids. And we wonder why so many kids today are unemployable?"

Salti's mother opened the first Save the Children office in Jordan in 1984. Save the Children worldwide had come into contact with supplemental education programs in the United States and elsewhere, like those created by a leading global nonprofit on workforce readiness called Junior Achievement. These classes not only emphasized enhanced academic skills for workforce preparation, but also self-awareness, requiring every child, from kindergarten through college, to speak their opinions. In 2001, when Save the Children wanted to launch a version of Junior Achievement in Jordan, they asked Salti to be country director of what they called "INJAZ Jordan," or Jordan Achievement. Holding her freshly minted MBA from Northwestern, Salti accepted, eager to return home and make an impact. She later would found a regional INJAZ office to spread the model across fourteen countries in the Middle East.

INJAZ was one of the earliest "private public partnerships," as they are commonly called today. Salti and her mother started with a USAID grant that matched contributions from local businesses, and chose schools in conjunction with the Ministry of Education. Their goal was to hold additional classes at the end of each day to not only supplement education, but also to focus on job-related skills and to push kids to think about entrepreneurship and develop their own ideas. Their first volunteers were friends ánd family, and they soon began to recruit local business leaders and their staffs to mentor and train local youth in after-school programs. Their first program held 300 students and ten volunteers. "In those days," she notes, "There was nothing written on demographics or the dysfunctionality of schooling. There was no sense of urgency about the challenges, and even greater skepticism about bringing in people from the private sector—teachers and communities thought all this was not their business."

It was slow going trying to win over every constituency—the private sector, the government, the schools, and the students themselves. "We constantly updated each group on what we were doing," she recalls. "We then convinced teachers to stay after school and join us, offering them little incentives and gifts to do so." Students loved it, and parents demanded it. Their curriculum today focuses heavily on encouraging entrepreneurship, and classes are often held during school hours. Local entrepreneurs teach students as young as middle-school age how to create business plans and compete in local and regional competitions, as well as basic professional skills like effective communication, teamwork, résumé building, and financial literacy. And it has grown to scale. INJAZ now exists in over 1,000 schools, spanning all economic demographics across the Middle East and North Africa. They have over 300,000 students enrolled in 2012 alone, and over 1.3 million alumni. They've even expanded to partner with entrepreneurship programs in over 140 universities.

The raw demographics, however, still keep Salti up at night. "We focused on entrepreneurship because the numbers require it," she sighs. "There will be 100 million new people entering the work force by 2012, and another 135 million who are under age 15. It is very clear that traditional industry can't grow fast enough to absorb all this—the youth will have to self-employ." She believes that, whether they become entrepreneurs or not, kids who absorb the job-training skills of the INJAZ program—even the soft ones—will become change agents for new, greater opportunity. But she is also a realist. "We are 300,000 kids this year, and millions need what we offer in the Middle East." She pauses for a long minute. "On some days the scale of the education challenge is daunting."

∾

When the goal is a thriving growth economy, let alone an ecosystem for innovation and entrepreneurship, the importance of educational infrastructure cannot be overemphasized. The best of the entrepreneurs in the Middle East are extremely well educated, often from abroad. My presumption, however, was that for most of the new generation, education was out of reach or subpar compared to other emerging markets. "No chance these guys have the commitment and skills focus like the Koreans," one U.S. venture capitalist said to me.

So I was surprised to find how much effort and money has in fact been directed to education throughout the Middle East. As a 2007 International Bank for Reconstruction and Development/World Bank report, revealingly titled "The Road Not Traveled—Education Reform in the Middle East and North Africa," found, on the whole countries in the region spend a higher percentage of their GDP on schooling than almost any emerging market with similar levels of per capita income. Middle Eastern countries average 5 percent of GDP on education (just behind North America and Western Europe, and above the averages of most countries in Latin American and East Asia), and often as much as 20 percent of the total government expenditures overall. Access to education is high, reaching almost every child at the primary school level, with rapid increase in attendance at the mid and higher levels. Perhaps most surprising, gender parity is almost complete and on par with Latin America and East Asia. Illiteracy has been more than halved in recent decade.[1]

Such a quantity of spending and improvements from a low baseline, however, mask the reality that the region lags where it matters most. Secondary and higher education enrollment, while growing, is still significantly lower than anywhere in East Asia and Latin America. Despite significant improvement in basic reading skills, illiteracy rates in the Middle East remain twice as high as in those other emerging markets. Most concerning of all, however, is that in more than half of the region's countries with functioning colleges, nearly two-thirds of students major in fields like social science and humanities rather than in science and mathematics. This enrollment pattern is the opposite of Asia, and, to a lesser extent, Latin America. In international tests like the Trends in International Mathematics and Science Study (TIMSS) and the Program for International Student Assessment (PISA), countries in the Middle East regularly fall below global averages, and well below growth economies in Asia and Latin America. "Given that technological innovation and adaptation is increasingly playing a prominent role in the development process," the World Bank concluded, "[Middle East and North Africa] schools may be producing the wrong mix of competencies."[2]

"This is the crux of the challenge," Dr. Sherif Kamel told me. As the dean of the American University of Cairo's School of Business, on whose advisory board I sit, and as a father who raised two children in Cairo, he knows whereof he speaks. His experience in Egypt, he believes, is common to the region. "There have been more studies on Egyptian education than any other societal issue," he tells me. "The good news is that there is a great agreement on the challenges which at least is an important place to start. But the bad news is that these challenges will take time—years—and brute will to fix."

He sees four related needs. First, he argues, policy strategy must be based around what students need to learn, as opposed to rote memorization geared toward passing statewide tests. "What do we want?" he asks. "What sectors do we need graduates prepared for and why? What are the clear deficiencies that we can systemically fix?" Second, even a stronger, more focused curriculum and infrastructure is only as good as the talent one attracts to implement it. "We pay teachers on average around $70 a month," he rails. "What signal do we send to society in that?" Third, classroom size receives scant attention. "In public schools, classes can be 60 to 70 students with minimal student engagement. Many kids simply don't attend, and there is no accountability, not even attendance taken." Finally, he argues that literacy statistics mask a false sense of quality. "At the University level, remember, I get to see the best kids, and the reading and writing skills are not good. And the gap between private schools and public schools are enormous. Of 16 million students in Egypt today, some few tens of thousands are able to go to private schools." The challenge is region-wide. One study indicated that universities in the UAE spend 16 to 20 percent of their budgets on remedial education in math and English. "The demographic math is simple," Kamel notes. "Unemployment is 20 percent in Egypt today, and we must create an incremental 800,000 jobs per year just to not lose ground. Education is everything."

Nafez Dakkak is one of a new vanguard of young education consultants in the Middle East. He is as pan-Arab as they come—a Palestinian with Jordanian citizenship who was born in Saudi Arabia and has lived in Jerusalem and Dubai. He studied at Yale despite an inauspicious presentation from one of their recruiters, who made his low expectations of education in the region clear. "I remember it seemed as if they were shocked that we used laptops regularly, and asked two questions: do we know what a liberal arts education is and what the SATs are?" he laughs. "I must have impressed them because I knew the answers to both obvious questions, and they encouraged me to apply early." He has a warm smile. "For all their global reputation, I thought, Yale must have a pretty low bar," he jokes.

In New Haven, Dakkak wrote his thesis on the obstacles to curriculum reform throughout the region. As a member of the Yale Arab Students' Association, he was approached by the consulting firm McKinsey and Company, who offered a grant to sponsor a gathering of a student's choosing that would be of interest to Arab youth. "I began to think hard about what to do, and talked to friends and it became clear that the most common theme was no one wanted to wait for anyone else to solve problems. Through technology, through entrepreneurship, big things could happen. So that was the theme we based our gathering around." He returned to the Middle East on a grant from Yale to dig further, seeking to marry entrepreneurial solutions with reform goals.

His findings map closely with Sherif Kamel's; he believes that three factors have hampered reform from moving fast enough. First, he was shocked to find a universal lack of continuity when reforms were actually tried. "The Minister of Education in both the UAE and Jordan seemed to get shifted out every six months—as if the powers that be felt it was the only way to prove they were doing something when reforms didn't get the results they wanted quickly." Second, he believes reform efforts did not take a holistic approach, focusing on different parts of the equation but never on all of them at once. "They focus on reforming standardized tests that emphasize rote memorization, while ignoring teacher training or vice versa. For example in Jordan, on average only 16 percent of questions on the college entrance exam test critical thinking; as such, learning how to think critically is not the best study tactic." Third, as the World Bank study suggested, there is little accountability for how money is spent. "Saying you are teaching technology skills by simply throwing money at the issues, and buying tablets, is not the answer without clear measured outcomes. A bad teacher with a tablet is still a bad teacher."

But while he expected these challenges to be met with resolved apathy, he actually found the opposite. Parents and teachers alike knew what was wrong. He recalled one English teacher in Jordan telling him, "I don't teach them English; I'm not surprised they don't speak it. I teach them to memorize words for exams, that is all I teach them." The system offers little incentive to innovate or go off the existing script. "They barely get rewarded for doing what they do," Dakkak says. "When I was doing my research, the best a teacher could hope for was a monthly raise of the equivalent of $5. That doesn't exactly spell 'We appreciate your work' or go out and innovate and problem solve."

Is it hopeless?

Sherif re-emphasizes that acknowledging and agreeing on the challenges is at least a start; that an executable vision, with measurable short- and long-term goals, is essential. And while he believes that substantive infrastructure changes, even if started now, may not yield results for years, two recent developments have encouraged him. First, businesses are taking corporate social responsibility more seriously than ever before—not simply as PR initiatives, but as a strategic way to engage and strengthen their societies. "Throughout the Middle East this is a discussion happening everywhere in the business, policy, and academic communities. People know that they have societal obligations, but that to reach our potential we need to bring creativity, new players, and resources to bear now. Businesses really for the first time are understanding that there is no choice but to find creative ways to help communities build for themselves." Second, he argues, there is significant potential coming from the bottom up, simply because today's youth have broader access to information technology. They can easily connect with others and supplement their skills. "Computer literacy is becoming so high, and not just in the main cities—everywhere someone has connectivity or a mobile phone. You'll see more and more interesting answers coming from new quarters. And you will see skills in commercializing answers and ideas through entrepreneurship."

I witnessed the combined force of these two changes in one improbable story from the poorest part of Amman.

An American venture capitalist once told me that when he makes a bet, he's actually betting on the entrepreneur's *next* company. Any idea can succeed or fail for a host of reasons, he believes. But when you find a natural entrepreneur—that rare combination of focused tenacity, creative ingenuity, humility, and unrelenting problem solving—you just know they will get it right at some point. Jordanian Ala' Alsallal is such a young man.

The twenty-something Ala' has a warm, ready, and self-effacing smile that makes him look about 16. One would not peg him as a driven business executive whose ambition is to build the largest online book platform in the Middle East. I first met him at the Oasis500 headquarters located in an ultra-modern, tightly guarded "Business Park" in Amman. Surrounded by the lush sales offices of global juggernauts like Microsoft and IBM, their simple, utilitarian space is a welcome relief. Ala' is unfailingly courteous and pleased to tell his story, but I got the distinct feeling that I needed to be brief so he could get back to work. His dark eyes narrow as he speaks of where he came from and what he is building, and he wastes few words. His story is as improbable as it is instructive.

Ala' is one of seven children born to Palestinian schoolteachers who came to Jordan after the formation of Israel in 1948. Such Palestinian refugees represent nearly a third of Jordan's population. Amman already has nearly three million people, and experts predict that number will double in the next decade. Aside from its Palestinian population, it has attracted over a million émigrés from Egypt, Iraq, and Syria. Continuous construction and a beautiful new airport have changed the face of the city over the last several years, especially on the western side. In the East, however, where Ala' and his family still live, time has stood still. As one West Amman tech entrepreneur sarcastically told me, "I think I need a passport to go from West to East."

Amman is a city of ring roads and hills, you can instantly infer anyone's wealth and prospects by which number ring road they live near, what hill or "Jabal" they call home. When Fadi Ghandour first explained to me that some of the hills in East Amman were "refugee camps," I pictured extensive tent cities. Instead I saw row after row of dark, low-rise, apartment buildings winding their way up the hill. There is power and plumbing, and small shops, but these communities are cramped, poor, and self-contained. Schools are run down, and there are few, if any, safe places for children to play. It is no surprise that both dropout rates and unemployment are staggeringly high. "Other than those with odd jobs outside the community, there is little contact with the western part of the city," Ala' told me. "Our world is pretty much our Jabal."

Ala' was lucky enough to attend one of the United Nations' Relief and Works Agency (UNRWA) refugee schools, an important but limited program started over 50 years ago to help the children of Palestinian refugees receive an education. Jordan leads the Middle East in public school enrollment, but the differences between the UN program and other schools in the community can be stark. Ala' told me, "We had some good teachers, some decent classes—especially in math—but we were taught mostly to pass the country's standardized tests. These tests were not necessarily about the skills that we needed to get the best jobs." In fact, as I visited schools and youth programs in very poor areas of Jordan and Cairo, the most common refrain I heard from students was that they had no sense of what the future realistically held for them.

"I actually saw my first computer in the ninth grade," Ala' recalls. "My father saved up forever to buy me a basic desktop. As I always loved math and science, I took to programming quite easily, self-taught. But more importantly, it opened up possibilities of what a future could look like." He read online about Bill Gates and the story of Microsoft. It dawned on him that the traditional paths to Jordanian society—to study medicine, or get a law or engineering degree—would never be open to him, since his parents couldn't afford it. But a computer literally opened up new worlds of opportunity at no cost beyond the machine itself. "Out of a class of 45 kids," he says, "only five of us had access to computers, and by the way, internet access in East Amman was barely existent and incredibly expensive—an unheard-of $60 a month." So they pooled their money and got online, one hour at a time. He laughs, "All of a sudden we looked very smart in school because we did homework searching on Maktoob, and most of our friends had never heard of it!"

His UNRWA school recognized his unusual talent and drive, and recommended him for a scholarship at the leading computer science college in Amman. On top of his programming studies, he audited every math class he could find. "No one could believe I wasn't a math student," he told me. "I liked the magic of mathematics. My favorite subject was numbers theory; it's like I connect them to computing." The university also had something he had never heard of: an incubator where science students could experiment and research. He built a simple website, and after discovering Google AdSense, he received his first check for $100. "My proudest moment was to be photographed with that check," he reflects. "But the learning was bigger. No one I knew yet thought you could make money on the internet, or knew what an 'entrepreneur' was. I now knew there was possibility; it was just a matter of time."

His life took a series of remarkable turns. Chosen in 2007 by his school to compete in a Microsoft tech competition, he got on an airplane for the first time in his life, visiting Colorado and Disney World in Florida. From the moment he received his visa at the U.S. consulate, he knew it would change him forever. "I'll never forget showing up, and the guy said, 'We want to have more people like you visit America.' It built my confidence." He came in sixth place out of 50 entrants from all over the world, and returned to Amman as a minor celebrity. Though eager to stay in the United States, he wasn't able to find the money, but he was awarded a fellowship to study in Greece with the Athens Information Technology Center, an affiliate of Carnegie Mellon. The fellowship covered everything but living expenses, which he soon learned were nearly 500 Euros a month, even at starvation levels. His father vowed to scrounge enough money to help at the margins, but he unexpectedly fell ill and died shortly after Ala' arrived in Greece. "It was extremely difficult," Ala' looks past me as he recalls this time. "Do I come home and help my family, or continue my studies? It was a tremendous responsibility on my shoulders, and it was very confusing for me." His mother pulled him aside at the funeral, however, and told him he had no choice: "Go back, I will take care of the family, we will manage."

Ala' returned to Greece but needed a job to pay his way and, he hoped, to send money home. He found one at a distinctly nontechnological business, Consolidated Contractors Company, a multibillion dollar multinational construction company with over 180,000 employees. He worked eight hours a day at their new IT support center on top of his studies, earning 800 euros a month.

Ala' also found time to dream. He had long been impressed by Amazon, and was vexed at how hard it was to find books in Arabic online in the Middle East. This was also around the same time that Samih Toukan's Maktoob exited to Yahoo!, and Ala realized a new world of opportunity was opening in Jordan. In fact, he remembers thinking that the idea of selling books in the Middle East was so obvious that someone else would soon jump on it if he didn't. He began to sketch out a business plan, and reached out to Fadi Ghandour, who he had met briefly in Amman. "You know, Ala' was kind of a pain in the ass, in a good way," Fadi laughs. "I knew the first time I met him that he was special. He was always asking me questions, and really came after me with his startup idea while in Greece. His 'business plan' was more of a case study, but I told him to finish his degree go back and work on it. He was relentless. Questions, push back, learning, refining."

Ala' also emailed Usama Fayyad just as Oasis500 was gaining traction. He knew that any great e-commerce company had to be heavily data driven, so Usama had the perfect background to help. Fayyad never returned his email, so Ala' simply signed up for one of Oasis' six-day training courses in the summer of 2010 on how to start a business. "I didn't even ask them for money, but the training changed my life. I got back to Fadi with a real business plan." Fadi and another friend decided to fund Ala's idea, now called Jamalon, with $14,000. His first employees were his mother, brothers, and sisters. He paid himself nothing, and his siblings invested their own pocket money in the company. At that year's ArabNet conference he won the people's choice award, but many other investors told him, "You'll never compete when Amazon comes; you'll never get enough titles to make it a marketplace." Ala' was undeterred. As he later told me, "Amazon knows a lot I don't know, but they don't know our market. If I move fast enough, we can be something different. I saw what the future could be, not only for Jamalon, but for the whole startup world in Jordan and the Middle East."

Usama Fayad doesn't recall Ala's initial email, but he certainly took notice of him during the Oasis training course. He offered him office space and an additional $15,000 to prepare for a more significant funding round. "The money was great and needed, but being in that environment of other startups, the access to mentors was everything." Fayad recalls, "He had two clear, fundamental missions at Oasis which were perfect. The first was to learn from everything around him, like a sponge. The second was to teach everyone he met about his business and its potential. When it was time to raise real money, he had laid the groundwork amazingly."

By the summer of 2012, Ala' Alsallal from East Amman had built Jamalon into a platform that offered not only the 7.5 million Arabic and

English titles earlier investors had told him he could never attain, but he negotiated deals with publishers for over nine million titles. This made Jamalon by far the largest online marketplace for books in the Middle East. And in addition to Fadi and Oasis500's investments, he raised $400,000 on a valuation of over $2 million. In the winter of 2013 he will be raising additional capital to open up warehouses in multiple cities in the Middle East, and is in partnership discussions with Amazon itself. Fadi notes, "This kid has kept his head about him because he knows that his challenges are getting only harder. E-commerce is an expensive proposition, and more competition will come. Whether and how he can scale are real questions. The Middle East isn't yet a huge market of book readers, at least outside of religious books. But I'll tell you, Ala' watches every dime so carefully, he didn't even give himself a raise in salary when he took new investment! Jamalon has real potential. I hope it will work. But Ala'—*he* will work today or someday."

That warm spring day in 2012 at Oasis500's offices, I asked Ala' if he thought his story was replicable. Was he merely the exception that proved the rule of how hard it is to overcome an educational infrastructure so ill-suited to the twenty-first century? He didn't skip a beat: "The successes of people like me will help drive other successes from all over the Middle East. The education challenge is enormous, but people aren't just waiting for government to fix all that. People are going at the problem bottom-up now—they have no choice—and there are new resources available to help." He paused, and his mouth curled into a curious smile. "We haven't even talked about it yet. If you want to see what I mean visit the one place that probably had more impact on me than any other. Visit Ruwwad."

∽

I already knew the Ruwwad story intimately. As early as 2005, Fadi told our U.S./Arab Young Presidents Organization subgroup about a youth center he was planning to build in a refugee camp near Ala's. Fadi knew the demographics as well as anyone: over half of Jordan's population, like much of the Middle East, is under the age of fifteen, and a large percentage of them lived in the marginalized communities. "They really have no vision of what opportunities might be available to them," he explained. "They think this is all they have, or maybe expect government to just give them basics to survive. Their education programs, even vocational training, were utterly inadequate at best." He believed, then and now, that government alone would not solve the challenges quickly enough, but that real public and private partnership, led by the local communities themselves, could change these dynamics sustainably. More importantly, Fadi holds that the role of the private sector is not simply to maximize profits but to invest in their societies where their well-being and future are inextricably tied. Knowledge, networks, skills, expertise, and entrepreneurial mindset are the resources all communities need as much as cash.

Ruwwad would not be a school, or a health clinic, or an after-school program—though it would have components of all these. It would be a hub, run by the community, to help its youth and families take ownership of their own challenges and opportunities. That sense of civic engagement and ownership—the same ownership that an entrepreneur experiences in her or his idea—would provide the foundation to build skills and knowledge not taught in their educational institutions. But there would be no handouts. The first and last rule would be that everyone who came to Ruwwad must give back in any way they could to build the center's relevance to the community. Businesses could contribute money, books, training, and computers. Professionals could teach job skills. And residents could give whatever they had in terms of time and labor. The goal was to empower local people to find local solutions to local challenges.

Ala' first heard of Ruwwad from his mother, during his second year of university. She thought he might benefit by engaging with it. "My first impression truly was, why bother? I was suspect of what I thought was simply 'voluntary work,' and I was so busy, who had time?" he recalled. "This feeling really was deep in growing up in places like I did. We did not believe much in bettering our communities for each other. Your problems were yours. Others' were theirs. I wasn't raised to think about how other workers were treated or how to better the environment. Mostly we are raised to think about how to get by for ourselves, how to take care of our own families, at most."

Yet Ruwwad changed everything for Ala', and for the dozens of people I met who participated in building it. Around the corner from the local public school—a gritty, barbed-wire-protected, drab and walled structure covered in graffiti—was something completely different. Ruwwad is housed in a small, freshly painted and immaculate building that has become a hub for the Jabal Natheef community. The services it has made available—from free English and IT classes to health care to legal advice to basic jobs skills like career training and résumé writing—are outstanding. There is an extensive library of children's and adolescent's books in Arabic and English; mothers with young children and teens come after school to enhance their reading skills. There are a dozen internet-enabled computers where kids can learn basic programming, do homework, and find games and entertainment from around the world. The essence of Ruwwad, however, is not its physical space and services, but its environment of inspiration and empowerment.

Ala' first came to help tutor kids in programming, but soon realized that the experience was educating him. "The kids pushed me with their questions," he recalls. "I learned from corporate mentors who came to speak to the community. They bused us out to Microsoft headquarters to get training on some of their latest technologies. But most of all, I got to participate in the youth group forums and discussions." He pauses and shakes his head in amazement. "I once thought *wasta* was everything; you need to know someone or pay someone to do anything. Through Ruwwad we had weekly gatherings where guests from business, or even government—people we may only see on TV—were talking to us as equals, teaching us the kinds of things they look for, the kinds of opportunities that could be available to us. We had all sorts of stereotypes of these people and how they viewed us. Now anything seemed possible."

Samar Dudin, who is now regional director and head of programs at Ruwwad, joined in 2005 as a volunteer who founded their youth dialogue platform and would be pleased to hear Ala's reaction. She is a remarkable woman who projects a serene but determined sense of purpose. She has been an educator, theater director, and community organizer throughout her long career in Amman, and has brought her entire rich background to bear in creating unique programs of community empowerment and youth development at Ruwwad. If she made nothing else clear to me it is that education starts when young people have a sense of ownership and purpose, that they can address their individual and community needs. "We start early on," she told me, "In creating a platform for citizenship-building that continuously challenges the mainstream values of nepotism versus meritocracy; leadership by lineage versus leadership by volunteerism and community service; human and women's rights versus traditional practices that disempower women and individuals. This is the most critical education paradigm in Ruwwad. It disrupts the traditional conservatism through a consistent, continuous, and intentional process. It creates a safe space for nonconformist, alternative thinking and respect for diversity and good traditional values." She believes it not only nurtures kids finding their own authentic, open voice but really partners with youth to be at the center, at the foundation, of their broader education journey.

By 2010, she had restructured the programs at Ruwwad to focus on what she calls "people power." By enhancing inquiry-based (not rote) learning, enabling communication in safe spaces and encouraging a commitment to the arts, scientific inquiry, and sports, she believes the experience is both educational and character-building. Her programs pay special attention to two elements. The first is a sense of ownership demonstrated through community-driven campaigns. These initiatives focus on critical social issues like literacy and physical abuse of children, and employ psycho-social support methods to inspire creative action. Every youth and participating family is expected to volunteer at Ruwwad, and last year alone they aggregated over 31,000 hours. The second is embedded in a remarkable program called *Dardashat*—weekly sessions every Saturday from noon until 2:00 PM where young people are encouraged to explore their notion of self, relationships, rights and citizenship, and career and life goals. "The sessions are usually run in a workshop style," she explains, "and we will bring in once a month a speaker on current affairs, entrepreneurship, or some question the youth are exploring. The discussions can be explosive, but the key theme that emerges is acceptance and celebrating diversity and pluralisms as a foundational value." In the end, she reiterated, the key to Ruwwad's model is that its volunteers "recycle." Whether they live in the community or leave to study as the recipients of one of the Mousab Khorma Scholarships, also created by Ruwwad, they stay constantly engaged.

When I asked members of the community what they valued most at Ruwwad, the teenagers in particular invariably mentioned *Dardashat*. I don't speak Arabic, but didn't need to in order to see the power of these gatherings. In a large room used for art classes during the week, dozens of teens arrive and break into groups of seven or eight and are given a scenario of people facing conflict. It can be as simple as how a young man addresses a woman, or a bullying situation, or a fight with a parent or teacher. The goal, though, is less to solve the scenario than to hone the skills to stop, listen, ratify another's perspective, and work together. The girls all wore headscarves, and the boys looked like the usual cocky adolescents. But once the session started, it was a room of self-confident equals. Ala' nodded when I shared my description. "In the first days, everyone is fighting, talking over each other, not trying to understand each other," he laughs. "Samar, and eventually other people who work at Ruwwad (often people from the community who are trained) build norms in listening, not jumping at your first reaction, seeing things from another's perspectives. This is great in our society. This is a kind of education that strengthens traditional academic solutions. The kids are developing skills and outlooks they never do in schools. It makes them more employable. It makes them leaders in society."

One of Ruwwad's many dedicated team members told me that she believes that sessions like these, along with art, music, and even acting, give these kids a voice they are not raised to believe they have. The issues of race, religion, and abuse are particularly intense in the close quarters of the Jabal, and the seemingly simple act of building trusted environments where teens have a voice is crucial to convincing them that they can build futures for themselves. "Supplementing school, creating resources for jobs, computing skills, and so on are crucial," she explains, "but the ability to talk about things that are normally taboo, to make it ok to express their experiences, to think of each other and respect each other is where so much of it all begins." One Ruwwad team member showed a movie to the group that touched on sexual themes—gently, by western standards—and all the students walked out. Samar told me, "So guess what. They all came back. They all said they should have voted on the movie. That the movie might have been fine if boys and girls were separate. We made a mistake that underscored the power of Ruwwad. They stood up, they debated, and they were respectful but showed their voice and took control of the issue on their terms." If there's one thing I took away from my time at Ruwwad, it was that while skills, coursework, and teaching were central to education in the short run, they're irrelevant without the strong foundation of self-confidence and ambition that comes from knowing you have both a voice and path to use it.

In only seven years, the numbers are impressive. In East Amman alone, Ruwwad touches the lives of more than 75,000 people. Their school outreach program has enlisted 1,500 primary school children in its literacy efforts. Mothers, teachers and youth in the community established a "Six Minutes" reading campaign to encourage regular short public readings that have touched over 5,000 people at over 6,600 events. Over 700 teens have received college scholarships. Ruwwad is now expanding to other towns in Jordan as well as some of the poorer areas of Budrus (Palestine), Cairo, and Tripoli (Lebanon). In 2012 they launched the Ruwwad Micro-Venture Fund specifically as a platform to encourage entrepreneurial initiatives. The fund's role is to support communities in translating their ideas into profitable business and create employment opportunities while addressing local needs. Micro and small ventures will benefit from financial and non-financial services through equity investment, as well as strategic added value services that are critical for such success—basic financial knowledge, marketing and sales in addition to access to networks and other markets. Fadi added, "We aim to provide communities with the ingredients to economic empowerment: access to knowledge, skills, capital, and networks to start and/or grow sustainable businesses."

Dina Sherif is a corporate social responsibility expert from Cairo, who has spent years working with nongovernment organizations and financial institutions in Africa. She believes that programs like Ruwwad hit on an essential truth that many overlook. "Too often people who are well intentioned don't spend enough time on the ground really observing what people are doing, and what they're capable of on their own terms and for themselves. Because youth is such a huge issue that could potentially impact the overall sustainability of our society, so many in government and business don't look at these youth as assets, but rather as problems. This is especially true in poorer communities. They don't look and see what their strengths are, what they are capable of. It means that then they're not a part of the solution." Organizations like Ruwwad presume that the answers to challenges are found and embraced by those with the greatest stakes in having them addressed.

According to Fadi, solutions *only* work when the people create and own them. "If there is any clear lesson from the Arab Awakening it is that people want to have a voice and want to solve local problems. This is about the guy who says, 'I'm going to solve the problem of garbage in our street.' Not big huge sexy development projects, but plenty of smaller guys who will think for themselves and act with their own hands." At the same time, however, he knew that resources, experience, and training are essential and the private sector has all three. "Look," he told me, "Ruwwad is not some hobby. I realized over my years in the private sector that we were out of touch, that trends in the region would not be sustainable. I'd get challenged by old guard for starting it. At first, they would say, 'What are you doing?' And my answer was 'I'm an entrepreneur, we do. *Now!*'" The challenge, he believes, is that even after the Arab uprisings too many businesses think they can get by with lip service. "The minute the heat lowers, too many in the region think the issues are resolved. But the heat is never low any more. People want better lives and will do what it takes to get them."

Reem Khouri works with Fadi Ghandour and Aramex on various initiatives and projects including Ruwwad and its expansion. The young Palestinian has learned early on that one always has a choice: surrender to frustration or initiate action. And she is all business. "I think of it as corporations renewing their social contract with society. Just as governments and societies are re-negotiating their social contracts, so are companies. Businesses cannot exist in isolation of societies and their woes; investments in community development, whether in education, health, and environment of any field will lead to healthier societies and healthier businesses. The need to do it is out of mutual benefit and mutual opportunity; not charity but continuity and interest." Dina Sherif is also cautiously hopeful, if for no other reason that it's in the interests of all parties to step up. "Businesses are doing it on their own because they realize that this could impact the sustainability of their business. Because they saw what happened after the Revolution, when all of a sudden everyone found a voice and companies were being attacked for corruption, poor governance practices. All these things came to the forefront so it wasn't just about our companies investing in their surrounding communities—it is a broader shift in mindset."

Ruwwad's successes are profound, so much so that I wondered aloud why there are not hundreds, even a thousand of them around the region. "You do what you can, with the abilities that you have, and attract as many people to be a part of it to scale," Fadi tells me. "Ruwwad is early stage, but it is also seven years old. We are now going regionally with it, elsewhere in Jordan, Palestine, Egypt, and Lebanon. The goal here is not to replace government, which must step up to its roles and services that only they can do. And some are. We don't fix schools anymore because the Queen of Jordan came up with an initiative to do so with 500 public schools. Similarly the government is stepping up with health clinics in these communities. The Ruwwads and companies other than Aramex are partnering with efforts like these as well. The ideal place is where those in the private sector push each other, and the private and public sectors push each other, to help communities take ownership of their lives and have visions and paths to their future. It may seem like a drop in the ocean, and maybe it is. But there is tremendous knowledge transfer in every success, new ideas coming from other places on their terms. Not years from now. Right now."

Fadi believes that Ala' is an extraordinary example, but hardly unique. "My view is that if you find someone curious, with the will, the ambition—no matter where he or she grew up—that person will do big things and will encourage others to do the same. They are out there. Same schools, same economic background, not a 4.0 student. They are curious; they want to do things and to make it happen. Business can mentor and help people like this, make them examples to their communities and other communities like them, make these communities proud of them and themselves." He stops and presses his finger into my chest. "In the end, who will these communities be proud of, me or their Ala's? One of their own brings more of their own. This is the most critical lesson of all. Ruwwad is about encouraging curiosity, inquiry, critical thinking in order to explore opportunities. These critical skills can be taught." And he adds the most recurrent theme I hear across the builders of the Middle East: "Success breeds success."

∾

Around the summer of 2010, Sawari Ventures founder Ahmed Alfi began to do some math in his head. He had heard that year that over one and a half million kids were entering first grade in Egypt and over two million were born. "You didn't have to be a math whiz to figure out that the government would have to build a few schools per day for the next five years to keep up with the numbers, and the odds weren't very high," he told me as we were, yet again, stuck in traffic in Cairo. Intrigued by the rise of online courses for kids around the world, like Khan Academy, Alfi decided to ask his driver about the concept.

He expected that the driver, like any working man, would simply be pleased to have supplemental education and not have to pay for private lessons. Private tutoring to compensate for mediocre schooling, I would learn, was an enormous business in the Middle East – a $2 to $3 billion market in Egypt alone. The driver, however, immediately asked three questions that stunned Alfi.

"So my wife can learn at the same time as the kids? I really want to talk to her more about things in life, but she doesn't read well, can't really read a newspaper."

"Can one of the women in our building use these videos and take the elementary school kids and help them with their lessons as a group?"

"Can my son really learn at home instead of going to school? Sometimes he gets beaten up and there is no place for him to sit."

Alfi paused in reflecting on this reaction and looked me straight in the eye. "I decided then and there I was going to launch my own startup out of Flat6Labs to offer supplementary classes in Arabic. This was going to be big, and reach every corner of society." His company Nafham. com, the only one where he is founder and chairman, pays over sixty teachers to make videos based on the current government curriculum. They have curated, created and posted by May 2013 over 4,000 video lessons as a base for what they hope will be a broader crowd-sharing model where hundreds, maybe thousands of educator, parents and even students will post educational videos and tools. Nafham is now working on curating additional courses to cover the Syrian and Saudi curricula.

INJAZ's Sorya Salti sees countless examples of the internet breaking down barriers during her company's annual country and region-wide startup competitions. I attended their finalist presentations at the Four Seasons in Amman in the spring of 2012. In one room, booth after booth of high school students from fifteen countries displayed their ideas, ranging from using recycled materials for crafts to mobile apps that would connect communities looking for safe drinking water. Five or six young women, stunningly attired in colorful flowing gowns, made a slight clanging sound as they walked, decked out in their traditional jewelry. They were Yemeni high school juniors from a mid-sized town. They loved science and wanted to solve the problem of bringing electricity to nearby tent villages. Fire was a regular hazard, as residents burned candles for light. They decided to start a small solar energy business. I almost fell

out of my chair when a judge asked them where they acquired the solar panels for their service. One young woman didn't skip a beat: "We
manufactured them ourselves. We went on YouTube and other sites on
the web, read everything we could on how to build solar panels, and we
built them." They also developed smaller panels attached to umbrellas
to power fans they had installed for people negotiating the summer sun.
They won the competition.

I asked education researcher Nafez Dakkak what technology can do
to speed up education and skills in the Middle East. "It allows anyone
to hack the culture," he said. "It could do, in many ways, what Ruwwad
does in bricks and mortar. Technology, however, can scale good ideas
across the region. Break through the learned helplessness while seeding
the belief that change can come from within, that we have what it takes
to do this." With the proper technology, at any age, people can see how
others solve problems that may seem unsolvable. "You never really know
how high the bar is, how much more you can do, until you see and engage
in what is out there."

He doesn't look at technology as a silver bullet, but rather a lib-
erating series of possibilities whose ramifications for teachers, adults
and kids are only beginning to be understood. "Technology, at its core,
allows very good ideas to scale. So if good teachers are scarce, the remarkable online teaching videos, like those on Khan Academy from
the States, allow great teaching to reach anyone for no cost." Dakkak
points out that the global nature of education is crucial, as literally any
parent or student with internet access (or even texting capability) can
find knowledge; it doesn't necessarily matter where it comes from. And
it removes the obstacle of age. "In fact, the exciting potential for solving problems now, not waiting for structural changes, is that people can
build skills at any age. An online tutoring website, Qayrawan, is enormous in Saudi Arabia. Guess who are by far and away the biggest users?
Middle-aged women!" He adds that, in the end, only education through
technology will allow adults to acquire new expertise at the pace globally competitive businesses will require. If you want a clear bellwether
of the future, look no further than the United States, where over the

past decade private investment in education technology has tripled, to a little under half a billion dollars—and there are over 70,000 educational apps on iTunes alone.

These are still the early days of Arabic and Middle East regional education technology, but Dakkak believes at least 20 percent of all startups there are education focused. Jordan's Rubicon Games, as an example, has created "edu-gaming" apps like Math Mage, a video game environment where kids destroy monsters by solving math problems. They expect another 2,000 online by this book's publishing. Easy access to English resources like Kindertown (a one-stop-shop education app reviewer for parents) Reading Bear, Storypanda, Hackety Hack, and Scratch are fun ways for kids to learn how to program. Coursera and Khan Academy are the largest of dozens of online class distributors for children and adults of all ages.

Salti contemplates the broader ramifications of youth connecting with youth through social media. INJAZ held an online competition with ten universities, asking them to identify a need in the community and potential solution. Fifteen groups were selected to upload videos and a report on their prototype on Facebook and kids would vote on it. The winner received over 370,000 "likes." "What social media is showing," she enthuses, "is that you can't remain silent, you can make a difference in your society, and *here's how*. You don't have to rely on government bodies and it doesn't matter whoever is in power, because there is less and less need of a middle man. You can take ownership and leadership in your own educational experience. This is happening now, with no need to wait. It has awakened the kids, and has awakened the private sector. It is our 'a-ha!' moment."

It was an intriguing young American, Eric Martin, who brought these issues of the role of the private sector and technology together for me. His encounter with technology in the Middle East was truly an accident. As a master's student in environmental science at University of California, Santa Barbara, the slight, fair-haired academic was viewed as "crazy enough" to consider studying at a recently formed research university in Saudi Arabia, called the King Abdullah University of Science and

Technology or KAUST. A gorgeous, rolling, ultra-modern campus outside of Jeddah, and backed by the Saudi Government, the university was reaching out to the best and brightest professors and students it could find. "The scholarship was extremely generous," Eric told me, "paying for the remainder of my education at UCSB plus a monthly stipend, sending me to multiple orientations, and of course school there, room, board, and a salary of $30,000 a year. To say it was a four-year adventure is an understatement."

The program was small and global, with 350 students from 70 countries and faculty from around the world. They were willing to be experimental, Martin having pitched and started a credited elective they called PlayLab Arabia. PlayLab was akin to the startup incubators beginning elsewhere in the Middle East. "I faced some harsh criticism from the decision makers citing the program as too 'transparent, fun, and open to the Saudi community.'" So they renamed it VentureLab and put serious focus on companies looking for $200,000 seed funding. He was stunned by the quality of entrepreneurs that came from around Saudi Arabia and their focus on solving problems. "I'm personally very excited for the day, five years from now, when the fruits of the top-down initiatives collide with those coming from the bottom up. Across many ministries, there are extremely interesting focus and efforts on entrepreneurship. The establishment of KAUST and other new tech-centric universities in the Gulf are bold statements governments can make. But the speed and diversity is all bottom up." He laughs, "I love seeing résumés in the region now because they are full of certificates they have earned through self-learning online—sometimes as many as fifty certificates!"

Chapter 7

The New Middle East

WOMEN AT THE STARTUP HELM

"Sorry to disappoint anyone," Alex Tohme said to me in an elegant, deep, last-century British accent, "My e-commerce startup is *not* focusing on 'sexy kinky lingerie' because that doesn't address the issue that women really want. They want advice, they want answers to their bra problems, and they want to feel like someone is focusing on their feelings and not their wallets. Every woman should be celebrated no matter the shape and size."

I met Alex first at Omar Christidis' ArabNet in Beirut in 2012, which she helped organize, and later in a café by her offices in Dubai. As a digital marketing executive at Western ad agencies like Ogilvy One in the Middle East, she has built a following as an at times shockingly blunt blogger on the startup ecosystem in the region. Lebanese born, Saudi raised, she was sent off to Britain for high school, and then in 1998 she passed the Regular Commissions Board for entry into Sandhurst, the United Kingdom's high school version of West Point. After studying psychology at the University of Manchester, she returned to the region in 2006, intrigued by the early days of the rise of the digital economy. One does not forget her.

She is launching amourah.com as the first underwear shopping blog and e-commerce platform in the Middle East. Her first blog post described bluntly how difficult it could be to find personal clothing that fit well, and not feel uncomfortable shopping in a public place. "I think it's the first time anyone actually showed their boobs in a bra in this region!" she laughs. "But I'm still alive and haven't been arrested. Women reached out with the same experiences and questions I had. If you take the risk it gives others confidence to follow."

Tohme has experienced significant pushback in what she acknowledges remains a heavily male-dominated retail industry. "I've even had some men tell me that women empowerment won't work," she pauses incredulously. "We are talking about a shopping experience for and about women. Women are more likely to admit where their skills are and where their weaknesses are and seek out people who can fill that gap." She believes that while the ecosystem is deeply challenged, something new is happening with women stepping up to lead. "Everyone says the Middle East isn't ready for X, Y, or Z but nobody knows until you try. Most of the time the market is ready, it's just that there isn't anyone around with the balls enough to do something about it."

Her anatomical analogy stayed with me later that day on my Arab-Net panel when I received the greatest reaction I ever received on any stage. Event founder Christidis, who is an exceptional, thoughtful, and provocative moderator, pushed us to speculate on why the Middle East seemed to be lagging behind other emerging markets in startups. "Do we not think big enough?" he asked with exasperation, and then channeling Alex, "Do we merely lack balls?" I looked over him and winked, "Well, the first thing you can do is promise never to ask about balls again. In my experience, some of the greatest innovation is coming from women." The room—all of the women and not a few, perhaps sheepish men—erupted in applause.

Like many of my fellow westerners, I once harbored the one-dimensional view of the Middle East that we often see on the news—a series of male-dominated societies where, in places like Saudi Arabia, women cannot even legally drive. After all, I often play a thought experiment with my friends in Silicon Valley, asking them to name five women general partners in venture capital firms or how many women engineers they have on their teams. Given how often such questions are met with silence here, I assumed female representation in the Middle East must be near nonexistent.

There is no question that men are more common on the tech scene in the Middle East. At the same time, one still sees a striking number of women at every gathering and meetup. Hala Fadel, who runs the Middle East MIT Business Plan Competition, sees the number of women applicants increasing each year, from an already surprisingly high base. In 2012, more than 4,500 teams of three people or more competed. "That means over 13,000 potential entrepreneurs," she told me. "Teams that included women were near 48 percent! How many Silicon Valley competitions can say that?"

The answer is none.

The rising role of women in the Middle East mirrors the rising role and impact of women across emerging growth markets. I wanted to understand the background of this rise more clearly, and to explore the opportunities some women entrepreneurial leaders are creating.

❧

One must be cautious about painting a region as rich and diverse as the Arab world with a broad brush. Saudi Arabia, the UAE, and the Gulf States tend to be significantly more restrictive than Egypt or the Levant, and they pay a significant price for it economically. According to a recent Booz study of women's role in Gulf region, women actually represent the better-educated talent pool than the greater population but a drastically higher percentage of the unemployed. "Women in Kuwait, Qatar, and

Saudi Arabia constitute 67 percent, 63 percent, and 57 percent respectively of university graduates," the study found. In countries like Kuwait, however, nearly 80 percent of the unemployed are women.[1]

Whether in the Gulf, Egypt, or Levant, however, one can find examples of both the old and new narratives just about everywhere. "Don't get me wrong," one twenty-something B2B CEO from Beirut told me, "too many men here, especially older investors, judge us in an old lens and it can be a problem." Another entrepreneur from Alexandria, who has developed a regional portal to connect mothers and their children, added, "Believe me, being a woman entrepreneur is very hard—being a wife, a mother, a daughter puts real pressure on us, we can feel real guilt under the weight of expectations. But at the same time being an entrepreneur is not mutually exclusive." And yet another social network founder from Cairo challenged why I was making any distinction. "We are *not* women entrepreneurs," she chastised me. "We are entrepreneurs who are women. We face all the same issues as any entrepreneur. If anything, as women, we probably work harder, are better collaborators, better at just getting things done than a lot of men."

Whatever one's perception of the Middle East, significant change has been well underway for years. And the crucial role of women in economic development is a global phenomenon. As every study of women's impact on society demonstrates—most recently the World Bank 2012 Gender and Equality and Development Report—that while gaps remain, women have an ever-increasing role in job creation, business creation, and consumer economic activity across every industry. It is no surprise that with access to technology, they are hungrier than anyone to create.[2]

Alyse Nelson, CEO of Vital Voices, Hillary Clinton's nongovernmental organization that trains and invests in emerging women leaders around the world, told me that she sees the change in the Middle East as part of a global shift. "We see women closing the gap with men in areas of economic development and girls' education," she told me, "but the greatest unfinished business in the twenty-first century is that women still lag significantly in leadership, power, and decision making."

She has found worldwide that women hold less than 20 percent of the seats in parliament and fewer of the C-level positions or board seats in larger corporations. "The exciting thing, however," she notes, "is that the power dynamic has shifted dramatically in recent years with access to social networks and mobile devices. Agency—real influence in making change—is no longer just wielded from the corner office, but also from a Twitter account. Technology is changing everything—breaking down cultural barriers that once held women back and creating innovative opportunities to make positive change."

In her book, also titled *Vital Voices,* Nelson tells the story of online activist Manal al-Sharif, who took on the Saudi "tradition" of not allowing women to drive. She not only began to drive, but she videotaped herself doing so and put it on YouTube, where it instantly went viral. As far back as 2008, Egyptian Esraa Abdel Fattah set up one of the first Facebook groups in the Middle East to promote a day of civil disobedience to protest low wages at a textile factory. It soon had 77,000 followers. The essence, Nelson told me, is, "One day women thought we have no voice—they see this and say, now we have a voice." The multiplier effect is profound. Vital Voices and Yahoo! partnered to host a "Change Your World Conference" in Egypt. Women by the hundreds who had never met before, except online, came together not only to share strategies and ideas, but also to push each other to make their voices heard.[3]

Ruth Messinger sees the multiplier effect of women active in their economies. Since 1998, she has served as chair of the American Jewish World Service, which has funded nearly 400 grassroots organizations working to promote health, education, economic development, disaster relief, and social and political change throughout the developing world.

"We in the west sometimes don't fully appreciate how women are the lynchpins of the family," she told me in her Manhattan office, which buzzes with her eager young team. "Women play an extraordinary role that keep the families together and functioning. When I think even in my home, I have to constantly remind my husband to call his family, it reminds me that throughout society things just get dropped when women don't step up."

She continues, "In emerging worlds, there are many ways women are codified as second-class citizens—how they dress, what education they are expected to receive. They see themselves as caregivers first and foremost—up (to parents); sideways (spouses and siblings), and down (children.) At the same time, most people underestimate their role as providers at the professional level. When you stop to think that there is something like one to two billion subsistence farmers in the world, and 60 to 80 percent of them are women, it should make us all rethink what their economic role already means." In addition so many women have viewed their roles—and thus their work—as not something one can get paid for. "Men all over the world presume they will be paid for their labor, but most women just do things even outside their homes—start a small health center, offer tutoring—and it doesn't occur to them they should even be paid for it. That is starting to change."

When women do become significant breadwinners in emerging markets, the first thing they do with their own income is invest it. "We know from all the work we do in microfinance, when women have disposable income they invest in the places that have the highest multiplier effect of getting their families out of poverty: in education and welfare of their kids. Men are more often likely to drink it up." Furthermore, women seem invariably driven to think ahead, weighing the ramifications of each step. "Again, look at microfinance. Ninety percent of the women tell us that the minute they receive a loan, $14 or whatever, it is the only shot to remove them from the wage slave thing. They will never *not* pay back what they owe, because if they blow this money they know they'll be handed a broom and paid 10 cents."

Technology is opening new problem solving throughout such communities. According to the International Finance Corporation (IFC), both mobile and computer usage in women-run businesses are about the same as men, approaching 90 percent, and over two-thirds regularly access the internet.[4] Access and outcomes are found in pretty surprising quarters. In fact, the young women in Yemen from the previous chapter are a few of thousands. Messinger explained to me, "Give a woman a cell phone and the capacity to recharge and watch them build a kiosk so people will pay them to make a call. Allow women access to an anonymous cell phone number where they can report abuse, have their stories anonymously vetted, justice can be offered. I know one entrepreneur in India who built this service, and they see themselves not only as protecting human rights, but offering a form of journalism to a community that has no newspapers. He's gathering reporting, checking it out, reporting it on mobile phones and making sure authorities follow-up. Others in Africa are offering similar services to combat corruption." Stories like these are unsurprising to Ghada Howaidy in Cairo, who runs institutional development at the American University of Cairo's School of Business. She explained to me that a large, informal, less tech entrepreneurial movement has been happening among young women in Egypt for over a decade. Many women may have come from other professions, but for other reasons—passion for an idea, lifestyle, raising kids—decide to start businesses from home. "Such businesses may start more traditionally—food catering, home accessories, or jewelry," she notes. "But it is no surprise that easy access to technology is not only driving those businesses but allowing women to create regional, maybe even global, online-only businesses."

The breadth of women-founded tech startups in the Arab world is stunning and inspirational, but also instructive as a window into the opportunities emerging in the region. They cross every corner of the *Improvisers,* the *Problem Solvers,* and the *Global Players,* but I examined four other common groupings: offering services in Arabic; helping other families achieve work/life balance; leveraging experiences from the Arab Spring to create collaborative crowd sharing platforms; and developing scalable women-focused retail and e-commerce platforms.

So Many Arabic Speakers, So Little Still Available Online

As a mentor and advisor to two remarkable ecosystem builders in the Middle East—the region-wide startup portal/angel investor Wamda and the Jordanian incubator Oasis500—I see, but take no economic stake in some pretty astonishing entrepreneurs. Through these efforts, I discovered three wonderful stories that look to solve the ecosystem challenge with which other Improvisers wrestle: the surprising lack of content in Arabic across the internet.

May Habib sat down with me at a classic bistro in downtown Beirut. The intensity and deliberateness of our conversation fit perfectly with how she built her company. A Lebanese-born, Harvard-educated wealth-fund manager in Abu Dhabi, she started getting restless about two years ago. She had reached an age when many of her friends were starting businesses, looking to solve problems. She wanted to make a difference in her region's development.

During a holiday in Europe, Habib began to fill a notebook with lists of problems and potential solutions in the region: everything from female disempowerment to religious radicalism to lack of college counseling in high schools. But it was something she read in the 2005 UN Arab Human Development Report that really hit her. Although over 80 percent of the Middle East's 350 million people spoke solely Arabic, shockingly few global information resources—especially online—could be found in Arabic. Even five years later, less than 1 percent of all content online is in Arabic.[5]

"By the end of the holiday," she recalled, "I had a model of how I could use a crowdsourced expert network to address this." Within two months she had written a detailed business plan, left banking, and returned to Beirut to seek funding. Qordoba, her first startup, was born in 2011.

Her team—now 14 full-time and three part-time engineers and over 500 freelance writers, editors, and translators—has built one of the largest Arabic-content creation platforms in the Middle East. Qordoba launched in the B2B space, largely because that's where the money is. "The region's multinationals, e-commerce startups, consulting companies, law firms all complain about the same thing: how hard it is to find Arabic language services that are high-quality, fast and convenient," she notes. By building a web-based platform that screens, tests, and employs freelance writers, editors, and translators, and distributes projects based on expertise and skill, Qordoba solves all three of these requirements. "Our customers were previously served by expensive global translation services companies and less-than-reliable local mom-and-pop shops," she adds. "We made the whole process easy and efficient."

Beating revenue forecast each month in a market place where star engineers cost a fifth of what they do in the United States, Qordoba is attracting significant investor attention, but wants to hold off their first Series A for the spring of 2013. By then, they also hope to enter the consumer space by offering Arabic translation of English language books.

Habib's roots help explain her dedication and determination. She was born in a small agricultural center in Akkar, in the northwest corner of Lebanon, and her family immigrated to Windsor, Ontario, when she was six. Her parents founded a machining tool company where she and her seven siblings were expected to help out while remaining focused on their education.

Entrepreneurship may have been in May's DNA, but her first job upon graduating college was at the investment bank Lehman Brothers and she eventually moved to Abu Dhabi to work in private equity. "I had a great two years there, in part because I was doing tech deals all over the world," she told me. "I kept seeing the problem of Arabic content everywhere, everyone talking about it, and no one was doing anything about it. Now no one has an excuse—we have built an awesome, affordable solution."

Habib worries about the same things as any entrepreneur—long hours, hiring the right people, finding customers and keeping them happy, spending every dime. "Being a woman, if anything, has been an advantage," she believes. "I work with an A-team, and they took pay cuts to join us. I think I was able to recruit them because of traits I see more frequently in female entrepreneurs. I have made my success their success, and I didn't take no for an answer. For cultural reasons (and this is true in both East and West), that's easier to do if you are a woman recruiting a man versus a man recruiting another man or woman." She is proud that online distributed platforms like Qordoba open up job opportunities for writers and translators throughout the Arab world.

The next day when I flew to Amman, I almost physically ran into Jordanian Samar Shawareb at Oasis500 headquarters—she had recently been selected to join the organization. Like May Habib she also knew early that she wanted to be an entrepreneur and found another large opportunity underserved in Arabic. Having graduated from the American University of Beirut with a business degree and then receiving her MBA at the University of Jordan, she landed a job at the British Embassy in Amman. She learned she had a passion for throwing events, and she was good at it, too. "I thought there was a need in the market for a professional event management company in Jordan," she recalls. "I decided to start my first business, Events UnLimited, in 2001 to organize exhibitions and conferences throughout Jordan."

Over the next decade, as the wedding category became one of her business's largest and most lucrative, she knew she could offer greater resources to brides-to-be throughout the region. Some of the most time-consuming, stressful, and confusing parts of wedding planning—identifying and selecting the right wedding suppliers; seeking guidance and inspiration on issues related to wedding planning, fashion, beauty and other tips; evaluating various offers and finding out what the bride and groom truly need and can afford—could ideally be served by an online content and social platform. To her surprise, few resources, especially bilingual ones, were available online in the Middle East.

In 2011, Samar launched Arabia Weddings, the first comprehensive bilingual wedding planning website to serve the Arab world. Originally launched in English, now also in Arabic, Arabia Weddings offers a unique combination of rich content (original, aggregated news and online directories of wedding suppliers in ten Arab countries); innovative planning tools (couples' wedding websites) and special deals. Her timing could not have been better. As one of the go-to executives in the industry—Events UnLimited ran the only bridal exhibition in Jordan, "The Wedding Show," for seven straight years—Samar's market knowledge gave her unique insight into the potential online. In addition, because Jordan's internet penetration and communications technology sector is one of the best in the region, Amman was the perfect place to build a region-wide footprint. Her team of seven is preparing to expand to the lucrative markets of the Emirates and Saudi Arabia next.

Samar concurs with Habib about the challenges and pressures of a startup. "Quitting a great job to set up my first business was one of the hardest decisions I had to make, mostly because of the loss of a monthly secure income. The risk was mitigated by the fact that I worked in parallel for a few years setting up the company and maintaining my day job. My new online company ties nicely to my offline businesses—seeing a dream becoming a reality is rewarding," she pauses and smiles, "Albeit it's always mixed with a sense of fear."

Jordanian media exec Fida Taher similarly plans to use technology to introduce the world to the best in Middle Eastern cooking. Zaytouneh, founded in late 2011, aims to become the world's largest library for short and illustrative cooking tutorials through multiple platforms, including websites and smartphone applications. Producing videos under three minutes showing step-by-step regional food preparation, she plans eventually to dub for every language in the world.

A television production major, Fida has long had a passion for regional cooking. Her mother was an entrepreneur establishing a leading catering company in Jordan. "Most video recipe content on the web is user generated and not very good quality—hard to follow," Fida explained.

"We film in full HD, and our videos are of excellent quality. Since only the hands are showing, dubbing our videos in any language is a minor operation and cost. Even in the best recipe websites, mostly English-based, it is hard to find 'good' oriental recipes in text, and near impossible to find good ones in video."

Starting as a woman entrepreneur brought with it clear three challenges, she recalled: "First, some men get intimidated by a strong woman. Second, others—and I will try to sound as proper as possible—think a business relationship with a woman should be a personal one. Finally, some men underestimate women in general, and believe that women are not capable of delivering good results."

"Of course, being underestimated in not always a bad thing," she continued. "I am proud to be a feminist and believe that we need to fight for equal rights on all levels, social, economic, and political."

Aside from garnering top recognition in regional startup competitions, Zaytouneh has nearly 35,000 followers globally on Facebook and is well underway to creating 120 video recipes per month. Having raised her angel round also from Oasis500, she is exceeding revenue targets and in line for her next round of funding in 2013.

Life Balance

Fear is not unfamiliar to any of the women I interviewed. Ask any woman in the Middle East startup community their greatest challenges and the first things you hear are painfully common to any entrepreneur in any country. Can I do this? Will anyone care? How do I choose among a seeming hundred priorities? When do I raise money? How should I hire? Can I move fast enough?

But press a little further and more woman-specific themes emerge, if with some regional sensitivities. As one online video founder told me, "Being a woman entrepreneur in general means that you have to overcome many cultural stereotypes, especially as wives, mothers or daughters. It is easy, in our cultural conditioning, to feel guilt for not being there for our kids as we have so much work to be done." Another agrees, "It is a very delicate balance. If you drop the ball, you are judged twice as harshly by society."

It is no surprise that great startups are offering platforms to help navigate this balance, and offer powerful resources for the Arab world and very possibly beyond.

Neither Yasmine el Mehairy nor her partner, Zeinab Samir, is a mother. But these Cairo-based entrepreneurs were stunned when Yasmine's sister-in-law became pregnant, and there was no online resource for new mothers in Arabic. "I come from a family of doctors so we were comfortable enough with English-language medical information," she told me. "But we wondered what other Arab women do." Having failed together in an earlier IT services venture, the two friends were looking for a new idea. The opportunity to create the first parenting portal was wide open, and they gathered a team of ten to launch, in 2011, a site that is quickly becoming the go-to parenting resource: Supermama.com.

After a year of researching the space, Yasmine and Zeinab concluded that the three greatest challenges for young mothers are finding information, finding the time to balance work/life issues, and creating financial plans for their families. Supermama became one part comprehensive resource, one part blog compiled by mothers who have "been there," covering basic questions around pregnancy and parenting, running a home, convenient recipes, and balancing their time between kids, husband, domestic duties, hobbies, and work. "Modern moms are online all the time," Yasmine notes, "but there is so little in Arabic, and so much information in any language is outdated or simply invalid."

Yasmine was a computer science major at one of the top universities in Cairo. "I started with the belief that technology is the way to make things happen. So for one year, we all worked from home, running the entire business on email and online tools and this allowed us to build a network of mommy bloggers and experts. They love working with us, since they are not required to be sitting in an office space all day."

They quickly gained attention in the growing regional startup community, being a finalist in the MIT Enterprise Business Competition last year (one of nearly 4,000 competitors). But it was the Europe-based Startup Boot Camp that changed their lives. "We were connected with experienced mentors, and could ask them anything," Yasmine recalled. "We learned not only how to think about mistakes, but also to understand we weren't just 'good' in an Egyptian context, but one of the best teams among the region and global participants."

As Supermama came out of beta last spring, with thousands of mothers already sharing experiences, investors agreed. They are finalizing their first $350,000 capital-raising round this week, which includes one of the leading local venture funds, MBC Ventures. "We think that there is global potential here—there are hundreds of millions of Arabic-speaking women around the world," Yasmine notes looking forward. "But we want to remain focused—diversify services around parenting—and grow from there."

Rama Kayyali Jardaneh and her partner Lamia Tabbaa Bibi were stunned by the absence of what they thought had to be high-demand early education resources online for Middle East audiences. Rama is Jordanian, Lamia Jordanian/Saudi, but both studied at university and received master's degrees in the United Kingdom and the United States. "We never thought of ourselves as entrepreneurs, per say," Lamia told me. "We were both working as freelancers in video documentary and news content production after university, but when we had our kids we felt there was an utter lack of responsible, high-quality Arabic educational products for them. We simply wanted to fill that gap." Little Thinking Minds, the region's first Arabic audiovisual educational company for children under seven, was born.

They started plotting, appropriately, virtually—Lamia was living in London and Rama in Amman, each with toddler sons—complaining that all they found for their kids were badly dubbed versions of Western programs such as *Barney* or Disney or religious content. At the same time, Disney's Baby Einstein was a huge hit all over the world, and their sons loved it. When Lamia came to visit Rama in Amman, they started asking each other, what if someone created the Arabic versions?

They soon began working on their first plotlines, which remain as popular today as when they were first screened in 2005. Back then, they hosted small cinema screenings for three year olds, who were invariably thrilled. Six hundred kids showed up to the first screening, and they had to expand it to six. "It dawned on me then," Lamia told me, "that what we are doing is quite revolutionary. By offering this eventually on digital platform, and by being first, we would become market leaders."

They started part time, with Rama overseeing production and DVD distribution while Lamia, still based in London, wrote scripts, consulted with child education specialists and pursued distribution deals. While offering videos on DVD and even VHS, digital access changed everything. "Parents simply want content delivered to their children that is culturally sensitive and reflects their values as Arabs, and they are willing to pay for it. By going digital, this will result not only in larger visibility for us in Jordan and the region, but we will also reach Arab expats around the globe more easily than we can now offline," according to Rama.

Today they offer their tools and content across an entire spectrum of media—DVDs and CDs online and in brick-and-mortar stores, including every Virgin Megastore in the region. Apps, music, video, and online games are available on the App Store, iTunes, and as YouTube rentals. They are in negotiations with regional airports and airlines to host their experiences for traveling families. Looking forward, Rama told me: "We plan to develop a portal on everything related to Arabic education to children under seven, as well as teaching kits for schools that will connect with our digital/electronic platform to enhance Arabic language learning for parents and young kids."

Alexandria-based Sara Galal just had her first child when she already saw a missing opportunity, even if a couple of years early. A hotel and tourism exec coming out of college, Sara's heavy travel schedule didn't allow her the time or ability to connect with her new baby. Switching to human resources at a local IT company changed everything for her. She learned about both the power of technology as a tool of connection and how important a company's culture was to the success of its mission. What, she wondered, could she create that would satisfy her passion for building things and allow her to be the best parent possible?

Alexandria has become one of the hubs of innovation in the Middle East, and two years ago Sara decided to attend the popular Startup Weekend Competition there—which attracted over 1,000 participants. "Over 90 percent of those competing were from technical backgrounds with very sophisticated ideas," she told me. "This pushed me to think, how can we utilize technology to support and strengthen the relationships between parents and kids? But it was also intimidating—my Facebook status then was 'Should I go, should I stay, should I come back another day?'" Her answer, however, was equally clear: "My deep inside feeling was that I have to prove that a working woman can also be a good mom and a good wife."

Sweety Heaven, beta available to anyone who signs up, is a web and mobile experience that helps parents and children set behavior expectations—keep your rooms clean, do your homework, be respectful—in a lovely, simple, game-like environment that also tracks their success. Based on a time frame and goals they set themselves, a parent and child create a reward system—this currently includes a toy or gift delivered right to their door, but will expand into additional privileges or even a gift to a local charity or cause. "The idea is quite simple, and it is what parents do every day already—but this platform really brings parents and children together to form closer and happier relationships, even if a parent might be traveling from time to time."

Galal was surprised that early investor feedback was enthusiastic, but also encouraged her to take the idea to Silicon Valley or elsewhere in the West. "With all the change in Egypt, I feel obliged to bring positive energy to my country, myself, my daughter," she explained. "I feel positive toward Egypt's future and as well as significant market opportunity in the Middle East." She adds however, "I think parents and children anywhere in the world might want to use our platform."

Her husband, Mohammad Badrah, is an IT engineer and, like Sara, quit his job to join her as tech lead and project manager. They have built out a local team of seven product specialists and engineers. "Having a supportive husband is like the kiss of life," Sara told me. "When you are so down, helpless and hopeless—and all entrepreneurs feel this at some point—a great spouse can lift you up in a magical way. We complete each other."

Sara speaks for many women in the region and around the world when she says: "Believe me, being a woman entrepreneur is very hard. It is an unusually a challenging thing for a woman to balance between taking care of home, husband, a child and even work outside—so many entrepreneurs cannot simply quit their 'day jobs' for financial reasons. But if you want to ask why we do this, it is because we have no choice. I won't be able to make my family happy if I am not happy, and in my startup I have found a great happiness. In using platforms like ours, women can feel connected, maybe have more time for them and possibly create and build their own ideas."

Connecting with Others to Build Better Ideas

These are the earliest days of crowdsourced storytelling, according to Perihan Abou Zeid, whose new multimedia startup, Qabila TV, took top awards at this year's MIT Business Competition in the Middle East. Like Yasmine Elayat of the collaborative social video capability 18 Days, she graduated from the American University of Cairo and became fascinated by both the power of social media and the performance analytics available to scale quality, useful content creation. But her roots as an entrepreneur started early. "My first entrepreneurial project was in grade 8, when I designed accessories and sold them to my classmates—I made a fortune for a kid at my age at the time." She is particularly interested in the power of marrying analytics and social media for effective advertising content.

Qabila, which employs over 30 engineers and curators, is a video content company that leverages crowdsourced media to provide any organization with cost-effective content. And they help clients engage audiences across any social network or online platform. "We guarantee that the message of our client reaches the target audience effectively," Perihan notes, sounding every inch the Google account strategist she once was. "By studying the audience behavior and adopting a crowd-sourcing model that actively interacts and engages the audience to better understand them. We believe we are revolutionizing the media production industry in Egypt."

The Revolution had a profound effect on the founding of Qabila. "The Arab Spring affected me greatly; in fact Qabila was inspired by the revolution in Egypt and the very first video we shot was in Tahrir square. The Arab Spring showed us the huge gap in the media industry and the opportunity presented itself at the time." At the time, the company thought no one, least of all themselves, understood the basics of civics and government. So they launched educational videos. According to the local media watcher, *Egypt Today*, "Using humor, simple language and even simpler animations, their videos reached out to the youth who recently found interest in politics but were bombarded with terms they didn't understand." This was the model and voice that they have subsequently brought to marketers across all industries.

Sabrine Assem was working toward her master's degree in innovation and technology at the German University of Cairo a year ago when she saw her colleagues posting questions and problems on Innocentive. The U.S-.based crowd-sharing platform has allowed over 200,000 experts in hard sciences to post R&D questions and projects to each other, and she was hooked. "Think of all the problems in Egypt that could be solved through technology, through connecting with expertise around the world," Assem told me. She decided to launch an Arabic version in her company, Fekkra—Arabic for "idea"—this past spring.

Sabrine was born in Alexandria, Egypt, her father an IT services consultant and entrepreneur in the late 1960s when few in Egypt knew what that was. "He always wanted to be his own employer," Sabrine recalled, "so he always encouraged me to start my own projects." Inspired by both her sister's active use of social tools in her youth empowerment initiatives, and her classmates at university, Assem was an early convert to the power of crowd-sharing. But even so, a startup wasn't easy. "Generally, it is very hard living alone in Cairo—hard financially, hard because some people don't think women should live alone, let alone start a business. But I learned that the only thing that mattered was my mission."

She too attended one of the many "Startup Weekends" and remembers one meeting at a Starbucks where her companions and the event organizers were riveted by her idea. "I partnered with another woman I met there and returned to Cairo to put together a team of students to build a platform and find if we could match in a beta some need to experts on the ground to solve it." She has convinced the university and one government energy department to post projects, and has already received a proposal from academics in Egypt.

Of course, the power of social media in Middle East startups is hardly limited to Egypt. Jordanian-based Abjjad is the first Arabic/English, Goodreads-like social network where book lovers log in, connect, and share recommendations and book lists with other readers, authors, and bloggers. Founder Eman Hylooz is a software engineer, MBA, and marketing research expert, and her team has built one of the largest databases of Arabic book titles. She believes this will stir audiences across the entire Arab world to read and buy more books.

"Apparently I am a bookworm," she told me. "I wanted since forever to start a project related to books." While covering Jordan and Saudi Arabia for KPMG, she heard that the new Amman-based startup incubator Oasis500 offered a six-day training class on how to start a business. "It was a turning point in my life," she believes. "I gained the knowledge of converting my idea into a real business plan. I pitched Oasis and won a seed investment to establish my ideas. That was May of 2012, had my beta up by June 18, and as of this week have more than 15,000 registered members and near 2,500 written book reviews by the audience." Built solely with freelancers, Eman will look to raise her first large investment round. Later this year she hopes to open an office, bring on full-time employees, expand beyond Jordan, and monetize through book sales and advertising.

"I have to tell you," she smiled, "I am proud to be a woman entrepreneur, as usually entrepreneurship is oriented more toward men in general. Currently, however, the ratio is changing as more women are tending to go through this journey. And maybe I am getting more opportunities from other women entrepreneurs as they love supporting other women more."

A New Day of Retail

Alex Tohme isn't the only woman leading the charge in e-commerce in retail in the region. I knew Jordanian Linda al Hallaq was a great entrepreneur, based on her focus and energy alone when I met her at a Wamda gathering specifically on e-commerce in Jordan, but clearly it was also in her blood. Raised in Saudi Arabia until the first Gulf War, she returned to Amman to study hospital management. At the tender age of seven, she would pick parsley from her grandmother's garden, wash it, remove the stems, wrap bunches in napkins, and sell them to her neighbors. In college, she organized student parties and threw children's events, and later, in 2004—knowing nothing about cars—she launched Jordan's first auto enthusiast magazine because she sensed a market need.

But it was in 1998, with fifty dollars and her sister Hana, Linda founded Hand Crafts—creating and producing painted handicrafts for friends and relatives. Their business succeeded, and they began to meet other women doing similar work. They eventually built a network of a thousand women artists working from home. They organized over 60 public shows and bazaars for local artisans, with over 200,000 people attending over time. And they knew that through technology, they could build an online store that would take the idea across the Middle East.

First Bazaar was launched in March 2012 to match designers and artists working from home to the enormous customer appetite for one-of-a-kind and beautiful handcrafted products. "We are providing hundreds of thousands—mostly women—with a portal to display and promote their products without the hassle of logistics, money transfers, high costs of store rentals," Linda told me. "Without us, they really would not have an opportunity to connect with each other." Thirteen years in the craft sales business is a significant barrier to entry. Linda notes, "We have the contacts, the know-how of how to reach and promote handmade crafts, and how to create awareness. We help buyers and sellers get exactly what they are looking for."

With two full-time employees, two part-timers and a team of trainees, Linda and Hana see no limits. They were proud when Queen Rania of Jordan visited one of their bazaars last year, admiring the quality of the products, and it inspired them to expand globally. "We absolutely will next year," Linda plans, "Though we already have had international sales, because the internet by definition is global." They currently have over 200 designers offering more than 3,000 unique products online, and 50,000 unique visitors last month.

And Linda and Hana are proud to pay it forward. "In 2010," Linda told me, "we created Hands Advocacy—a nonprofit organization that provides a platform for women entrepreneurs working from home and women interested in owning their businesses." Hands offers free confidential advice, connection to mentors, and guidance on influencing the policy environment for business formation and growth. "Our vision is to empower working women nationwide to achieve economic security."

Rasha Khouri is a global mix—she was born in London to Lebanese Palestinian parents, raised in New York City, and studied at Brown and INSEAD. Her commitment to the region never wavered. "When I was at INSEAD," she recently recalled, "I realized I wanted to combine my interest in retail and my love for the Middle East. Through my research, I realized that no one was offering luxury goods online specifically catering to the region. I knew this was an enormous opportunity to create something new and exciting."

DIA-Style was launched two years ago as the definitive online destination for on-trend luxury shopping in the Middle East. Commuting between London and Beirut, Rasha appreciates the size, velocity, and global nature of her opportunity. "Even in 2010, there was an explosion of users online in the Middle East as well as an increased consumer confidence to online shopping," she notes. "We became the only site that offers the most comprehensive selection of on-season and on-trend women's ready-to-wear and accessories in both English and Arabic." Surprisingly, leading luxury brands already in e-commerce—such as Ralph Lauren and Burberry—do not have sites in Arabic, concentrating their e-commerce efforts on European languages, Chinese, and Japanese. She believes that they are missing a $7 billion market opportunity in the Middle East. More than an e-commerce site, DIA-Style helps "fashionistas" learn their best options by offering popular virtual styling tools for users to create their own fashion "mood board," and a "Lifestylizer Quiz" they can share with their friends and receive feedback.

Rasha is proud that she is building a broad-based Middle East e-commerce enterprise. "At one level, we are giving an online fashion voice to a region that is finding its voice politically and socially," she believes. "But moreover, the business itself is linked to all parts of the Middle East—our translators are in Lebanon, our developers are in Palestine, we are working with a marketing agency in Saudi Arabia and a PR agency in Dubai. It is very exciting to work with this region during this time of change."

∽

A piece of every one of these remarkable women's stories is embodied in Randa Ayoubi. Her multiplatform on- and offline content production house is one of the most respected in the world. But Amman-founded Rubicon Group Holding is in its eighteenth year. With over 500 employees spread across Amman, Dubai, Manila, and California, her privately held company is rumored to be valued at over $200 million. She has partnerships with global media players like MGM, Sony, and Turner Broadcasting. They have created content and computer-generated imagery for television, online, and in areas as diverse as entertainment, education, and training, and soon the billion-dollar Red Sea Astrarium theme park planned to be opened in 2014. Everything this new generation has experienced and expressed she lived, though she smiles, "in 1994 there were no entrepreneurs except for Fadi Ghandour in Jordan, no VCs or even much culture to start your own business. The idea of digital was foreign to most people."

She looked out her office window and grew quiet and asked me to look at all the cars parked in the parking lot and driving on the bustling Amman streets. "I know you are thinking "big deal," but you have to understand that most of the kids you are talking to today never thought having a car and all this was possible. The men and women you meet, possibility is the determining factor, not politics. They see success, they see those cars or others creating their own ideas, and its empowerment to know they can do the same. What they see now is that they can drive their own futures."

She believes she had it easier than many women despite all the challenges of being alone not only as a woman but as an entrepreneur. She lived in a more cosmopolitan center where women did go from university to the workforce, and her family was very supportive especially as she began to raise a young family. But she is aware that the Middle East is at a turning point. "It has nothing to do with the law," she tells me, "nothing to do with religion. It is about broad-based cultural perceptions about what women can do here. Nothing will change that but education and experience."

Was I hearing "success will breed success" yet again? "Of course," Randa said, "If every year there are 10, 15, 20 examples on any of our concerns, society will change. But I think the entrepreneurs need to also set their own expectations about themselves. In the market they should not worry about limits, they will persevere. But I'm often asked how I handle work life balance, and I always say you can't, it is a myth." She pauses noting that women are making real choices now in the region about whether to work, stay at home, or do some of both. "But when we learn and accept that we can't be super human beings, but are open with our expectations—today or this week I travel, tomorrow or the next week I am at kids' school activities, there is a balance."

Salwa Katkhuda, the investment manager at Oasis500, agrees and is encouraged by what she sees daily across the spectrum of local, regional, and global potential for women-led startups in the Middle East. Having been an international financial analyst, a Jordanian investor, and founding franchisee for a global children's fitness center, she brings a broad perspective.

"Women have had real challenges—male bias, life style balance, limited role models, and even limited access to basics like a proper transit system," she told me. "But the internet has transformed our opportunities. It has allowed for more flexible work options (freelance, remote, and home-based work). It requires low capital needs and allows women to more easily be their own bosses. All kinds of resources are literally at their fingertips for free or low cost."

Randa, however, wrapped my inquiry succinctly: "this isn't about men. Bad behavior is bad behavior and we should call out bad behavior. But we should acknowledge that we are different, we have different emotions, experiences, even paces." She agrees with something almost every founder said to me in some form: "These differences and how we balance them are why we are such good and impactful entrepreneurs."

Chapter 8

Religion and the Ecosystem

It was a breezy Cairo evening in the comfortable, historic section of Zamalek. I sat with my dinner companion, a young tech entrepreneur on the outside patio of a hotel restaurant an arm's length from the Nile. In the distance, the well-lit skyline was punctuated by the occasional passing tourist or shipping boat. The sounds of live traditional music played in the background, and the smell of fresh Egyptian bread baking in an open kitchen drifted toward us. My dinner partner was full of questions and ideas, and clearly committed to exploring the full potential of e-commerce in the region. We talked about technology and business issues for hours. As we parted, he thanked me for my "mentorship," but I was confident I had learned more from our discussions than he possibly could have.

The next morning I had breakfast with one of his investors, who greeted me saying, "I cannot thank you enough for the time you spent with him; it really helped his thinking and opened his mind, not only to ideas for his business but how he views Americans like you." He paused and gave me a big smile and a wink: "Did you know that he is a Salafist? A pity he also thinks you will spend eternity in Hell."

Having been raised a strict Italian-American Roman Catholic, I noted, only partially in jest, that this was hardly the first time someone had come to that conclusion. But his comment, also only partially in jest, stayed with me. I wasn't offended; after all, and sometimes to my own personal regret, I no longer considered myself part of any organized religion. I also understood that not only do most Muslims differ with the very strict and conservative Salafi perspective but neither the investor nor I could possibly know what the entrepreneur left thinking. But it did make me stop and reflect about how in any discussion of the Middle East in the United States, even in business and startups, religion is never totally removed.

As I share my experiences in the region with friends in the United States, I am invariably asked if Islam and sectarian tensions make a thriving ecosystem difficult, if not impossible, in the Arab world. Not one of these same people has ever asked me about how Hinduism in India or Judaism in Israel affects those remarkable ecosystems. Interestingly, the reaction seems selective even toward different Muslim-majority countries. Religion rarely comes up even when I discuss the great growth markets of Turkey, Malaysia, or Indonesia, all with large and rich Muslim populations and traditions. I have never met a venture capitalist who would hesitate to invest in a great individual entrepreneur in the United States or abroad due to their faith.

It was tempting in writing this book to ignore religion altogether. It is a rich, complex, and sensitive subject, and I am no theologian or expert. But three questions are important to consider specifically in the rise of startups in the region. First, knowing that I am regularly asked in the United States about Islam in the Arab world, I wanted to examine directly why. Second, knowing equally that religion informs not only so much of daily life in the Middle East, but historic, often violent political struggle, I wanted to understand what distinct impact, if any, Islam has on the growing startup ecosystem. And third, I wanted to see whether startups were rising as a direct result of that impact.

The why, no doubt, is not only that we in the United States are unfamiliar with Islam, but that so much of our contemporary consciousness of the Middle East was formed by September 11. "For so many of you," a Lebanese television journalist once said to me, "Islam is mostly about the praying, protesting, and terrorism you see on cable news." That acts of terrorism were justified by a tiny minority of individuals using *a* language of Islam, have had many Americans believe this is *the* language. But if truth be told, I suspect very few in America actively seek a wider understanding. When I wrote about a related issue for the *Washington Post,* I was struck by the number of people in the United States that I interviewed—from all points on the political and economic spectrum— who were uneasy even talking about Islam. To a person, they spoke passionately about the importance of religious tolerance, the separation of church and state, and the Bill of Rights. But there was inevitably some click, some hesitation, in their voices when it came to how Islam fit into these beliefs.

A 2010 Gallup survey seemed to confirm this observation, as it found 43 percent of Americans admit to feeling at least "a little" prejudice toward Muslims, as compared to 18 percent who say the same of Christians and 15 percent of Jews. Nearly one-third of Americans say their opinion of Islam is "not favorable at all."[1] This bias means, as dean of the Johns Hopkins School of Advanced International Studies and Middle East expert Vali Nasr told me, "that in American society there is a need at a human level to understand more, to demystify Islam, and take it out of the cross-political name calling."

In my own journey to understand more, I certainly have learned that Islam is not a monolith. Throughout Muslim communities around the world, as is true in any faith, for some their religion is core to their self-identity. For others, it is not the only or even defining aspect of their lives. And even among those for whom it is core, the spectrum of interpretation is wide. I saw this play out with the same students back at the American University of Beirut who taught me about *wasta.* They found it frustrating when, on a campus of higher learning, the first question the upperclassmen asked them was, "What sect are you?" One student told me, "Though my parents had lived through the Civil War in Lebanon where sect was everything, I had never thought in those terms before.

But I knew what they were doing. They were going to lump me into one category in their minds of who I was based on my answer. I love my faith and who I am, but I refuse to be categorized by someone else's interpretation."

In the context of the startup ecosystem, Egyptian venture investor Ahmed Alfi was a great place to begin connecting some dots. Alfi is as devout in his faith as he is proud of his years in the United States. We had a long breakfast in Manhattan at the height of the 2012 presidential campaign, and discussed how religion and faith played a significant role in both U.S. political conventions. Christianity was a central refrain in most of the Republican speeches, and the Democrats had to backtrack when a reference to God was pulled from their party platform. I asked him what he thought Americans most misunderstood about Islam in the Middle East.

He looked almost wistful in his answer. "Throughout my entire life it has been clear to me that Islam, at its essence, and America are perfect together. Every core ideal Americans value—individualism, individual accountability, calling out lying, cheating, stealing—are all there." I looked at him with curiosity, and he shrugged at me. "There is no question that much in Islam is subject to debate and will be debated. There is no Pope; there is no final answer. Responsibility lies with the individual, with their families and with their local communities. Islam is one of the few religions between you and God directly, no middle man, even if some try to claim there is." He added: "My wife always taught the kids, on judgment day, no one else is on your report card—no parent and no sheikhs. It's all you."

He then explained the two fundamental economic principles present in Islamic business transactions. The first defends individual property rights. "What is mine is mine, and it cannot be seized by a rule or the government. It is, in fact, protected by God's law," Alfi noted. The second is an Arabic word, *reda,* which requires the informed consent of both parties and defends free trade down to the simplest transaction. Alfi continued, "but what many people don't understand is *reda* also means the 'informed *contentment* of both parties.' Both utterly coincide with any libertarian economic thought. If I had one wish for governments in the region, whether the Muslim Brotherhood or any other, it is that they would simply enforce these core Islamic financial principles."

As interesting and true as this may be, it left me with a nagging question. The most successful and innovative ecosystems require transparency—the ability to question paradigms; the openness to embrace diverse perspectives and backgrounds. How could entrepreneurs thrive if so many governments in the Middle East seemed to demand a hierarchical discipline around religion—such that one was unlikely to rise in the ranks without toeing the party line—and if rigid inflexibility to alternative views was allowed to limit the contributions of huge and talented segments of society like women?

Alfi's partner, Hany Sonbaty, believes that this is one of the central questions the new Middle East is wrestling with today. "We debate less about the forward-thinking questions, like what we need or want from our institutions and ecosystem," he argues. "We often get stuck, instead, on two factors: our own worldview, which drives a desire to constantly look back, and our willingness to sidestep questions we don't like to ask ourselves."

Many westerners are unfamiliar with the history of the region, but when Europe was immersed in the so-called "Dark Ages" of the late tenth century, Islam was leading the world in science, math, and philosophy. Less than two centuries after Islam's founding, its influence spanned the globe, from today's India through North Africa to Spain—a reach greater than that of the Roman Empire. Hany noted the profound role this has played in the regional psyche. "Our place vis-à-vis the West has created a lot of frustration from the fall of that level of world influence a thousand years ago, leading to colonialization and European-led, post-war carve-up of the region in the last century. Religion in politics took on a real significance, both in yearning for the 'glory days of yesteryear,' but also a very real and legitimate concern about a demise of Muslim values. There was and is a lot of soul searching as to why we have regressed. Many have concluded we have tried everything and failed—except turning back to God."

There is a strong desire in the post-Arab uprising world, he contends, to believe that what once made the Arab world great will make it great again in the future. "Therefore, as a 'battered people,' we crave a strong leader to drag us out of the mire. We seem to be currently predisposed to accept the notion that we are one great leader away from glory. It is a very hard argument to combat against given the climate." The result, he says, is a great focus on what is "un-Islamic," rather than a more personal discussion of what it means to *be* Islamic. Too much attention is paid to the technicalities of the faith (e.g., does one perform the five prayers a day or not) versus what kind of person one is, how he or she engages with and treats others, which, Alfi points out, was always meant to be the core focus of the faith.

Muhammed Mekki, the co-founder of the Zappos-like Middle East fashion and e-commerce company Namshi, spent over a year after university examining similar issues on a Fulbright fellowship. He taught me about the concept of *riba*, and how it, too, shifts the debate in the region from its core purpose. Roughly meaning "usury," or collecting oppressive levels of interest on loans, *riba* is expressly banned in the Qur'an. It also implies unwarranted taking advantage of others, especially a weaker party, in any business dealings. "Despite the popular understanding of *riba* as simply being interest of any kind, to me *riba* is really about being financially oppressed," Mekki told me, "The Qur'anic injunction banning it in the starkest of terms was meant to protect people from being caught onto a path of effectively indentured slavery to the people they owed." An entire industry of banks and consultants has risen over the years to determine what is "Islamic Finance"—how to identify and promote an economic order that conforms to Islamic scripture and tradition. Yet religiously compliant financing structures without interest, but for "fees," to Mekki, can seem like *riba* in and of themselves. "Ironically, getting an 'Islamic loan' can cost devout people more money—maybe even a few percentage points—than a conventional loan. This is technically done in the name of our faith, but is it, at its essence, what our faith is about?"

Alfi, Sonbaty, and Mekki all strongly believe that a secondary challenge is the Middle East's unwillingness to talk transparently about the
very real challenges it faces. Alfi notes, "It is the insular nature of our
society. We are not yet comfortable with that level of transparency; yet,
bluntly, it is a perversion to look the other way. We have flaws in our
societies that need to be fixed. All societies do. One of them is our looking backward instead of forward. We need to think of the glory of the
future, not the past." Wael Fakharany of Google Egypt and the driver of
the Ebda2 startup competition put it to me more bluntly: "I am a good
Muslim who prays five times a day, but I want to live in the world and
accept everyone. I want to take the work ethics I see in the West. I want
to adopt a scientific approach when I am thinking about my country and
its people. We have been downgraded because of autocratic systems and
dictators empowered by religious scholars to get the people hypnotized
by what they call 'religion' and in reality it's just about power."

But as these men know all too well, in a world of personal computers and smartphones, technology puts these debates and conversations
back in the hands of individuals. Alfi notes, "Think about it: all that is
being unleashed by our entrepreneurs fits perfectly with the essence of
our faith. In a world of social networks, there is a presumption that the
community can and should solve problems. There is a sense of immediate accountability where your actions and ideas are for all to see and
your weaker moments are kept in check. Islam is the perfect thing to
disaggregate—'dispower'—aggregated, central solutions that rarely address specific often complicated needs. Islam instead allows enormous
collective innovation. It brings people together, but the responsibility is
back on you." He pauses for emphasis, and makes a point that seems
consistent with Fadi Ghandour's and others' belief that there can be no
wasta on the internet: "In social media, you can't participate *and* hide.
It fits perfectly into the Islamic idea of full individual accountability."

Sonbaty is even more passionate: "There is more in Islam in the end
to encourage entrepreneurship than almost any religion, and it inspires
social entrepreneurship when the region most needs it. To do less than

embrace these opportunities in technology is to squander our wealth, even corrupt our morals. People will live, businesses will grow, but they will all be poorer than we have to be." As he sees it, what is happening today is a series of very clear tradeoffs. If there is no respect for private property, there will be no ecosystem. If regulations are too complex, there will be no startups. If governments attempt top-down economic control, any given country will lose its dynamism just when it is showing its most promise. If there are inflexible labor laws, there will be less hiring, more unemployment and a loss of productivity. "Most importantly of all, talent has never been more mobile," he notes. "Tech entrepreneurs will change societies in the Middle East, but how governments act and interpret faith may decide where exactly that happens."

Given all this hope that transparency will allow a more direct discussion of regional challenges, I asked Hany why he and Alfi implemented their "no religion, no politics" rule at their Flat6Labs incubator. "It was just about time and place," Hany said. "It is a mechanism, as we are getting off the ground, to minimize heated debates and keep the entrepreneurs building product. We started this right as the parliamentary elections were underway, so things were particularly sensitive." At the same time, anyone can—and many do—pray in the Flat6Labs auditorium each day. "I admire them and their dedication, but want the focus of our mission clear in everyone's minds," Hany clarifies.

We turned back to that young Salafist I had had dinner with. Hany agreed with my other friend. "He may think you're eternally damned, but he also knows the value of exchanging ideas. You probably have had conversations with evangelical Christian entrepreneurs in the States who equally worry for your soul. What is happening today is that as more people do business with each other, they are also having conversations and making connections. A hardcore Salafist would not even talk to you, but whenever any touch happens like this, a stereotype might be broken. Perhaps even a few of yours as well?" And what about those who aren't flexible enough to deal in close proximity with women, I asked. "Any entrepreneur who limits his or her connection to the best talent won't be globally competitive, period." He looks away and says, as if to himself,

"Do these people forget that the Prophet's wife, as a leading merchant at the time, was an extremely successful entrepreneur?"

∾

Of course, many startups have found great opportunity in engaging in faith and building community among the faithful in the Arab world and beyond. Yousef Ghandour (no relation to Fadi) is a Palestinian entrepreneur who created AnaBasalli, a mobile app and web platform for tracking daily prayers. It is a reminder alert tool for those wanting to pray the required five times a day, combined with a movement tracker to help the devout measure how long they pray and in what position. It is also a social network wherein community members can share when they pray and any related thoughts or content that might be inspiring them. There are a series of e-commerce companies that facilitate buying halal foods and other items of the faithful. Around significant holidays, like Ramadan, many sites offer special services. For instance, mindful that people spend the Ramadan month mostly at home with family, reflecting but also seeking entertainment, Rasha Khouri, founder of e-commerce site DIA-Style, launched a "Ramadan Lifestylizer." This limited-time experience showed artwork with Ramadan-relevant themes and tied it to a temporary shopping section with products tailored to the holiday, including *abayas*. Rasha told me, "There was a marked increase in traffic and repeat visits, in both Arabic and English, driven—interestingly—by sharing on social networks like Facebook."

Mohammed Donia, with fellow Egyptian/Silicon Valley entrepreneur Youssri Helmy, created a particularly powerful tool in their company, Ideal Ratings, which was also part of his journey in faith. Born in Egypt and residing there through his university years, Mohammed worked for Proctor & Gamble's regional arm. In the mid-1990s he joined another Egyptian friend in a startup in Silicon Valley that helped people buy insurance policies online. After it went public in 1999, he co-founded a second company to help hedge funds and investors view, on one screen, multiple data and research capabilities across their portfolios. Yet he found his success unfulfilling. "I had gotten to know many wealthy and successful people, and they just valued things I did not value," Donia told me. "My clients were very successful hedge funds who got very, very rich but did not add much to society, or even to smaller investors. I wanted a different system, a different way to think about business and investing."

In 2006, Donia decided he would invest only in businesses that were "Sharia compliant"—companies that lived by the core values of his faith in their dealings with their employees, clients, and communities. But to his surprise, it wasn't easy to determine which companies were. "I have always been fascinated by the U.S.," he recalls, "I love being here and became a citizen. I never faced any direct harassment, even in the days of 9/11. But when I wanted to find out if AT&T is Sharia-compliant or not, there was no way of doing it. In fact, I had no idea what Sharia-compliant was all about, but I knew millions cared and wanted to find out and understand more."

Donia began reading and interviewing friends, and realized that accurate research and stock reviews on Sharia compliance, though widely desired, were basically nonexistent. What little information there was out there was mostly definitional, academic, and disconnected from what was actually happening in the business world. With over 70,000 publicly listed companies, and a larger Muslim investor base around the world, he saw an opportunity.

But he had his work cut out for him. Even settling on a clear definition of "Sharia compliant," given the various interpretations and the complexity of the companies in question, was very hard. "Can a company be compliant if it has debt? What if a McDonald's sells pork or beer? I went and studied this. What if a company's revenue was 2 percent in pork and alcohol and I invested and then gave 2 percent of my investment away? There is no one view, so it is an individual's interpretation." He studied every document he could find, and assembled a review process to rate any publicly traded company. He created a massive database, covering 160 countries, of both information and potential investors. His goal was that institutions with ample capital, like local college education funds, would now have a way to participate in global investment opportunities more easily. Individual investors in the Middle East and elsewhere could also save through better investments and have greater liquidity. Such individual investors could enter the broader economy and become less isolated in understanding the world around them. The potential for impact was real.

Ideal Ratings began to sell to institutions and fund managers worldwide. Donia laughs, "I remember when I first pitched a Saudi firm; the guy's jaw dropped when I showed my card. A company that offered Sharia compliance investing with Silicon Valley innovation captured his attention." Today, his reports marry Sharia-compliance ratings and research with state-of-the-art data from partners like Bloomberg and Reuters. The company has fifty people, forty of whom are in Egypt, and an extensive network of research consultants around the world. Their database comprises 60,000 companies, and Donia has clients in twenty countries, with offices recently opened in Saudi Arabia and Singapore. "We don't tell people what is or is not compliant *per se*, but in the spirit of our faith—in the transparency and individual interpretation our faith embraces—we offer them a perspective and the information so that they can decide."

In their next iteration, Ideal Ratings will reach out to individual investors as well. They recently launched a free iPhone app in ten countries, including the United States, Saudi Arabia, and Egypt, as a beta test. One can look up a stock for a quick thumbs up or down, and then pay for an in-depth report, if desired. He notes with some irony, "I know that some people have told me that Apple itself is not compliant, because some of the lyrics on the songs it sells are not appropriate. But I have no doubt that it is. Any Muslim can benefit from having access to this platform for music, reading, and videos. An individual song may be inappropriate, for sure, but anyone who uses the services knows there are already screens in place for porn and gambling." He adds that what his company does is analogous to the screening others do for social responsibility. "Investors can disagree or agree; what I'm providing them with is transparency."

He could not be more enthusiastic about the rise of startups in the region, from an investor perspective. Despite the lingering debate about the roles of debt, *riba*, and compliance, venture capital and equity investment is wide open, constrained only by whether the operations may conflict with one's individual view of faith. "The bottom line is that if cash in our region is sitting in the sidelines in a small bank or under the mattress, or put in real estate, how will we build the opportunity? The region is ready for greater engagement in global economic sectors at all levels of society."

~

"That," said ten-year-old girl, with the dramatic pause and furrowed brow of a seasoned film critic, "was *awesome*."

She had on her best dress to attend the New York Film Festival debut of *The 99*, a new television cartoon series featuring 99 superheroes, each connected by ancient stones with distinct powers, creating missions to save the world. Based on a comic book series, it has all the artistry, action and music that American kids have come to expect from their screens, large and small.

Yet the creator is not a Hollywood whiz kid, but Kuwait-born, New York–licensed clinical psychologist Naif al-Mutawa. The superheroes are not Americans alone; they hail from nearly every country in the world. The storyline builds on the history and culture of Islam and the Middle East.

Al-Mutawa first had the idea for *The 99* while riding in a London taxi not long after September 11. What would happen, he wondered, if he could create a children's show of and for the Middle East that could instill pride in local heroes but also show universal values and connect with audiences around the world? "My conviction is that the only way to beat extremism is through arts and entertainment—they often prove the best ways to get people to rethink culture," he told me.

The PBS Independent Lens documentary *Wham! Bam! Islam!*, aired in 2011 and 2012, tells Naif's story of starting a media company in

Kuwait, based on the first major local comic book series. He struggled to find support in a religious and political environment where any connection between cartoons and Islam raised suspicion. "I knew there'd be resistance in my region," he noted, "and slowly built the confidence, as people saw and understood what I created." Over several months, he and his team of designers and writers of all faiths and creeds got to work creating storylines. Meanwhile, Naif was out meeting with other media companies and ministries of information throughout the region, convincing them that what he was doing was in no way a threat to their faith.

Through his product, Naif attempts to connect two seemingly conflicting paths. On one hand, he has designed his superheroes around the tenets of Islam. Each hero represents one of the 99 core values of the faith. But by having no overt religiosity in his stories, no expression or encouragement of faith, he has created a global platform for children of all backgrounds to understand how many values they share with Islam, such as generosity and mercy. Naif personally sees no conflict. "We came out in the middle of the Danish cartoon controversy, those riots and threats spawned by the cartoonist who drew a representation of the Prophet. We could have laid low then, decided to just be another 'cartoon,' but we would have never reached the level of success. I thought we could go along to educate and inspire not just religious communities but all communities."

His greatest struggle, he says, is that everyone defines their own elements of religion slightly differently. His answer was to keep religion *per se* at bay, because any discussion of a specific faith quickly deteriorates into an argument about who is right. "It is the human nature," he tells me, "So *The 99* never talks about religion. We never discuss God, we never address the mechanics of any religious law. Our superheroes are archetypes—blueprints—of values we all aspire to, the values we all share with sensitivity to other cultures we all need to understand."

Like Alfi and Sonbaty, he sees the core values of his faith as perfectly matched with the unprecedented opportunity in the current ecosystem. But he is also blunter: "People don't like to say it this way, but there are religious and political leaders in Islam who are simply hijacking the faith for their own purposes. Do they want people to rise in society based on their ability to memorize verses of the Qur'an or to be prepared for the opportunities of the technology age, the twenty-first century? If children's textbooks don't emphasize tolerance, if they have some magical mystery tour of faith and mystify our Prophet instead of making him understandable, how does this reflect our faith? According to the Holy Qur'an, The Prophet himself made mistakes like we all make mistakes, and this our own journey of faith more accessible, more real to us."

Naif found himself facing the buzz saw of religious controversy in the United States when he tried to launch there through the Discovery Channel and Hasbro Toys partnership, "The Hub." Several bloggers suggested that he had a secret agenda to convert American children to Islam. When others complained that one of *The 99* characters wears a burka, Naif was incredulous. "*One* character in the entire 99—*one* percent of the characters—wears a burka," he explains. "A central character of the Marvel comic series *X-men* 'Dust,' has worn a burka since 2002! In *The 99*, each character represents a different country and background. I'm not advocating for anything, but wearing a burka is part of our world. We are about inclusivity, not exclusivity."

It's hard to measure the true extent of American resistance to these ideas, because it's not always explicit. Al-Mutawa, who was once singled out by President Obama as a model Middle East entrepreneur, came under fire from conservative bloggers during the 2010 congressional election. Two years after signing an U.S. television distribution agreement with The Hub, *The 99* has still to see the light of day on cable television in the United States. Isaac Solotaroff, Director of *Wham! Bam! Islam!*, attended a planning meeting with The Hub in March of 2011, and has no doubt that blog pressure has delayed U.S. distribution. "The Hub clearly expressed that as a relatively new network, they simply could not afford any risks. This was not something they had initially anticipated when they bought the rights to *The 99*, but it was, in fact, an unfortunate reality of the current political climate in America." The Hub's communications executive, Mark Kern, would only note, "At this point no scheduling decisions have been made."

Conservative columnist and former Under Secretary for Public Policy at the Department of State under President George W. Bush, James Glassman, believes Naif's critics miss the central point. "If America stands for anything, it is universality, community, working together, diversity. Why would we not want to celebrate accomplishments any community has had and will have? Any heroic, positive act should be embraced and re-enforced. The values, articulated in *The 99*, are exactly the kind that should be supported on the merits, are in all of our interests. Why would we ever *not* want to support the kind of 'good guys' captured by *The 99?*"

Lewis Bernstein, Executive Vice President of Education, Research, and Outreach for *Sesame Street*, counsels Naif to push forward. In the first year, he recalled, *Sesame Street* was banned in Mississippi, since it depicted one of the first African American couples on children's programming. A year later the ban was removed. "*Sesame Street* came at a very difficult period and the issues were charged and complicated," he says. "In the end, the question really is, is the programming strong enough, good enough to break through any resistance? And in today's technology, web, and mobile programming, there are more channels and choices."

The internet opens the door to clearing up longstanding misconceptions in the Middle East. "In the region, historically our cultures have focused on happenstance—we have been peoples thinking our destinies are in others' hands, that it was OK to wait around for things to happen. Technology is showing us that the opposite is the case. It strengthens not only our impact, but also our understanding—of us and our relationships to our faith," Naif notes.

Like Alfi, Naif wishes that followers of Islam would focus more on what it is, rather than what it isn't. "We are tired of people who co-opt God to do terrible things, and leaders who don't condemn the obvious. People bomb things and decapitate in the name of Allah, but my own kids need something to relate to in all that is positive in our faith and values. A hundred people told me not to take this all on, but things are changing, I believe." He laughs as he sets up a line I've heard him use in his many speeches and TED talks across the world: "We need to stop asking for permission and start asking for forgiveness if and when we make the mistake. In the words of the great comedian Emo Phillips: 'Every night until the age of ten, I used to pray to God for a bicycle. Then I realized that God didn't work that way. So I stole the bicycle and started praying for forgiveness.' Emo is saying be proactive and make the mistake. These are the words I leave to tomorrow's entrepreneurs. Steal a bicycle."

The surest sign of how technology is changing his business arrived in the fall of 2012. He had long wrestled with The Hub over their retaining television rights in the United States without using them; in November, their additional internet rights expired. The next day, Naif announced a deal with Netflix, instantly reaching 25 million subscribers in the United States alone. In his tenth year since he founded *The 99*, he is now in 70 countries, from South America to Ireland, Australia, and the Middle East—reaching the entire Arab region through the children's channel of the broadcasting juggernaut MBC and the global Arabic audience through none other than Yahoo!'s Maktoob online, which has already driven nearly a quarter of a million streams. Their YouTube channel launches in February 2013, when anyone with a browser will be able to see *The 99*.

∿

In November 2012, one of the most widely debated articles from Egypt was a blog post from a young former member of the Muslim Brotherhood. Osama Dorra is a freelance columnist who writes for the *Egypt Independent*. Once devout in his faith and unwilling to reject the role of faith in political life, he passionately wrestles greater connectedness to what he believes Islam is and can be, rather than what it limits. Some of the entrepreneurs I spoke to agree with his overall argument and others disagreed, but they all thought he nailed the truth in his last sentence: "Here is the message that my generation sends to those who control this country: Purify religion from all the jurisprudential horror and elevate it above political misuse, or else we will reject you and your beliefs altogether." Proud of their faith, these entrepreneurs and their investors often see their startups as extensions of their personal values, and they are wary of the ongoing debate in their midst. Yet, as in everything they do, they also see opportunity.

Chapter 9

Not a Matter of Whether, but When

As I write this in early February of 2013, I have been up much of the night reading Twitter feeds. Some of my friends—some of the people in this book—have been reporting from the streets of Cairo and Alexandria. Three months previous, Egypt's President, and Muslim Brotherhood leader, Mohamed Morsi issued a decree effectively putting himself above judicial accountability. Crowds—hundreds of thousands, even millions of people, cell phones in hand—gathered then in almost every Egyptian city in demonstration. In December 2012, they voted on the new Egyptian Constitution, or in many cases abstaining from voting as a protest. Now they await Parliamentary elections in a few weeks, and wonder if violence will break out as it just did on the second anniversary of the first Tahrir protests. Other Twitter reports argue whether Syrian dictator Bashar al-Assad will hang on with unyielding brutality or may be on his last legs. There have even been suggestions that his regime may have armed missiles with chemical weapons for potential use on his own people. The final outcomes may not be fully known in either countries even when this book is published.

Several weeks previous to all this, the seemingly never-ending battle of Gaza erupted once more. Several weeks before that extremists attacked the U.S. consulate in Benghazi, Libya, killing four Americans, including the U.S. ambassador.

Beyond the deep sorrow and uncertainty that accompanies all of these events, I also have had two interconnected reactions.

The first is that before the Celebration of Entrepreneurship in 2010, I might have glossed over, even dismissed, these kinds of incidents as evidence of the seeming intractable, unchanging and unfixable narrative of the Middle East. Today, however, I see two distinct narratives—both at odds with each other but also coexisting: the top-down entrenched powers' desire to control their societies' agendas; and the bottom-up, often tech-enabled problem solving and opportunity building that is happening regardless. I note, in addition, that every growth market is wrestling in some form with its own version of this tug-of-war.

This first reaction leads to my second, which is to think of Saed Nashef. He is a venture capitalist who, in the last months of 2012, led a $1 million round in a travel startup and committed outright another $1 million in a hot new mobile-text, eventually app-based, job matching company. This would be unexceptional on the surface, except that both he and these companies are based in Palestine. If anyone anywhere is testament to the unstoppable power of technology in the hands of entrepreneurs, it is Nashef.

Palestinian-born Nashef is the co-founder of Sadara Ventures, a $30 million venture capital fund whose limited partners include some of the brightest names in global technology and investment: Google Foundation, Cisco, the George Soros Economic Development Fund, the Skoll Foundation, and the European Investment Bank among others. Sadara's offices are located on the Palestinian side of the Separation Wall—the 25-foot-high barrier between Israel and the West Bank begun in 2002—in the city of Ramallah. It invests in Palestinian tech startups.

Nashef is not a wild-eyed optimist but has fought through long odds his whole life. Born and raised in East Jerusalem, the former computer engineer came as a teen to the States in the late 1980s helped by an aunt living there. He paid his way through Cal State, Long Beach, by working long hours driving taxis and in a gas station. Self-taught in computing—he would visit computer electronic stores and spend hours at the demos—he caught the eye of Microsoft before graduating and spent the next five years in their Redmond, Washington campus.

Five years of programming at Microsoft taught him all the basics, and he spent the first years of the new millennium launching his own tech startups in the United States. He decided to take a one-year sabbatical to return to Palestine and was astounded by what he saw. "I started meeting people and saw this stunning, potential, nascent pool of tech talent. There weren't hundreds of thousands, but it was more than I expected, and they were doing very interesting things and were extremely good. All they missed was exposure and opportunities others take for granted. If I could help them to access some networks, guidance, mentoring—something different could happen here."

The answer came in 2008 from the man who would become his co-founder in Sadara, Yadin Kaufmann. The successful Israeli–New York venture capitalist had already put together a plan to invest in Palestine. He, like Nashef, was intrigued by the surprising tech opportunities in corners of the world most people had written off. They agreed then, as they believe now, that looking at the ecosystem in a place like Palestine would certainly have a social mission, but they were committed first and foremost to the business of making money. With these parameters, and after assessing the growing talent, they concluded that they could. Their partnership was born.

"Part of the reason we focused on technology specifically," Saed told me, "Is that it is more resilient to geopolitical volatility. Traditional Palestinian business like masonry, stone work, agriculture, and tourism are all sensitive to geopolitical change. Tech is much less so. It was clear that the next wave of economic growth, not only in Palestine but in the Middle East and the world, would be tech based." I asked him whether there were opportunities to connect with the remarkable tech-center that is Israel, and he paused. "Maybe one day. For Palestinian entrepreneurs who are interested, we can make these connections happen. Cisco and several Palestinian companies have experimented in building Israeli-Palestine partnerships in areas like software development. What matters first and foremost is investing in exceptional entrepreneurs and building great businesses. The rest will take care of itself."

I asked him via Skype how things are on the ground after the then recent violence in Gaza, and he became very quiet. "I would be lying to you if I said this does not affect things here. Palestine is often only seen through the prism of conflict and occupation—both of which are real and stifling." His voice rises, "But despite it all, Palestine has talent and economic opportunity. Oasis500 from Jordan came and did sessions here that lit up the community more than I can say. Aside from Sadara, there are two other active funds focused on Palestine. Bottom line, this is a bet on the long term."

He continued: "So much is happening despite occupation and political challenges. A solution not based on parallel progress in both the political and the economic tracks will be hard to sustain." He pauses again, and says, "But if it can happen in Palestine, it can happen anywhere. And once entrepreneurs taste success, they don't stop."

Saed was on my mind when, right after the terrible events in Benghazi, a journalist called me to ask if I was now ready to give up on the idea of startups in the Middle East. I asked him how many people were involved in the attacks on the consulate and protests that had happened there and simultaneously at the U.S. embassy in Cairo. He thought around two thousand (in fact, it was likely around two hundred). I told him that several months ago between four and five thousand young women and men from around the region had applied for and competed for an MIT startup competition—one of dozens, maybe hundreds of such competitions big and small over the past year in the Arab world. Violence and instability are realities in the region and in many emerging growth markets. However something different is happening at scale concurrently. What he sees and what I see are both present in the world. The real question is, which group do we want to bet on going forward?

Almost on cue, I heard from Youssri Helmy. Helmy is an Egyptian who has had outstanding success in several Silicon Valley startups, including as a co-founder of Ideal Ratings, the Bloomberg-like resource of Islamic Finance with Mohamed Donia. He, with yet another fellow Egyptian-Valley success story, Dr. Ossama Hassanein, also successfully chaired TechWadi—the leading nonprofit group to connect entrepreneurs in the Middle East to the San Francisco Bay Area. He was in Cairo during the heart of the December 2012 protests in a very different vantage point. Nearly 1,400 entrepreneurs were attending the Cairo TEDx—one of the thousands of global sessions spun out from the famous annual TED gathering that attracts some of the best innovators in the world to Long Beach, California, each year.

"My time in Cairo was the perfect dichotomy of what is going on today," he told me. "People live normally and do business as usual, then go to Tahrir Square or the Presidential Palace to do their political participation. On TV we see one million people, but Cairo is nearly twenty million, so the rest are at work or school or at TEDx," he laughed. "TEDx was incredible. On top of the 1,400 in the room or outside on bean bag chairs watching the presentations, over fifty thousand viewers were watching the sessions streamed. Speakers were very eclectic, with a doctor talking about telemedicine in Egypt, a lawyer talking about women's rights, thinkers, writers, innovators. The youth have dropped their fear, and that is reflected in their demands for freedom, career choices, and the wave of entrepreneurship. There is no going back."

There is no going back.

∾

*For one last reality check, I turned back to the founder of the Celebra-*tion of Entrepreneurship, where my journey began. Arif Naqvi is among the largest global growth market private equity investors in the world, and I wanted to hear where his chips are laid and why. He has seen it all.

Those who believe linear careers are linearly predictable might suggest Arif Naqvi has had consistently bad timing. The Karachi-born investor studied Soviet Economic Systems and National Planning at the London School of Economics a few years before that nation collapsed.

He decided to move from London to Saudi Arabia on a date that would turn out to be three days after the Iraqi invasion of Kuwait. He led and funded the Celebration of Entrepreneurship event two months before the Arab uprisings consumed the Middle East. His private equity firm, the Abraaj Group, launched a series of multi-hundred-million-dollar and country-specific Middle East and North Africa growth funds at the same time.

But there is nothing linear or linearly predictable in this remarkable entrepreneur except his performance. He arrived in Dubai in 1994 with a total savings of $75,000 and set to work to find investment opportunity by making contrarian bets. Over the subsequent 15 years, his Abraaj Group effectively gave birth to the private equity industry in the Middle East. Today it manages over $8 billion, and in the summer of 2012 acquired London-based emerging market private equity fund Aureos Capital, making it one of the largest growth market investors in the world.

Reframed, Naqvi's career has mirrored the rise of emerging growths markets and the impact from entrepreneurs and technology perfectly. I have sat with Arif countless times as part of our Young Presidents Organization U.S.–Arab subgroup and in his activities around the globe. In the late fall of 2012, while he was in New York City to meet with President Clinton at the Clinton Global Initiative summit, we sat in a quiet antechamber of his suite in the Four Seasons. His dark hair and features make him appear younger than his fifty-two years. While he looked tired from recent near-endless flights and meetings, I knew it meant he was plotting a next move. Throughout our time together, it seemed that whenever he fantasized about slowing down, he would shortly increase his new activities. His eyes were alert and his tenacity ever present as he described where he sees the world today, and the unstoppable trends coming our way.

"The mistake that so many people make looking at the world today, especially when they consider the Middle East," he explains, "is that they paint it all with one brush as opposed to understanding the nuances within each of the different countries. It is one of the main drivers of 'misunderstandings.' Especially regarding the Middle East, the

West—particularly Western media—doesn't seem to be able to discuss the region in any other way than as to suggest it is simply one big war zone. Events that happen in Syria should not detract from what the region can accomplish. But they do."

In fact, he believes that the issue is not so much of what the West misunderstands as it is at least three realities they are missing all together.

The first is that the narratives of war blind the West to equally clear economic trends in the region. For over a decade, in macro terms, countries like Turkey, Egypt, and Saudi Arabia have been consistently ranked in the top ten growth markets in terms of potential across almost every survey. "Even today," he notes, "these countries are expected to grow at 5 percent per annum over the next five years. So the next question should only be what this means in terms of the investment requirements in specific various sectors." He notes, for example, that the demand for more than a million houses to be built in Saudi Arabia over the next three years is good for construction; that the growth opportunity in credit and debit card penetration in the larger regional economies means greater consumer spending; that the fact that demand for hospital beds will double in the Gulf countries over the next 15 years means real opportunity in health care. "These are trends and markets that not many investors really get to feel or understand from afar. That's why we remain very local in the markets in which we operate."

Second, what is happening in the Middle East is part of a significant and clear shift in global economic and, to some extent, political power from West to East. As Abraaj's story has been predicated on the global growth driven from this shift, his firm is now operating out of seven hubs across 35 cities worldwide, investing in global growth markets that span from Latin America to China, from Kazakhstan to South Africa. "Africa is a new frontier for some," he notes, "But we have deployed over $1.5 billion across over 50 companies in the continent and continue to be very optimistic about the prospects there." McKinsey, he adds, estimates that by 2060 there will be 600 million middle class consumers on the African continent, and seven out of ten of the fastest growing countries in the world today are found there. "Most people don't think of Africa this way, but for us it's not a new frontier but a growth market in which we are extremely well positioned." The Middle East not only has its own significant growth prospects, he notes, but sits at the very center of this broader growth. "The Middle East is what connects China and India to Africa. It is for this reason that the Middle East is home to one of the most profitable airlines, Emirates Airlines, and one of the largest ports in the world, Jebel Ali. As Asia and Africa continue to grow, I only see a greater role for the Middle East in the global economy."

Third, the desires of the new generation in the Middle East and how they are expressed are equally a global phenomenon. "Fifty percent of the population here is below 25, and many are currently underprivileged. This is very challenging, but at the same time virtually all have aspirations for social mobility." What needs to be highlighted is that the youth in the region are fighting for the same things as are their Western counterparts. "The events of the Arab Spring and what caused them—the reaction to inequality, and these aspirations for mobility—are no different from what we saw with the Occupy Wall Street movement or the uprisings in Greece." Arif beliefs that what the new generation is doing with technology, and in the startup businesses he and his team see every week, is a new expression of their taking control of their own mobility. "This is going to scale," he adds. "The Arab youth, all youth, will not let it be any other way. The genie is out of the bottle."

As clear as these three realities are for Naqvi today, one does not need a crystal ball to see equally three additional and predictable trends for the future brewing now.

First, with over 50 percent of the world's population living in cities today, growing over one million per week, greater urbanization is inevitable. "Every year cities are expanding in growth markets to the tune of eight New York cities. Twenty-five cities in these markets represent more than the entire population of the United States. This represents a potential middle class of 1.4 billion people, which is larger than the entire [34-country Organization for Economic Cooperation and Development] OECD," Naqvi adds.

Second, and concurrently, community will continue to replace hierarchy in business and politics out of necessity and desire. With size and urbanization comes greater complexity, and traditional institutions have less ability and fewer resources to solve problems. This means at one level, that cities in aggregate will take increased ownership of their challenges, but more importantly that individuals and entrepreneurs will increasingly lead from the bottom up. Arif observes, "What it really means is that everyone will be drastically more empowered in the way we deal with governments, or business or any institutions." Technology is already facilitating this change as people are becoming more technologically dependent on each other. "Over time, this will blur lines of nation-states. Community is in the ascendance, and is coming into conflict with the hierarchical base on which government, society, and business were previously organized."

Finally business itself will have to redefine its role and engagement in society. "Companies that transcend borders in many respects need their own foreign policy. It doesn't matter if it is a global giant like Coca Cola, a small company in spare parts, or a new tech startup. Companies will compete with people on the ground, and in their connections will know what they stand for, how they interact with other global companies, countries, and individuals as responsible citizens." For Arif, "corporate social responsibility" is not a term of public relations but as important a component of a company as making a profit. All stakeholders today and increasingly in the future—including traditional ones like customers, investors, and employees, but also the communities where they live or that they touch virtually—will simply demand a sense of inclusiveness. "Inclusiveness doesn't come naturally to human beings," he argues, "but in a storm when the waves are up all boats must rise, not just the strong ones."

Consistent with an entire career marked by looking beyond the most immediate and commonly accepted narratives, it is no surprise that Naqvi takes a different view than those who think the Arab uprisings have increased the risk of doing business in the Middle East. "Of course the events in the region have resulted in uncertainties coming to the fore in some countries," he tells me, "but when you look at those realities and trends, clearly that does not mean that the potential for an entrepreneur to succeed in a commercial endeavor has dissipated."

For Arif the man, the fundamental unknowable question for the intermediate term—the fundamental choice really—is whether governments and institutions will embrace these realities and trends. "I don't think anyone can deny that people asserting their rights to seek a better life, participatory governance, and more accountability from governments is a good thing in the long term." The point of disagreement may be in the differences of twentieth-century institutions moving at a different pace toward the "long term" versus individuals who want and are making changes more quickly. "It is not a matter of whether governments adapt, in my view," he shrugs, "but when and how. Will the benefits of a democratic platform in the Middle East result in positive changes within five years, ten years, or twenty years?"

For Arif the investor, the fundamental question in the near term is, will there still be good investment opportunities where he can deploy more capital? "I certainly don't want to be facetious about this, but I'm more concerned that the Eurozone and the U.S. are able to put their house in order. One can't be an island of excellence in an ocean of turbulence. We are living in an increasingly interconnected and complex world—where problems in the Eurozone and the U.S. could end up resulting in what International Monetary Fund president Christine Lagarde calls the lost decade."

He pauses and looks over my shoulder at the New York City skyline. "Where we are today, and the central trends in and demands from societies, could not be more clear." He pauses and looks hard at me, "I am, on balance, optimistic about the Middle East's contribution to global growth increasing over the next five to ten years. My bet is with the entrepreneurs who will make it so."

$\sim$

Will the new governments and societies taking shape make the same bet?

The power of technology has, in many respects, made this question less relevant. If anything marks the rise of startups in the Middle East and around the globe, it is that entrepreneurs build, bottom-up, around obstacles and succeed despite them. At the same time, however, while there is no going back, governments have a distinct ability to slow this talent in ever faster-moving, globally competitive markets. In fact with progressively universal access and adoption of technology worldwide, anything slowing an ecosystem can have significant, even generational, consequences.

In all the focus on political instability in the region, less examined is that many countries have adopted restrictive internet access and privacy laws. This includes business-friendly Dubai and lean-forward tech center Jordan. Often described as necessary steps in areas like press-and-publications law in order to protect libel concerns, these restrictions are usually vaguely worded and subject to wide and opportunistic interpretation. On the ground, entrepreneurs and investors alike view these as moves that risk chilling business development in their promising ecosystems.

Jordan's 2012 legislation, as an example, among other things, holds online news sites accountable for comments left by readers, requires the sites to archive all such comments, and forces them to obtain licenses from the government or risk being shut down. This, for a tech sector that has grown 25 percent annually over the past decade and now accounts for 14 percent of gross domestic product—up from 2 percent in 2000.[1] A leading regional news and research group, Sindibad, notes that in 2011 nearly half of all startups funded in the Arab world were based in Jordan.[2]

Backlash from regional tech communities against such strictures was immediate. Hundreds of the country's most popular websites periodically take themselves offline in protest (akin to protests in the United States earlier this year against the Stop Online Piracy Act then being considered by Congress). Twitter was replete with entrepreneurs warning that, as one recently wrote to me, "The government may be about to ensure one of the greatest brain drains in our history."

But will the ire of the tech sector change the government's policy? Internet restrictions, after all, are commonplace in countries where central control is paramount. China regularly wrestles with Google. Saudi Arabia and Russia have many restrictive laws—and even democratic Turkey and India have plenty of online restrictions. In late 2012, the Philippines tried to severely restrict social media use before the courts intervened. In the short term, these countries weather protest, and business seems to move apace. The king of Jordan has wisely reached out to the tech community to reinforce his commitment to support the tech community.

Internet clampdowns, however, present a larger and longer-term economic paradox for all emerging nations. The internet today is not merely a mode of communication but the defining platform by which businesses innovate and transact around the world. How can governments restrict this platform when its very success is based on transparency, openness, and access?

"More and more major businesses and industries are being run on software and delivered as online services—from movies to agriculture to national defense," wrote internet pioneer and venture capitalist Marc Andreessen in the *Wall Street Journal* in 2012. "Many of the winners are Silicon Valley–style entrepreneurial technology companies that are invading and overturning established industry structures. Over the next 10 years, I expect many more industries to be disrupted by software, with new world-beating Silicon Valley companies doing the disruption in more cases than not."[3]

If this book has shown anything, it is that becoming a force in technological innovation or disruption far beyond Silicon Valley has never been easier than it is today—but unimpeded access to the internet is essential. New entrepreneurs worldwide are creating ways to collaborate and solve local, regional, and even global problems. And governments should note that while these innovators are passionate about their homes and culture, they have also never been more mobile. If pushed, they can seek out other countries that embrace their talent.

In addition to losing their best and brightest, emerging nations will have trouble competing if their legal environments squelch innovation. Even in China, where stunning growth has seemed to suggest that the government is surprisingly adept at managing technological transitions, the engine appears to be slowing. For newer economies in the early days of technological adoption and struggling for growth, the damage could be much worse. Once behind, how can they hope to catch up and compete over time?

History is a story of governments constraining capital in order to maintain political control, with the Soviet Union as the most egregious example. Oppressive regimes have survived for decades by allowing a select few to aggregate wealth while impeding others' access to capital. However, this strategy has not been sustainable—as the Middle East has shown especially in recent years. It is unimaginable that constraining technological access, all but impossible in any event, will have better outcomes.

Nitin Nohria is the dean of the Harvard Business School, and was my professor two decades ago. His life has both touched on and mirrored the shifts, challenges, and opportunities of our time. Born and raised through university in India, Nohria studied at MIT and subsequently joined Harvard, and he has lived the combined rise of technology and emerging growth markets. No one pushed me harder to think about the ramifications of this paradox than he.

"People greatly underestimate the psychology in all this," he told me in his office in Boston. "The power of 'I want to be a part of that because I *can* be a part of that.' It is what drew so many people to the Arab Spring. We are in a moment of conceptual change where no one needs to live in a world in which our lives are totally determined by dictators. This is a political expression, but also an economic one that is behind the entrepreneurs you are seeing." He pauses. "And with every example of success, it will inspire so many more to then have the courage to say 'I don't need to be a salaried man. I don't need to be in the military to be successful. I don't need to ride the coat tails of some religious organization. I don't need to be from a prominent family. I don't need to go to the West. No longer is my only hope to escape and find some opportunity abroad.'"

He drove the point home, in reminding me of all that we in the West take for granted. "It's not a trivial thing. It's easy for us to sit here in my office and say, 'Well of course anyone should imagine an idea and act upon it.' Truly for me this mindset is the greatest asset that the U.S. has; that one's psychological space can also be a real space. We in the

States don't have to grow up actually wondering whether it's a huge leap to decide to do something entrepreneurial, it's taken for granted. For the first time, it is becoming a reality in many corners of the world, and it's hard to suppress once it's out there. Governments are afraid to embrace it because it brings uncertainty—not understanding that in this expression are the answers to a lot of their own concerns."

Nohria continued, "It's just mindboggling, the fact that you have super-open access to the internet and all it offers—this platform means that kids in college can dream about stuff and make it so because it is so open." He pauses. "How much ingenuity are governments willing to choke off? Because if we've learned anything about what makes societies better, it is in respecting, philosophically and in action, the sovereignty of the individual above everything else—that every individual is sovereign, in some sense, over his own life. That's the only way to honor the fact that every life has an opportunity for self-determination."

The paradox of whether top-down institutions can successfully achieve the growth they require by controlling the internet and its entrepreneurs—a platform and people who by definition thrive on transparency, flexibility and rapid innovation—is not a paradox at all. They can't. They assure their own continued marginalization and risk that their best entrepreneurs will build somewhere else.

Instead, what governments in emerging growth markets have, in fact, is an unprecedented and unique opportunity in history to embrace the internet as their central business platform. Singapore, South Korea, and Israel did so and became world-class technology players. These countries have had their own challenges with political liberalism, but their embrace of open, globally competitive access to technology has meant that businesses can grow and college students can dream of building new enterprises at home.

∾

If I have any one hope for Startup Rising, *it is that it will inspire* people to rethink our conceptions of the Middle East and engage.

Rethinking is proactive, not reactive. It requires regular effort to question conventional wisdom, not to dismiss it but to check it and look forward. The great hockey legend Wayne Gretzky, when asked what he thinks about on the ice, is said to have paused and answered, "I think about where the puck is going, not where it is." I can think of no better skill to hone in the times in which we are living.

Rethinking also means reframing. There is a temptation in the West to think of the emerging growth markets as requiring top-down aid or assistance. In some venues, this is not entirely untrue. Even in the startup worlds, the most common "ask" I hear from regional entrepreneurs and investors is for knowledge sharing. Lebanese-born, Dubai-based Loulou Khazan launched Nabbesh, a social network platform that matches available talent to part-time work and projects, in 2012. She soon won the first region-wide reality TV show competition *The Entrepreneur*. She could not feel more passionately about what she and others can learn in connecting with the United States. "The startup ecosystem there is obviously much more advanced and sophisticated, and we can learn from the failures and successes as well as your best practices on key issues of how to scale. There is also a great opportunity for Americans to see what we're doing and find interesting investment opportunities while our ecosystem develops."

At the same time, in the great, global, connected, and transparent worlds of technology, the first question should be less what can you do for someone, or what can they do for us, and more what can we do for each other? We in the United States too often engage in growth markets thinking "larger market cap—gotta be there" and/or "cheap labor—gotta outsource there." We don't think enough about what we can learn and co-author together; that the "innovation" of the future will come from unexpected places and will push us to embrace unique experiences, locations, and cultures; and that selling and transporting virtual and physical goods to once-hard-to-reach customers has never been easier or more cost effective. The puck of history is going toward bottom-up collaboration where everyone has something to add to the problems and opportunities we collectively experience.

For all the power of communications technology, there is no substitute for human interaction. And there is no greater first step we in the West can take toward understanding emerging markets than to simply visit them. Entrepreneurs and ecosystem builders in these markets love to have people come not just for some dog and pony show, but to have serious conversations about finding mutually beneficial ways to connect. I was thrilled in the fall of 2012 when the great, if not peripatetic, 500 Startups founder Dave McClure toured the Middle East with a group of tech investors and returned with a very different view of the ground for doing so.

Similarly, the impact created by making it easy for startups from emerging markets to come here—plotting in advance to bring delegations of hundreds, even thousands, of young startups to the great gatherings in Silicon Valley, New York City, Austin, and beyond—is profound. It takes significant time and work, which we easily forget, for them to accomplish this on their own (to get visas, to find money to cover trips, to coordinate connections/meetings in person, etc.). This is already increasingly happening ad hoc, as young entrepreneurs I meet have been visiting the United States individually. Imagine what great ideation and innovation could happen at scale where hundreds, perhaps thousands, of entrepreneurs regularly and repeatedly connect with global counterparts, explore and do business.

What we must keep in mind is that while entrepreneurs are tech savvy as a result of daily engagement with world-class software, and their hunger is often as strong as, or better than, what we are used to, these ecosystems are still nascent. As I have shown, the challenges around tech infrastructure, education, skills, and mindset are real, but so is the innovation with which they are being engaged. I remember one conversation with a kid on term-sheet best practices; he knew significantly more than I did simply by looking online and asking questions. The sheer desire and self-taught aspects of these markets have a lot to teach us. Understanding this is a key step to understanding great potential connections to mutual benefit. What often stands in our way in underestimating the global shifts like the ones happening in the Middle East is our bias.

I'm in my forties, yet my journey toward understanding these historic and universal changes in the Middle East and beyond is only beginning. There is no doubt that the next company I build or buy will be global in nature. It will embrace the broader definition of innovation I have discovered in the region. It will cultivate old and new friendships abroad as real partners not only for the traditional purpose of market access and outsourcing, but as a regular, continuous, mutual co-authorship of learning and fresh thinking.

And among the many circles in which I wander—my own startup ecosystems around the country, the broader investment communities, the news and blog communities, and the policy makers here in my home of Washington, D.C.—I will push for everyone to seek out the "unobvious" and engage with it. I will strive to shine light on these remarkable entrepreneurs and their stories as they take their futures into their own hands and change their societies.

Everything I have described in the Middle East is happening now. That there will be pain and setbacks, some severe, is certain. Where the greatest successes will come from and how long they will take is less so. Whether it is next year, five years from now, or ten doesn't matter. Quoted by great thinkers from Arthur C. Clarke to Bill Gates, the late futurist Roy Amara noted that we tend to underestimate the effect of a technology in the long run at our own peril.

The long run is now.

Notes

Chapter 1: Celebration of Entrepreneurship

1. Vali Nasr, *The Rise of Islamic Capitalism* (New York: Free Press, 2010), 15.
2. David Sheff, "Interview with Steve Jobs," *Playboy Magazine*, February 1985.

Chapter 2: Work-Around

1. Derived from the World Bank and European Bank for Reconstruction and Development database, Business Environment and Enterprise Performance Survey (BEEPS).
2. International Monetary Fund, *Regional Economic Outlook: Middle East and Central Asia Report*, November 2012, 88-90. See also: IMF World Economic Outlook online database, October 2012.
3. Rina Bhattacharya and Hirut Wolde, *Constraints on Growth in the MENA Region*, International Monetary Fund, February 2010.
4. United Nations Development Program. *Arab Development Challenges Report 2011*, December 2011.

Chapter 3: The New Breed

1. Karim Sabbach, Mohamad Mourad, Wassim Kabbara, Ramez Shehadi, "Understanding the Arab Digital Generation," Booz & Company/Google (Fall 2012), http://www.booz.com/media/uploads/BoozCo_Understanding-the-Arab-Digital -Generation.pdf.
2. Glen Palakian, "25 Essential Stats on e-commerce in the Middle East," *Wamda .com*, October 16, 2012, http://www.wamda.com/2012/10/25-essential-stats -on-e-commerce-in-the-middle-east-stats?goback=%2Egna_2778360%2Egde _2778360_member_190563641. See also Philip Hampsheir, "Mall v. Internet. Can e-commerce Conquer the Middle East?" *BBC.com*, January 17, 2012, http:// www.bbc.co.uk/news/business-16581980.
3. *Op. Cit.*, "Understanding the Arab Digital Generation."
4. Email conversation with Aramex, Lyad Kamal, November 27, 2012.
5. *Op. Cit.*, "Understanding the Arab Digital Generation."
6. The World Bank, "Cairo Traffic is Much More than a Nuisance," August 21, 2012, http:// www.worldbank.org/en/news/2012/08/21/cairo-traffic-much-more-than-nuisance.

See also: *EgyptToday*, "Raging about Road Safety," February 7, 2012, http://www
.egypttoday.com/index.php?url=news/display/article/artId:506/Raging-About
-Road-Safety/secId:12/catId:2 ; Ahram Online, "20 Egyptians Die Per Day in
Traffic Accidents: CAPMAS," September 9, 2012. http://english.ahram.org.eg
/NewsContent/3/12/52385/Business/Economy/-Egyptians-die-per-day-in-traffic
-accidents-CAPMAS.aspx ; Naeema Al-Gasseer of the World Health Organization, "Road Safety in Ten Countries: Egypt," 2012. http://www.emro.who.int/media
/news/improving-road-safety-egypt.html.

Chapter 4: Leap Frog

1. Vijay Govindarajan and Chris Trimble, *Reverse Innovation* (Boston: Harvard Business Review Press, 2012), 8.
2. *Ibid.*, 15-19.
3. *Ibid.*
4. Tonny K. Omwansa and Nicholas P. Sullivan, *Money Real Quick: The Story of M-
   Pesa* (London: Guardian eBooks, 2012), 9.
5. The European Photovoltaic Industry Association (EPIA*), Global Market Outlook
   for Photovoltaics Until 2015,* (Brussels: Renewable Energy House, January 13,
   2012). See also, Padron-Fumero, Noemi, "A Regional Mitigation and Adaption
   Approach to Climate Change: Technology Transfer and Water Management in the
   MENA Region," Universidad de La Laguna, Spain, 7.
6. Janet L. Sawin and Lisa Mastny, eds., *Prospects of the Renewable Energy Sector in
   Egypt,* (Cairo: Egyptian-German Private Sector Development Program, 2010), 7.

Chapter 6: Startup/Turn-Around

1. International Bank for Reconstruction and Development/World Bank, "The Road
   Not Travelled—Education Reform in the Middle East and North Africa (Washing-
   ton D.C., 2007), 3-6. See also Pauline Rose, "Education for All: Global Monitoring
   Report 2012" (EFA Global Monitoring Report Team, Commissioned by UNESCO,
   Paris, 2012).
2. *Ibid.*, 4.

Chapter 7: The New Middle East

1. Ramez Shehadi, Dr. Leila Hoteit, Dr. Kamal Tarazi, Abdulkader Lamaa, "Educated, Ambitious, Essential: Women Will Drive the GCC Future" (Booz & Company, 2011), http://www.booz.com/media/uploads/BoozCo-Educated-Ambitious
   -Essential.pdf.
2. Bruce Ross-Larson, principal editor, *World Bank 2012 Gender and Equality and
   Development Report* (Washington, DC: International Bank for Reconstruction and
   Development/World Bank, 2011).
3. Alyse Nelson, *Vital Voices: The Power of Women Leading Change around the World*
   (San Francisco: Jossey-Bass, 2012), 134-135.
4. International Finance Corporation/World Bank Group, *Women Entrepreneurs in
   the Middle East and North Africa: Characteristics, Contributions and Challenges*
   (Washington, DC: Center of Arab Women for Training and Research, 2007), 6.
5. United Nations Development Program, Arab Human Development Report 2003:
   Building a Knowledge Society (2003), 50, http://www.arab-hdr.org/contents/index
   .aspx?rid=2.

Chapter 8: Religion and the Ecosystem

1. Gallup Center for Muslim Studies, "In U.S., Religious Prejudice Stronger Against Muslims," January 21, 2010, http://www.gallup.com/poll/125312/religious-preju dice-stronger-against-muslims.aspx.

Chapter 9: Not a Matter of Whether, but When

1. September 2012 Sector Presentation and email interview with Abed Shamlawai, CEO of int@j—Jordan's Information and Communications Technology Association.
2. *Ibid.*, and Oasis500 and Sindibad-business.com (in Arabic translated by Wamda. com): *Investment Report on Internet and Technology Startups*, October 2011.
3. Marc Andreessen, "Why Software is Eating the World," *Wall Street Journal*, August 20, 2011, http://online.wsj.com/article/SB1000142405311190348090457651225 0915629460.html.

Acknowledgments

Startup Rising is, if nothing else, a story—or many stories—of cour-
age, determination, and not-so-little craziness that marks great entrepreneurs anywhere. My greatest fear throughout writing this book is been
failing to do them justice. My greatest regret is that I could only tell a
fraction of their stories.

Whether named or not in the narrative, well over 150 individuals sat
with me in often extensive one-on-one interviews and follow-up Skype
conversations. Everyone quoted here was offered the opportunity to
check their quotes, and nearly all did, and most read and commented on
their relevant sections. Many of those quoted read entire chapters, even
the entire book draft; they taught me countless lessons in the region's
rich history and culture; they pushed me to rethink technology and innovation in new ways; they forced me to write and re-write until my facts
were correct and language passable; they taught me the definition of patient generosity and hospitality with their time, tours, homes, and meals.
In over a dozen other multi-hour group settings at the American University of Cairo, the American University of Beirut, Oasis500, Flat6Labs,
and conferences and competitions I learned from countless others whose
names and full stories I never learned.

∾

My appreciation, thus, starts with the entrepreneurs themselves, in
alphabetical order:

Amer Abdulghani and Wasseem AG, of a Syria/Dubai based computer animation and gaming company; Sarah Abu Alia, Jordanian founder of art and music startup Art Medium; Abed Agha of Dubai digital entertainment agency Vinelab; Mohammed Al-Ajlouni of Jordan/Dubai broadcast and internet media services ABS Network; Ala Alsallal of Jordan online book e-commerce company Jamalon; Ziad Aly, of the Cairo Mobile company Alzwad; Wael Amin of Cairo IT professional software services ITWorx; Sabrine Assem co-founder of Cairo-based crowdsource project system Fekra; Selcuk Atli, founder and CEO of social marketing firm SocialWire; Wael Attili of new media company Kharabeesh; Randa Ayoubi of the global media company Rubicon; Mohammad Badrah, co-founder at a Alexandria rewards site Sweety Heaven for parents and children; Edward Disley of Egypt-based Ogra Taxi; Mohamed Donia of Islamic finance/research company Ideal Ratings; Yasmin Elayat of Cairo-based video and social network 18 Days; Ahmed Essam of Cairo Twitter Mobile company Neatly; Haytham el Fadeel of the Egyptian mobile answers startup Kngine; Ahmed Fathalla of mobile TV startup Gyro Labs; Sara Galal, co-founder at Sweety Heaven; Yousef Ghandour, serial entrepreneur in Palestine; Mohanad Ghashim of the Houston/Aleppo/Amman e-commerce platform ShopGo; May Habib, Beirut/Dubai founder of translation services Qordoba; Linda Hallaq of crafts e-commerce company First Bazaar; Mostafa Hemdan of Cairo recycling services RecycloBekia; Hind Hobeika, Beirut founder at Butterfleye's Instabeat; Eman Hylooz of Jordan-based books social network Abjjad.com; Khaled Ismail, Cairo founder of SysDSoft, now Intel Mobile, Egypt; Loulou Khazen Baz of the Dubai skills management platform Nabbesh; Rama Jardaneh and Lamia Tabbaa Bibi, co-founders of Arabic children's online content center, Little Thinking Minds; Fawad Jeryes, Jordanian serial entrepreneur; Rana el Kaliouby of Affectiva ; Elie Khoury of woopra; Rasha Khouri, founder, DIA-style.com & DIA-BOUTIQUE.com; Yasmine El-Mehairy, co-founder of SuperMama; Muhammed Mekki, co-founder of fashion e-commerce play Namshi; Ronaldo Mouchawar of e-commerce platform Souq.com; Cairo-based Ahmed Naguib; Amr Ramadan of Alexandria weather/app company Vimov; Ziad Sankari of Cardio Diagnostics; Mohammad Shaaban of Cairo e-commerce app Eshtery; Samar Shawareb Ashqar, managing director at Arabia Weddings; Ahmed Soliman of Cairo-based city guide app Circle-Tie; Dan Stuart, founder of Dubai-based group-buying site GoNabit and country manager, Canada at LivingSocial; Fida Taher, Jordanian founder of recipe media company Zaytouneh; Alexandra Tohme of Dubai-based women's clothing/lingerie site Amourah.com; Samih Toukan, founder of Maktoob.com and Jabbar Group; Martin Waldenstrom of payments company cashU; David York, senior vice president of U.S. KarmSolar partner WorldWater & Solar Technologies; Ahmed Zahran of solar energy/water pump company KarmSolar; Perihan Abou-Zeid of Google and co-founder at crowdsourced media company Qabila.

I am equally grateful to their many partners in ecosystem building: Henri Asseily, investor; Rashid Al-Ballaa, CEO of N2V; Emile Cubeisy, managing director of IV Holdings; Omar Christidis, founder of Arab-Net in Beirut and his head of entrepreneur outreach Racha Ghamlouch; Nafez Al Dakkak, Jordan-based education reform consultant; Karim Fahmy, director, Global Business Development at Intel; Elias Ghanem, general manager, PayPal Middle East and North Africa; Mazen Helmy founder of Cairo-based space sharing the District; Youssri Helmy, co-founder of Ideal Ratings and Techwadi; Ossama Hassanein, chairman of Techwadi; George Khadder, co-founder, board member (Steering Committee) Abdelrahman Magdy Founder & CEO at Egypreneur; Pecks Eric Martin, formerly of Kaust and now consultant, Koltai & Co.; Ali Matar, head of LinkedIn MENA; Muhammad Mansour (known as TripleM on Twitter); Sherif Nagui of Wharton School of Business; Rony El-Nashar, founder and managing director of SeedStartup; Ramez Shehadi of Booz&co.; Saed Nashef and Yadin Kaufmann co-founders of Sadara Ventures; Nadia Oweidat, studying at Oxford; Sahar Sallab, Egyptian executive and active supporter of the Google startup competition; Soraya Salti of INJAZ al-Arab; Orlando Vidal, Dubai-based partner with SNR Denton; Hashem Zahran, co-director of the Alexandria Chapter of the Founder Institute and regional StartupWeekend; Fawaz Zu'bi of Jordan's Accelerator Technology Holdings.

Reading, commenting, and pushing across multiple chapters were Sawari Ventures' founder Ahmed Alfi and his partner Hany Sonbaty,

Aramex Group founder and chairman, Fadi Ghandour, and Abraaj Group founder and CEO Arif Naqvi. They were generous with their time and hospitality, and have been central in their leadership of change in the Middle East and introducing me to these new narratives.

For many courtesies, readings, and counsel, I thank: at Wamda.com Habib Haddad, Nina Curley, Roland Daher; Sawari's Flat6Labs founder Ramez Mohamed, Ahmed Essam, Heba El-Habashy, Yasmine Kamar, and Dina El-Shenoufy, Ali Darwish, and Ahmed Rayan of Sawari Ventures; Aramex's e-commerce lead Hassan Mikail guided me through the changing e-commerce landscape, read drafts, and answered innumerable questions, and Aramex's Lina Shehadeh and Diana Masannat were my go-to help in both Amman and Dubai. Abraaj's CEO Mustafa Abdel-Wadood, CEO of Aureos Capital Tom Speechley, partner Fred Sicre, senior vice president Ghizlan Guenez, and senior vice president Ovais Naqvi and Walid Bakr. Pradeep Ramamurthy, who I first met in his service at the White House and then at USAID, and who later joined Abraaj, patiently had many provocative conversations about and important edits to my drafts; Usama Fayyad, head of Oasis500, spent many hours with me and commented on drafts, as did his dedicated team, especially Amy Lute; Salwa Katkhuda, and Serene Shalan; Wael Fakharany of Google Middle East spent hours with me helping me to understand many aspects of the ecosystem in the Middle East, and Maha Abouelenein and Najeeb Jarrar at Google were regular resources. At the American University of Cairo School of Business, dean Sherif Kamel has been an extraordinary leader, friend, and reader, and Ghada Howaidy, Ghada Hafez, Sandy Iskander, and Ayman Ismail read, wrote, and were there for me in a moment's notice.

Four women stand out for teaching me more about the culture, history and changes in the Middle East, and keeping me honest around my own biases about the region. They were extraordinary guides and candidly commented on multiple chapters: Beirut-based Amal Ghandour, author of one of the most important and best-written blogs on the Middle East and global affairs generally, ThinkingFits.com; Amman-based Reem Khouri, who has pushed Aramex into new thinking about corporate social responsibility and has actively supported Ruwwad; Cairo-based Dina Sherif who has dedicated her life to thinking through bottom-up solutions among entrepreneurs, social entrepreneurs, and the private sector more broadly; and Hala Fadel, investor, founder of the MIT regional startup competition and leading efforts to create a Ruwwad in Tripoli Lebanon.

In three visits to Ruwwad in Amman and many interviews, Samar Dudin and the entire staff were exceptional and are simply changing the world one person, one community at a time.

My dear friend Kamal Shehadi, his remarkable wife Natalie Honein, and their children extended me a thousand courtesies and Kamal patiently sat through many interviews and drafts on mobile history and technology. Generous with their time on mobile innovation are: Khalifa Hassan K. AlForah AlShamsi, chief digital services officer for the Etisalat Group; Mohammed Al Ayouti, Vodafone Egypt of Vodafone, Egypt; Jim Cicconi, senior executive vice president–external affairs at AT&T; William Hague, executive vice president–international, AT&T Mobility; Chris Locke, managing director, GSMA Mobile for Development; Glenn Lurie, president—Emerging Enterprises and Partnerships, AT&T Mobility.

Ben Horowitz of Andreessen Horowitz and Michael Moritz of Sequoia Capital have been friends and teachers in countless ways, and were generous with their time for this book. My old professor and dean of Harvard Business School, Nitin Nohria has long given me time and teaching which resonate throughout this book. The great public activist and CEO of American Jewish World Service, Ruth Messinger, has had extraordinary insight and impact on the role of women in growth markets, as has Alyse Nelson of Vital Voices. LinkedIn Founder Reid Hoffman and Premal Shah, president of Kiva, offered great insight on the power of crowd-sharing and technology to drive change around the world. Linda Rottenberg, the tireless co-founder of Endeavor understands the power of high-impact entrepreneurship better than anyone, and on her team including co-founder Peter Kellner, President Fernando Fabre and SVP of International Expansion Walt Mayo, and on the ground Ismail Alatrash, Tamer Alsalah, Ahmed El Bedawy, Brian Chen, Tyler Gwinn, Joanna Harries, Baily Kempner, Rasha Manna, Lucy Minott, Travis Marchman,

Rhett Morris, Daniela Terminel, Tarek Sadi, Shaun Young, and their teams throughout the region extended every possible courtesy. Great leaders in global entrepreneurship Carl Schramm and Jonathan Ortmans were generous resources and in offering insight and friendship.

I am deeply grateful for the support, wisdom, and comments from some of the great journalists of our time: The *Washington Post*'s David Ignatius, Kevin Sullivan, and the former *Post* managing editor and Pulitzer Prize-winning author and writer for *New Yorker* Steve Coll; formerly of ABC News John Donvan, and formerly of CNN Frank Sesno, now director at George Washington University School of Media and Public Affairs; and author/freelance journalist Ben Kerschberg, who painstakingly edited multiple chapters, line by line. A day didn't go by where the counsel of and exclamation by the great foreign correspondent, author, and editor, the *Washington Post*'s and *Foreign Policy*'s David Hoffman, rang in my ears: "Stop trying so hard in your writing. Let go; show, don't tell."

Much of my thinking for this book came together when I wrote over a dozen columns for great news groups and blogs during this journey. The extensive feedback about this writing from the editors simply made this book better. I thank: Fred Hiatt, page editor at the *Washington Post;* Frances Sellers of the *Washington Post*'s Style; Daniel Henninger, deputy editorial page director, Mark Lasswell, editorial features editor, and David Feith, assistant editorial features editor, all of the *Wall Street Journal;* Kara Swisher, co-executive editor of *All Things Digital,* and their senior editor Beth Callaghan; Sarah Lacy, founder *Pando Daily,* and author of *Brilliant, Crazy, Cocky: How the Top 1% of Entrepreneurs Profit from Global Chaos,* which chronicles the great shifts in innovation and startups across many emerging markets, and her editor Nathan Pensky and artist Hallie Bateman; Tim Sullivan, editorial director of the *Harvard Business Review,* and their assistant editors Courtney Cashman and Kevin Evers; *Fortune* senior editor Adam Lashinsky and managing editor of Fortune.com, Megan Barnett; Henry Blodget and his team at *Business Insider;* Larry Roberts of Bloomberg and Ian McCarthy of LinkedIn led the charge on their new content initiative and asked me to be one of their thought leaders which literally opened this conversation to thousands; he and Francesca Levy and Dan Roth have been central in making it so. Entrepreneur Sandi MacPherson's new platform Quibb. com, to which she invited me early, has allowed me to get feedback I would never have found. Many journalists on the ground were unwavering helpful, including Kristen Chick of the *Christian Science Monitor,* Nancy Messieh, formerly of The Next Web and now with the Atlantic Council, and Chris Dickey of the *Daily Beast* and *Newsweek.*

Other great readers who had significant impact on my thinking from the proposal days on include: Will McCants, Randy Castleman, Sarah Chayes, Mohamed El Dahshan, Parag and Ayesha Khanna, Samir Khleif, Raphe Sagalyn, and Jeremy Shane. Former ambassador to the OECD Karen Kornbluh not only read the entire book with an outstanding critical eye, but also supplied me with data and insight especially on women in emerging growth markets. Naif Al Mutawa, founder of The 99 who sat for countless interviews over many components of the book should appear in my list of great entrepreneurs, but I single him out here.

❧

I am indebted to Marc Andreessen for the many lessons he has taught me across just about every issue, the friendship and laughs we have shared over the years, and for kindly agreeing to write the foreword of this book. Marc's remarkable wife, Laura Arrillaga Andreessen, has been a dear friend and advisor to me and for this book in countless ways. I am similarly indebted to Herb Allen III for all his wisdom, humor, and support over a decade, and for graciously bringing all of it to reading an entire draft. He has been equally gracious in introducing me to his father, Herbert Allen Jr., and the entire Allen & Company family (with a special shoutout to John Griffen, John Josephson, Kaveh Khosrowshahi, Leroy Kim, Gillian Munsen, Meg Kelty Lawler, and Mandy Tavakol), who not only supported my business ventures but taught me more about the world than I can articulate here. Ilana Mair, also of Allen, is an extraordinary editor and patiently weeded through and repeatedly fixed many chapters wonderfully.

Others who have supported my thinking in countless ways include Nada Abandah, Ahmed Abdelwahab, Omar Alfi, Rafat Ali, Brad Aronson, Ronit Avni, Durriya Badani, Hoda Baroudi, Sarah Baxter, Nick Beim and Piraye Yurttas Beim, Frias Ben Achour, Jeff Berman, Lewis Bernstein, Gina Bianchini, Paul Bragiel, Brenda Butler, Jason Calacanis, Ian Cameron and Susan Rice, Steve and Jean Case, Mike Cassidy, Rama Chakaki, James Chan, Andrew Chen, Beezer Clarkson, Sean Cleary, Brooke Coburn, Cameron Cook, James Crabtree, Henry Crumpton, David Dean, Barry Diller, Peter Dornan, Sara Dudin, Neveen El Tahri, Andrew Exum, Bruce Feiler, Nate Fick, Alan Fleischmann, Richard Fontaine, Said Francis, Maurie Gelfman, Julius Genachowski, James Glassman, Seth Goldstein, Paul Gompers, Jim Goldgeier, Don Graham, Catherine Halaby, Lorraine Harriton, Bob Hayes, Abdulsalam Haykal, Heather Henyon, Auren Hoffman, Jim Hornthal, Julia Hurley, Martin Indyck, Joi Ito, Bedriye Hulya, Dima Jamali, Riyad Abou Jaoudeh, Zem and James Joaqin, Mary Jordan, H.E. Marwan Juma, Maher Kaddoura, Rami Al Karmi, Tarek Kettaneh, the Kauffman Foundation, Juliette Kayyem, Andrew Keene, Saad Khan, Yelena Kadeykina, Basel Kilany, Robert Kimmitt, Jay Koh, Ambassador Karim Kuwar, Rob Lalka, Korina Lopez, Kristin Lord, Nancy Lublin, Andrew McLaughlin, Dave McClure, Eric Martin, Ed Mathias, Cathy Merrill, Nancy Messieh, Christopher Michel, Ranit Mishori, John Nagl, Sherif Nagui, Ahmed Nassef, Peggy Noonan, Michael O'Hanlon, Dan Olszewski, Ahmed al Omran, Denis Ozerov, Jim Pinkerton, Dan Prieto, Sulan Sooud Al-Qassemi, Mehrunisa Qayyum, Sally Quinn, Hooman Radfar, Andrew Rosenthal, Kevin Ryan, Rob Schroeder, Lara Setrakian, Amr Shady, Deena Shakir, Maha Shami, Faysal Sohail, Cem Sertoglu, Isaac Solotaroff, Alan Spoon, Ryan Spoon, Mark Stencel, Andrew Stevens, Mark Stein, Nafeesa Syeed, Shouq Tarawneh, Nate Tibbets and Suzy George, Rock and Jill Tonkel, Gayle and Joel Trotter, Elizabeth Ulmer, Oltac Unsal, Elizabeth Weingarten, Katharine Weymouth, Fred Wilson, Joelle Yazbeck, Ahmed Younis, and Rahilla Zafar. No one person has had more impact on my thinking about the world, and of late especially of emerging growth markets, than Robert Zoellick.

Technology executive Leslie Jump, U.S.–based partner of Sawiri Ventures has been a remarkable support to the Middle East startup ecosystem and to my thinking about it. Her husband, former Assistant Secretary for the Middle East Ned Walker, an Ambassador to Egypt and Israel who served throughout the region and is now professor at Hamilton College, taught me more about political context in the Middle East in one hour than I often got in months of my own reading. Everything written about the Middle East by Vali Nasr is a revalation, a meal with him is a tutorial.

I decided to focus *Startup Rising* primarily on the stories of the Middle East, but in so doing left out some of the amazing pioneers and ecosystem supporters in the U.S. government. Woefully under-budgeted, often a second thought to the major aid, investment, loan and loan guarantee programs government has historically focused upon, these "intrepreneurs" have tried to smartly move programs to better connect great startups in ecosystems around the world to opportunities, investments, and friendships with great ones across the United States. I thank Steven Koltai, now with the Koltai Group, who drove for many years one of the leading connectors of U.S. and emerging growth market ecosystems, the Global Entrepreneurship Program (GEP) of the Department of State; his successor Shelly Porges, a great former executive with American Express and Bank of America, who has expanded GEP extensively; Brenda Rios at GEP who seemed to make everything look easy; Mike Drucker, who is on the ground in Cairo as a consultant to USAID and their efforts in entrepreneurship; U.S. Ambassador to the UAE, Michael H. Corbin; Toni Verstandig and Maysam Ali, and Mickey Bergman at the great private-public Partnership for New Beginnings (PNB) has made more executives and investors aware of opportunity in growth markets than anyone; Cathleen Campbell, CEO of CDRF Global who with Natalia Pipa, Ovi Bujorean, Yoritzi Acosta, and their staffs who among other 24-hour-a-day obligations, host outstanding startup competitions around the world.

Cristina Fernandez tirelessly did research and fact-checking for me throughout and was there on a moment's notice, as was Dana Stuster, now at *Foreign Policy* magazine. Jeanne Murie patiently transcribed a third of my longer interviews.

∾

I want to thank my YPO Arab American forum for all they have taught me over the years, and to the great Washington, D.C.–based entrepreneur and venture investor Cal Simmons and West Coast entrepreneur/investor Jim Hornthal who introduced me to the group. Seif Fahmy was also a great host to me in Cairo and elsewhere in Egypt, and as much as anyone spends each day building a better Egypt. My YPO Forum in Washington, D.C.—David Eisner, Sean Greene, Dean Graham, Stuart Holliday, Tom Monahan, John Rice, Rob Wilder—helped my thinking and plotting and patiently absorbed my absences due to travel.

∾

When I first thought of writing Startup Rising, *a friend and expert* in the book publishing world smiled and said to me, "The two least-selling books are those on entrepreneurship, and those on the Middle East. You are quite a contrarian to write about both in one shot." In a time where the glow of the Arab uprisings seemed to dim, very few in these worlds were willing to take a risk on a hopeful narrative that seemed so against the grain of daily news. Two women stand out not only for their courage in taking this on, but for their incredible patience and support of me, and outstanding editing throughout.

My agent, Alia Hanna Habib of McCormick and Williams, understood the power of this story immediately. Through months of painstaking editing and re-editing of my proposal, and her entrepreneurial energy and tenacity, she sold the concept to the other brave soul. My editor, Emily Carleton of Palgrave Macmillan, believed in this book from the beginning. In giving me time, counsel, and wisdom all but unheard of for first-time authors, she kept me focused, on task, and upbeat in more ways than she will know. On an impossible deadline, she edited every chapter more than once, asking the tough questions and making my writing consistently better. I cannot thank them both or their staffs enough. In particular I thank Leslie Falke of McCormick for her outstanding copyedits of my proposal and Laura Lancaster of Palgrave Macmillan for juggling, it seems, a hundred balls all the time. Carla Benton and Joel Breuklander of Palgrave Macmillan stepped in to be an outstanding editors as well. The Palgrave Macmillan marketing team, including Lauren Dwyer and Elisabeth Tone in New York and Verity Holliday and Jamie Forrest in London, is doing amazing work in getting this new narrative of the Middle East out. Mark Fortier and Punja Sangar of Fortier PR and Amy Gonzalez and Cameron Cook of Blueprint Interactive are best in class in public relations and interactive marketing respectively, and became central team members.

The great writer Bill Murphy was a remarkable friend, confidante, storyboarder, reader, editor, butt-kicker, and moral support from the book's first outlines, through each chapter and final product. His impact in clarifying my thinking and writing cannot be described.

My dear friend, and author, Tom Mueller, has taught me how to write since college and was a constant support in ways big and small throughout.

Blair Hoffman who was my executive assistant at HealthCentral patiently stood by me throughout the logistics of this process with great humor and support.

It seems almost a cliché to thank one's family at the end of acknowledgments, but I know now firsthand how central they are to it all. My wife, Sandy Coburn, is writing her own novel while being an extraordinary mother and having her hands in a dozen other activities. She too often put aside her own priorities while I made over a dozen trips to the region in less than two years, and holed myself up like a hermit for months of writing and Skype calls: she made invaluable edits and suggestions. My parents, Ed and Elaine, were never a hundred percent comfortable with my travels when news turned difficult in places I was visiting, but were incredibly supportive throughout and they taught me wanderlust. Sandy and my kids, Jack, Julia, and Ben, not only asked remarkably insightful questions when I reported back from my travels, but were never shy to ride me to stay focused if I took a day off. They are entering a fascinating world of turmoil and uncertainty, but of great opportunities—and I hope in their own ways, like the great entrepreneurs I have been lucky to get to know, they will grasp at them and, in whatever form, make a new and better world.

Annotated Bibliography

The literature on startups in the Middle East, and all emerging growth markets for that matter, remains relatively nascent. The best resources unsurprisingly remain in the blogs, new research groups, and the dozens, maybe hundreds, of related social network groups. Virtually everyone I acknowledged and interviewed is a regular resource on the latest information, data, and insight through Twitter.

Having said this, I gained invaluable insight and context from the following:

Historic Context and Current Shifts in the Middle East

Abdel-Malek, Anouar. (1968). *Egypt: Military Society.* New York: Random House. Holds up surprisingly well as an early look of the ramifications of Nasser and Egypt on Egypt.

Abou, El Fadl. (2007). *The Great Theft.* New York: HarperCollins. Provocative history and analysis of Islam, its relationship to the West, and step-by-step argument against extremist interpretations of the faith.

Akyol, Mustafa. (2011). *Islam Without Extremes.* New York: W. W. Norton & Company, Inc. A thoughtful historical survey of the political rise of Islam and views on how Islam should and does co-exist with liberalism and democracy.

Bishara, Marwan. (2012). *The Invisible Arab.* New York: Nation Books. Thoughtful overview of what led to the Arab uprisings, the internal and external forces that had impact upon them, and what may come next.

Dhillon, Navtej, & Yousef, Tarik (Eds.). (2009). *Generation in Waiting: The Unfulfilled Promise of Young People in the Middle East.* Washington, DC: The Brookings Institution. An outstanding collection of articles, country-by-country, on the state of, challenges facing, and opportunities among the youth in the Middle East.

Lynch, Marc. (2012). *The Arab Uprising.* New York: Public Affairs. Excellent reporting and analysis of the Arab uprisings and the issues yet to be resolved.

Ghonim, Wael. (2012). *Revolution 2.0.* Boston and New York: Houghton Mifflin Harcourt. The first and most comprehensive, first-hand description of the Arab uprisings in Egypt in English.

Haddad, Bassam. (2012). *Business Networks in Syria.* Stanford: Stanford University Press. A definitive study on Syria's current political economy and business environment.

Mahajan, Vijay. (2012). *The Arab World*. San Francisco: Jossey-Bass. An outstanding history and overview of shifts in consumer behaviors happening in the Middle East, how businesses broadly are both addressing and leading these shifts, and where the new generations are focused.

Nasr, Vali. (2009). *The Rise of Islamic Capitalism*. New York: Free Press. A definitive overview of the history and trends in Middle East business and economies.

Rizk, Nagl, & Shave, Lea, (Eds.). (2010). *Access to Knowledge in Egypt*. London: Bloomsbury Publishing. An outstanding overview of Egypt's history and future centers around connecting to the best resources of experience, information, and information technology, not only in Egypt, but also around the region and the world.

Rivlin, Richard. (2006). *Desert Capitalists*. London: Bladonmore Media, Ltd. A definitive history and future look at the Middle East's financial, investment, and trading landscape and its most impactful leaders.

Vatikiotis, P. J. (1961). *Egyptian Army in Politics*. Bloomington: Indiana University Press. Like Abdel-Malek, a classic in its time and an interesting perspective through the lens of the early 1960s.

Drivers of Changing Ecosystems

Banerjee, Abhijit V., & Duflo, Esther. (2011). *Poor Economics*. New York: PublicAffairs. *Financial Times'* "Book of the Year"; research-rich analysis that shines often-shocking light on our premises around traditional development efforts and bottom-up initiatives on the ground.

Gleick, James. (2011). *The Information*. New York: Vintage Books. A sensational history and look forward at how access to and the creation of new information changes societies and ourselves.

Govindarajan, Vijay, & Trimble, Chris. (2012). *Reverse Innovation*. Boston: Harvard Business Review Press. A provocative raising of what we mean by the term "innovation," its ramifications in emerging societies, and how Western businesses miss new opportunities both in internal processes and markets by being locked in dated outlooks.

Hwang, Victor W., & Horowitt, Greg. (2012). *The Rainforest*. Los Altos: Regenwald. While I am not persuaded that building the "next Silicon Valley" is the right way to look at new growth markets, the authors are provocative in what makes for great ecosystems.

Ibrahim, Lethem, & Sherif, Dina H. (2008). *From Charity to Social Change: Trends in Arab Philanthropy*. Cairo: The American University of Cairo Press. An excellent country-by-country overview of philanthropy and shifts to bottom-up, public-private partnerships to solve regional challenges.

Lacy, Sarah. (2011). *Brilliant, Crazy, Cocky: How the Top 1% of Entrepreneurs Profit from Global Chaos*. Hoboken: John Wiley & Sons. A definitive first look at the rise of startups, technology and innovation from some of the most overlooked regions of the world.

Nelson, Alyse. (2012). *Vital Voices*. San Francisco: Jossey-Bass. Excellent overview with remarkable stories of how women around the world and particularly in emerging growth markets are leading change in their communities, their regions, and globally.

Nielsen, Michael. (2012). *Reinventing Discover*. Princeton: Princeton University Press. Meticulous and fascinating overview of how interactive technologies and the impact of collective expertise and knowledge is changing innovation and science.

Saxenian, Annalee. (1996). *Regional Advantage.* Cambridge: Harvard University Press. This is the classic description and analysis of the rise of Silicon Valley and the concurrent decline of Route 128 in Boston.

Schramm, Carl L. (2006). *The Entrepreneurial Imperative.* New York: HarperCollins. From the recent president of the Kauffman Foundation, one of the leading institutions in entrepreneurship, this is a passionate call to action in the value of startups and how ecosystems can support them.

Related Global Shifts

Acemoglu, Daron, & Robinson, James A. (2012). *Why Nations Fail.* New York: Crown Business. Historically supported, extensively researched analysis of the impact of governments, individuals, and institutions on why some nations prosper and others do not.

Diamandis, Peter H., & Kotler, Steven. (2012). *Abundance.* New York: Free Press. Provocative account on how scientific innovation is and will address a wide array of global challenges in energy, education, and health care, among others.

de Soto, Hernando. (2000). *The Mystery of Capital: Why Capitalism Triumphs in the West and Fails Everywhere Else.* New York: Basic Books. A classic on what has allowed for success in economic ecosystems and structural challenges in emerging markets. De Soto has written and spoken (much available online) and developed these ideas with the changes brought by technology.

James, Harold. (2002). *The End of Globalization.* Cambridge: Harvard University Press. A historical overview of previous periods of rise globalization and ramifications of their backlashes.

Kaplan, Robert D. (2010). *Monsoon: The Indian Ocean and the Future of American Power.* New York: Random House. A definitive account of how economic and strategic growth and power has shifted to a region often all but ignored in the United States today.

Kaplan, Robert D. (2012). *The Revenge of Geography.* New York: Random House. Ties together geography, history, culture, and politics to outline tomorrow's core areas of conflict.

Khanna, Parag. (2008). *The Second World.* New York: Random House. Smart overview of the rise of emerging growth markets, and how larger players like the United States, China, and Europe engage in them differently and may miss central and new trends.

Omwansa, Tonny K., & Sullivan, Nicholas P. (2012). *Money Real Quick: The Story of M-Pesa.* London: Guardian eBooks. Definitive account of the remarkable mobile payments company in Kenya.

Sharma, Ruchir. (2012). *Breakout Nations.* New York: W. W. Norton & Co. Provocative and concise overview of the most important global shifts and dynamics among emerging growth markets.

Studies

Abou, Ehaab, Fahmy, Amina, Greenwald, Diana, & Nelson, Jane. (2010, April). "Social Entrepreneurship in the Middle East: Toward Sustainable Development for the Next Generation." Wolfensohn Center for Development (Brookings), Silatech and Dubai School of Government.

Aguirre, DeAnne, Hoteit, Leila, Rupp, Christine, & Sabbagh, Karim. (2012). "Empowering the Third Billion Women and the World of Work in 2012," http://www.booz.com/media/uploads/BoozCo_Empowering-the-Third-Billion_Full-Report.pdf Booz&co.

Arab Development Challenges Report 2011. United Nations Development Programme. (2011).

Bhattacharya, Rina, & Wolde, Hirut. (2010, February). "Constraints on Growth in the MENA Region," http://www.imf.org/external/pubs/ft/wp/2010/wp1030.pdf International Monetary Fund.

Chamlou, Nadereh, & Nabli, Mustapha K., supervised. (2007, October). "The Environment for Women's Entrepreneurship in the Middle East and North Africa Region," http://siteresources.worldbank.org/INTMENA/Resources/Environment_for_Womens_Entrepreneurship_in_MNA_final.pdf The World Bank.

Dakkak, Nafez. (2011, October). "Obstacles towards Curriculum Reform in the Middle East: Using Jordan and the UAE as Case Studies," http://www.dsg.ae/en/Publication/Pdf_En/DSG%20Policy%20Brief%2028%20English.pdf Dubai School of Government Policy Brief.

Ducker, Mike, in collaboration with Deloitte for the USAID_funded TAPR II Project. (2012). "Egypt Entrepreneurship Final Report: Where are all the Egyptian Entrepreneurs." USAID.

The European Photovoltaic Industry Association (EPIA). (2012, January 13). Global Market Outlook for Photovoltaics Until 2015. "Global Market Outlook for Photovoltaics Until 2015."

Galal, Ahmed, et al. (2007). "The Road Not Travelled: Education Reform in the Middle East and North Africa." http://web.worldbank.org/WBSITE/EXTERNAL/COUNTRIES/MENAEXT/0,contentMDK:21617643~pagePK:146736~piPK:226340~theSitePK:256299,00.html International Bank for Reconstruction and Development/World Bank.

Galloway, Scott, & Guthrie, Doug. (2012). "Digital IQ Index: Brazil, Russia, India," L2 Think Tank and the *International Herald Tribune*.

International Monetary Fund. (2012, November). "Regional Economic Outlook: Middle East and Central Asia Report." http://www.imf.org/external/pubs/ft/reo/2012/mcd/eng/mreo1112.htm

International Monetary Fund. (2012, April). "Regional Economic Outlook Update."

International Monetary Fund. (2012, October). "World Economic Outlook Database."

International Monetary Fund. (2012, November). "Regional Economic Outlook: Middle East and Central Asia Report." http://www.imf.org/external/pubs/ft/weo/2012/02/weodata/index.aspx

Jaruzelski, Barry, Loehr, John, & Holman, Richard. (2012, November). "Global Innovations 1000: Making Ideas Work." Booz&co http://www.strategy-business.com/media/file/00140-The-Global-Innovation-1000-Making-Ideas-Work.pdf

MENA Private Equity Association, VC Taskforce (multiple contributors). (2012, August). "2nd Venture Capital in the Middle East and North Africa Report." MENA Private Equity Association, KPMG and Zaywa.

Nakat, Ziad, & Herrera, Santiago. (2010). "Egypt—Cairo traffic congestion study—phase 1." The World Bank. http://documents.worldbank.org/curated/en/2010/11/16603168 /egypt-cairo-traffic-congestion-study-phase-1.

Palakian, Glen. (October 16, 2012). "25 Essential Stats on eCommerce in the Middle East," 1." Wamda. http://www.wamda.com/2012/10/25-essential-stats-on-e-commerce-in -the-middle-east-stats.

Revenga, Ana, Shetty, Sudhir, et al. (2012). "Gender Equality and Development 2012." The World Bank http://econ.worldbank.org/WBSITE/EXTERNAL/EXTDEC/EXTRE SEARCH/EXTWDRS/EXTWDR2012/0,contentMDK:22999750~menuPK:8154981~ pagePK:64167689~piPK:64167673~theSitePK:7778063,00.html.

Rose, Pauline. "Education for All: Global Monitoring Report 2012," *EFA Global Monitoring Report Team,* Commissioned by UNESCO (2012). http://www.unesco.org/new/en /education/themes/leading-the-international-agenda/efareport/reports/2012-skills/.

Ross-Larson, Bruce, principal editor. (2011). "World Bank 2012 Gender and Equality and Development Report," International Bank for Reconstruction and Development. http://site resources.worldbank.org/INTWDR2012/Resources/7778105-1299699968583/7786210 -1315936222006/Complete-Report.pdf.

Sabbagh, Karim, Mourad, Mohamad, Kabbara, Wassim, & Shehadi, Ramez. (Fall 2012). "Understanding the Arab Digital Generation." Booz&co. http://www.booz.com/media /uploads/BoozCo_Understanding-the-Arab-Digital-Generation.pdf.

Sawin, Janet L., & Mastny, Lisa (Eds.). (2010). "Prospects of the Renewable Energy Sector in Egypt." Egyptian-German Private Sector Development Program. www.jcee-eg.net /download.asp? . . . / . . .

Shehadi, Ramez, Hoteit, Leila, Tarazi, Kamal, & Lamaa, Abdulkader. (2012). "Educated, Ambitious, Essential—Women Will Drive the GCC Future," Booz&co. http://www.booz .com/media/uploads/BoozCo-Educated-Ambitious-Essential.pdf.

Shehadi, Ramez, Kassatly, Fady, Karam, Danny, & Cherfan, Michael. (2012). "Digital Spring—MENA Governments Must Speak the Language of Social Media," Booz&co. http://www.booz.com/media/uploads/BoozCo-Digital-Spring-MENA-Governments -Social-Media.pdf.

Stevenson, Lois. (2012). "Women in Business: Policies to Support Women's Entrepreneurship Development in the MENA Region." Organization for Economic Cooperation and Development (OECD). http://www.oecd.org/daf/privatesectordevelopment/womenin business-policiestosupportwomensentrepreneurshipdevelopmentinthemenaregion.htm.

USAID. (March 2012). "Gender Equality and Female Empowerment." http://transition .usaid.gov/our_work/policy_planning_and_learning/documents/GenderEqualityPolicy .pdf.

World Health Organization. (2012). "Road Safety in Ten Countries: Egypt." http://www .who.int/violence_injury_prevention/road_traffic/countrywork/egy/en/index.html.

Index